D0787107

Latin and Greek
in Current Use

PRENTICE-HALL CLASSICS SERIES

Caspar J. Kraemer, Jr., Ph.D., Editor

Latin and Greek

in Current Use

by ELI E. BURRISS, Ph.D.

and LIONEL CASSON, Ph.D.

Professor of Classics • Washington Square College
New York University

Second Edition

COMPLETELY REVISED

by LIONEL CASSON

PRENTICE-HALL, INC
Englewood Cliffs, N. J.

Preface

THE first edition of the textbook for this course appeared in 1939. Its aim was to organize and present in teachable fashion the classical element in English for the student who had had little or no Latin or Greek and who, in all probability, would never study these languages. Ten years of successful use have justified the book's general approach to, and presentation of, the material. They also revealed weaknesses, chiefly in the exercises that accompany each lesson. What the present revision offers first of all is a set of new, classroom-tested exercises.

Our primary aim is, not to teach the student to form or coin words from classical elements, but rather, when he meets in context words so formed, to recognize their meaning and appreciate their flavor. The heart of each exercise, accordingly, consists of sentences, generally taken from well-known authors, and short expressions containing words that, as experience has shown, students cannot fully grasp out of context. Other sentences illustrate particularly felicitous uses, in which the author has deliberately retained the flavor of a word's etymology. Still others, from older writers, show words used in their basic Latin or Greek sense, usages which are so common in classical English literature that, with the passing of Latin and Greek from the modern curriculum, not only the student but even, very often, the teacher of English is unable to read Milton and Shakespeare unless aided by elaborate glossaries.

Wherever possible, each exercise includes more material than can be covered in a single class-hour, thus enabling the instructor to make his own selection in assignments.

In the first edition insufficient attention was paid to scientific vocabulary. We have filled this lack, first, by introducing into the exercises those scientific words that have entered

into common usage and, second, by including in the General
Vocabularies virtually all Latin and Greek words that are
important in the formation of English scientific and techno-
logical terminology.   For students majoring in any one of the
sciences these vocabularies offer rich supplementary material.

The General Vocabularies, in addition to the feature just
mentioned, contain the ultimate source of every English word
in the exercises.   By referring to these vocabularies and by
applying the principles and forms learned in the lessons, the
etymology of most of the words assigned can be worked out.
The student should be required to have a standard English
dictionary, such as *Webster's New Collegiate Dictionary*.   In
those cases where an additional clue to a word's etymology is
needed, he will find it in the dictionary's etymological note.
He will, of course, always rely on the dictionary for determining current meanings.

We have had considerable success with collateral reading
assignments in Greenough and Kittredge, *Words and Their
Ways in English Speech* (Macmillan, 1901).   The material
in our introductory chapter may be supplemented by assignments in A. C. Baugh, *History of the English Language* (Apple-
ton-Century, 1935) and Mary Serjeantson, *A History of
Foreign Words in English* (Dutton, 1936).

Professor Burriss was unfortunately prevented by other
commitments from full collaboration in the revision, and the
responsibility for the rewritten portions, accordingly, lies with
me.   Every line of these, however, has benefited from his
advice and criticism.   There are many acknowledgments to
be made to the members of the Classics Department of Washington Square College.   Professor P. E. Culley supplied the
sections on the art of definition and learned and popular words,
as well as a number of questions for the exercises and valuable
advice for the treatment of the vocabularies.   Many of the
words included in the Etymological Notes were suggested by
Professor J. Johnson.   Professors C. J. Kraemer, Jr., E. L.
Hettich, J. A. Kerns, A. G. C. Maitland, Dr. C. Benedict,

Dr. W. Grummel, Mr. A. Holtz, have all contributed useful
material and suggestions.   A number of illustrative sentences
were contributed by Miss Gloria Weinstein of the Graduate
School of New York University.   The invaluable assistance
of my wife lightened immeasurably the onerous task of preparing the manuscript and of compiling vocabularies and
indices.

L. C.

Contents

PART TWO

GREEK

PART ONE

LATIN

CHAPTER ONE

Latin and English

TO STUDY the history of every word in the English language would be interesting and rewarding. It would also be a task of heroic proportions, for to do it we should have to dip into almost every language under the sun. To trace the history of *cot* and *loot* we should have to turn to Hindu; to trace *cotton* we should have to go to Arabic; *candy* and *lilac* would take us to Persian; and so on. If, however, we put aside *cot*, *loot*, *cotton*, and other words which come from less familiar languages, we find that the bulk of the English vocabulary can be divided into two classes: the Anglo-Saxon element, and the Latin and Greek element.

In this course only the second class, the Latin and Greek element in English, concerns us. There is justification for this limiting of the subject. The Anglo-Saxon element includes for the most part words familiar to all of us—we don't have to spend time over the meaning of *go*, *been*, *ride*, *through*, and so forth. But *desideratum*, *tergiversation*, *intransigence*, *supposititious* do demand study. These belong to the Latin-derived portion of English, the portion that contains most of our complex, our "hard" words. Moreover, when new words are coined today, especially in the sciences, they are coined from Latin and Greek, not from Anglo-Saxon elements.

Now, the words that we shall study have all been *borrowed* from Latin and Greek. For one language to borrow from another, some form of contact must take place between the two. We shall, in due course, review for you the history and the

3

nature of the contact between English and Latin.[1]   Before we do that, however, we want, by way of historical background, to give you a brief account of the origin of Latin, Greek, and English.   Where did these languages come from? How did they develop?   Are they at all related?

The Indo-European Family of Languages

The origin of English, Latin, and Greek goes back to a period from which we have no written records, a time about which we have no historical facts but can only make conjectures.   The account we are going to give, consequently, is not proved history but a reconstruction built up by scholars on the basis of all available evidence.

When you examine the oldest known words of English, Greek, Latin, Welsh, Irish, Lithuanian, Russian, and certain other languages of Europe and Asia, you quickly find that there are resemblances among them which are more than coincidental.   The English word *father*, for example, is not unlike the Latin word **pater,** the Greek word *patér,* the Sanskrit word *pitá.*   The English word *nine* is similar to the Latin word **novem,** the Sanskrit *náva,* the Old Irish *nōi*[n].   Our *two* and the Latin **duo,** the Greek *dýo,* the Lithuanian *dù* seem to have something in common.   Examples, of which there are thousands, show that these resemblances follow certain fixed patterns.   What is the answer?

The explanation offered by linguistic scholars is that all the languages containing words that show these patterns of resemblance come from a common source.   The story, as they reconstruct it, runs this way.   At some time in the prehistoric past a certain people lived on the shores of the Black and Caspian seas.   Having no written records from them we do not know what they called themselves; for the sake of convenience we call them "Indo-Europeans."   Possibly around 3000 B.C., possibly earlier, this people migrated to most parts

---

[1] The contact between English and Greek is dealt with in the introduction to Part Two.

of Europe and many parts of Asia. Wherever they went they brought with them their language, "Indo-European," as we call it. In each part to which they migrated they must have found local languages, but somehow their language managed to supplant these. In each part the original inhabitants gave up their local language and adopted Indo-European, just as, for example, the native population of many Central and South American nations over the course of centuries have given up their native Indian tongues and today speak Spanish. Now, the kind of Indo-European that was spoken in one part differed somewhat from the kind spoken in another, just as the Spanish spoken in Cuba differs from Mexican Spanish, and that, in turn, from the Spanish of Spain. As time went on, these differences grew greater and greater, until a point was reached at which the Indo-European spoken in each section was so unlike the original tongue as to deserve the name of a separate language. In the Italian peninsula, for example, Indo-European supplanted whatever native languages previously existed there. With the passing of time, the Indo-European spoken in this region acquired certain characteristics that distinguished it from the Indo-European spoken, say, in the Greek peninsula, or in south Russia, or in north Europe. Finally, these characteristics grew so marked that the language spoken in the Italian peninsula differed enough from the original Indo-European to be considered a distinct language; thus arose the Italic branch of the Indo-European family, the most important member of which is Latin. In the same way the Hellenic branch grew up in the Greek peninsula, the Indo-Iranic branch in India, and so on. A whole group of "daughter tongues" arose out of Indo-European, the "mother tongue."

The following chart shows the most important branches of the Indo-European family of languages. Under each branch are listed the important daughter tongues.

I. *Indo-Iranic:* Sanskrit and later vernaculars (Hindu, Bengali, etc.), Persian

II. *Armenic:* Armenian
III. *Albanic:* Albanian
IV. *Hellenic:* Ancient Greek, Modern Greek
  V. *Italic:* Latin which, in turn, is the ancestor of the Romance languages: Roumanian, Italian, Provençal-Catalan, French, Spanish, Portuguese
VI. *Celtic:* Welsh, Irish, Scotch Gaelic, Breton
VII. *Germanic:* Gothic, Swedish-Danish, Norwegian-Icelandic, English, Dutch-Flemish, German
VIII. *Balto-Slavic:* Lithuanian, Lettish, Bulgarian, Serbo-Croatian, Slovene, Russian, Polish, Czech (Bohemian), Slovak

The languages on this chart are related or "cognate," to use the technical term. They are daughter tongues of the same mother tongue, Indo-European. You will note that English, Latin, and Greek appear on the chart. These three languages are cognate. The English word *father*, the Latin word **pater,** and the Greek word ***patér*** resemble one another because they come from some one Indo-European word. Words so related are also said to be cognate.

In reconstructing the development of the Indo-European family of languages, linguists had the help of a similar development that took place in historical times—namely, the example of the Romance languages. At one time the area where Spanish, Portuguese, French, Provençal-Catalan, Italian, and Roumanian are now used was under the domination of the Roman Empire, and its inhabitants spoke Latin—not the cultured language of Caesar, Cicero, and the other great literary figures, but a colloquial form known as "Vulgar Latin." Over the course of centuries the Vulgar Latin spoken in the various sections of the empire developed each its own characteristics. Just as, thousands of years earlier, the growth of such local characteristics had produced the Indo-European languages from Indo-European, so the same sort of growth in the Dark Ages produced the romance languages from Vulgar Latin. The local Latin of the Iberian peninsula became Spanish, that of Gaul became French, and so on.

History of the Contact between Latin and English

English, Latin, and Greek, then, arose from, or are daughter tongues of, Indo-European. From Indo-European, by the evolutionary process described above, English inherited the group of words which is known as the Anglo-Saxon element. But that group of words was not sufficient for its needs. English has steadily added to it by *borrowing*. To do this it has turned, as we pointed out, to many languages, but to none so much as to the great classical languages, Latin and Greek.

There is only one prerequisite for borrowing words: the languages concerned must, somehow, through trade, cultural intercourse, even through war, be in contact. English established contact with Latin as early as the first century B.C. and has never broken it off. The history of their relationship falls into six periods.

1. *The Roman Occupation of Britain* (ca. A.D. 43–410). Although Julius Caesar had invaded Britain in 55 and 54 B.C., the island did not become Romanized until almost one hundred years later, when the Roman emperor Claudius sent an expeditionary force against it. Within forty years the Romans had penetrated to the borders of Scotland—as far as they were ever to go.

The people of Britain in this period spoke not Anglo-Saxon but a Celtic tongue. Latin, although the official language under the Roman occupation, had little effect on the Celtic of the natives. Words were borrowed by the natives, of course, but not many. Among those which we are fairly sure were taken over in this period are:

LATIN	EARLY FORM	MODERN ENGLISH
mīlia (passuum) 'thousands of paces,' 'miles' [singular, mīlle passuum 'a thousand paces,' 'a mile' (1,618 yards)]	*mīl*	*mile*
castra plural of castrum 'fort'	*ċeaster* 'city'	*-chester* (cf. *Rochester*, *Winchester*, etc.)

2. *Anglo-Saxon Invasions* (First Century B.C.–ca. A.D. 600).
In this period of borrowing, Latin was in contact with people
who spoke Anglo-Saxon.   As the dates given show, this period
overlaps the whole of the first.

From the first century B.C. on, the north German tribes
known as the Anglo-Saxons had been in contact with Romans,
particularly with the soldiers of the legions guarding the Roman border in North Germany.   As time went on, many of
the members of these tribes became Roman soldiers themselves.   Naturally, they picked up Latin words—Vulgar, not
literary, Latin—especially military terms and the names of
objects used in camp and in town.

In A.D. 449 the Anglo-Saxons began their great invasions
into Britain.   They brought with them not only their native
tongue, Anglo-Saxon, but all the Latin words they had borrowed in the previous centuries on the Continent.   They
drove out the native Celtic of the Britons but picked up at
least some of the Latin words that Celtic had previously borrowed.   For over one hundred years these invasions, and with
them the passage of Latin words into Anglo-Saxon, continued.
Here are a few examples of words borrowed in this period:

LATIN	ANGLO-SAXON	MODERN ENGLISH
vāllum 'wall set with palisades'	*weall*	*wall*
calx 'stone,' 'lime'	*cealc*	*chalk*
postis 'pillar'	*post*	*post*
vīnum 'wine'	*wīn*	*wine*
pix 'pitch'	*pic*	*pitch*

3. *The Period Marked by the Introduction of Roman Christianity* (ca. A.D. 600–1066).   In A.D. 597, the first monastery
was established in Britain, and within a century all England
had embraced Christianity.   Churches and monasteries were
built and schools set up, and the use of Latin, the language of
the western Church, spread considerably.   As a result English borrowed several hundred more words, most of them having to do with religious matters.   Since the Church was in its

early days a Greek institution, many of these go ultimately
back to Greek. A few examples of the words borrowed in
this period are:

GREEK	LATIN	ANGLO-SAXON	MODERN ENGLISH
monachós 'monk'	**monachus** (**monicus**)	*munuc*	*monk*
monastḗrion 'monastery'	**monastērium**	*mynster*	*minster*
	nonna 'child's nurse,' 'nun'	*nunne*	*nun*
pápas 'father'	**pāpa**	*pāpa*	*pope*
	crēdo 'I believe'	*crēda*	*creed*
eleēmosýnē 'compassionateness'	**eleēmosyna**	*aelmysse*	*alms*

4. *The Norman-French or Anglo-French Period* (A.D. 1066–
ca. 1200). In 1066, by his victory at Hastings, William the
Conqueror took possession of England for the Normans, and
Norman-French (Anglo-French) became the language of the
court circle and of cultured people generally. Now, Norman-
French was little more than a slightly modified Latin; thus
any word borrowed from it can be considered a borrowing
from Latin. Norman-French and English for the most part
existed side by side without either greatly affecting the other.
The new language, however, did introduce a few words into
the English vocabulary, for example:

LATIN	NORMAN-FRENCH	ENGLISH LOAN WORD
caldārium 'hot bath'	*caudron*	*caldron*
cancer 'crab,' 'cancer'	*cancre*	*canker*
castellum diminutive of **castrum** 'fort'	*castel*	*castle*

5. *The Old French Period* (ca. A.D. 1200–1500). It is in
this period that English begins to borrow on a large scale:
more words were taken over than in all the previous periods

together. As in the preceding period the borrowing is indi-
rect: English is in contact not with Latin itself but with Old
French, which, being a Romance language, was essentially
Latin. Old French had a richer, far more cultivated vocabulary than English, at this time still a rough and limited instrument. From Old French, then, English borrowed to fill out
its lacks. Words associated with every phase of life were
taken:

LATIN	OLD FRENCH	ENGLISH LOAN WORD
bonitās 'goodness'	*bontet*	*bounty*
calumniārī 'to slander'	*chalenger*	*challenge*
cōnsuētūdō 'habit'	*costume*	*custom*
dīgnitās 'dignity'	*dainté*	*dainty*
gaudium 'joy'	*joie*	*joy*
poena 'penalty'	*peine*	*pain*
praedicāre 'to proclaim'	*prechier*	*preach*
radius 'spoke of a wheel'	*rai*	*ray*

6. *The Revival of Learning* (ca. A.D. 1500–   ). This is
the period in which the vast majority of the words we are to
study was borrowed. It is the period in which English first
comes directly into contact with Classical Latin. Borrowing
now takes place not from Vulgar Latin, not through Norman-
French or Old French, but directly from the pages of Latin
authors.

The Renaissance brought to Europe the writings of Greece
and Rome in the original. To any cultivated man of the time
Latin was a second language. In England those who preferred to write in their mother tongue rather than in Latin
felt that the English language, as it existed then, was inade-
quate to express thoughts which Latin or Greek could phrase
with ease and felicity. To rectify this, thousands of words
were borrowed with but slight change in form, sometimes with
no change, from Latin and Greek. Moreover countless new
words were produced by the use of Latin and Greek elements.
Latin suffixes and prefixes and bases were put together in

combinations which, although linguistically possible in Latin, had never actually been formed by the Romans. *Independence*, for example, contains two Latin prefixes (**in-** and **dē-**), a Latin base (**-pendent-**), and a Latin suffix (**-ia**). This word looks as if it came from a Latin word spelled **indēpendentia**. Actually, there is no such Latin word: the four elements were put together by some English borrower.[2] Frequently, in making up words in this fashion, the borrowers mingled elements from more than one language, adding a Latin suffix to an English base, a Greek suffix to a Latin base, and so on. *Talkative*, for example, is half English (*talk-*), half Latin (*-ative*). Words so formed are known as *hybrids*. Sometimes the borrowers took over a foreign word that had already been borrowed in an earlier period. For example, the Latin noun **dīgnitās** had been borrowed through Old French in the form *dainty*. A later borrower took over the same word again, this time in the form *dignity*. Such pairs of loan words, which go back by different courses to the same word, are known as *doublets*.

The major borrowing was done from Latin and Greek. But other languages were not forgotten, especially French (modern French, no longer Old French as in the preceding periods) and, to a far less extent, Italian.

The wholesale borrowing that started during the Revival of Learning continued for centuries. Loan words from the classical languages are still being added today. We need give you no examples of the words borrowed during this period; you will start meeting them in Lesson 1.

EXERCISES

1. Read the Explanatory Notes in your dictionary (pages xviii–xx in *Webster's New Collegiate Dictionary*).

2. Look up the nouns *cannon* and *mode* in your dictionary. Determine the meanings of each abbreviation used in the etymological notes.

---

[2] Such combinations will be marked hereafter by an asterisk, e.g. *indēpendentia.

3. The English noun *father*, Latin **pater**, Greek *patér*, Sanskrit *pitá* come from the same Indo-European word. What name is given to words so related?

4. The English noun *charm* has come into English through Old French *charme* from the Latin noun **carmen**. What is the relationship between **carmen** and *charme*? between *charme* and *charm*?

5. Answer the following questions and state the reasons for your answer:

(a) Which words are the older words in any given language, inherited words or loan words?

(b) Can a native English word be cognate with a native Russian word? French word? American-Indian word? Hebrew word?

(c) Can a native German word be cognate with a native Irish word? Latin word? Arabic word?

6. *Poison* and *potion* are ultimately derived from the same Latin noun **pōtiō** 'drink.' What name do we give to such words?

7. The English noun *martyrdom* consists of a Greek-derived element *martyr-* and an English element *-dom*. What name do we give to such words?

8. Distinguish between "doublets" and "cognates." Give examples of each.

9. In which period was the largest number of words borrowed from Latin?

10. What is the chief difference in the way in which Latin words were borrowed before and after the Revival of Learning?

Latin Pronunciation

The following are the rules for the classical pronunciation of Latin, the pronunciation in use in the first century B.C. and first century A.D., when Latin literature reached the peak of its development. It must be borne in mind that Latin, unlike

English, has no silent letters: all consonants and vowels are pronounced.

Vowels. These may be long or short and are pronounced as follows:

LONG VOWELS	SHORT VOWELS
ā as in *father*	a as in *adrift*
ē as in *they*	e as in *eh?* (clipped short) or as *é* in French *été*
ī as in *machine*	i as in *pin*
ō as in *note*	o as in *obey*
ū as in *rude*	u as *oo* in *look*

Note: **y** was introduced at a comparatively late period to represent the sound of *upsilon* in words borrowed from the Greek, and has a pronunciation between that of Latin **u** and **i**, like the French *u* or the German *ü*.

Consonants. These are like their English counterparts, except for the following:

b before **s** and **t** is pronounced like *p*. **Urbs** is therefore pronounced **"urps"**; **obtineō, "optineō."**

c always has the English hard *c*- (*k*-)sound (as in *can*), never the English soft *c*- (*s*-)sound (as in *cider*).

g always has the English hard *g*-sound (as in *gun*), never the English soft *g*- (*j*-)sound (as in *gem*).

j is always pronounced like *y* in *yolk*.

qu is pronounced like *kw*.

s is always pronounced with a sharp hissing sound (as in *sun*), never with the *z*-sound (as in *ties*).

t always has the sound of *t* in *ten*, never the sound of *t* in *nation*.

v is always pronounced like *w* in *way*.

ph, th, and **ch** were probably pronounced like *p, t, k*, respectively, followed by an aspirate, or "breathing," *h*. For convenience, we may pronounce **ph** like *f*, **th** like *t*, and **ch** like the German *ch*.

Diphthongs. The diphthongs are pronounced as follows:

ae as *ie* in *pie*
au as *ou* in *house*
ei as *ei* in *eight*
eu as *e* (short) plus *oo*, pronounced in rapid succession
oe as *oi* in *oil*

Note: In later Latin, **ae** and **oe** came to be spelled and pronounced ē.

Accent. Words of two syllables are always accented on the first syllable. Words of more than two syllables are accented on the penult (last syllable but one) if it contains a long vowel or a diphthong—for example, **a-rḗ-na, in-caú-tus**—or if it is followed by two or more consonants or by **x**—for example, **per-féc-tus, dē-fléx-us;** otherwise they are accented on the antepenult (the third syllable, counting from the end)—for example, **ex-ér-ci-tus, sen-tén-ti-a, for-tís-si-mus.**

Anglicized Pronunciation of Latin Phrases, etc. The numerous Latin phrases and words that have been borrowed without change and made part of English are not pronounced in the fashion described above. These, as well as Latin proper names when used in English contexts, are pronounced as follows:

VOWELS—In general the long and short vowels are pronounced like the corresponding English long and short vowels.

CONSONANTS—In general the consonants are pronounced like their English counterparts. Note carefully that *c* and *g* are soft before *e*, *i*, *ae*, *oe* and *y*, otherwise hard (for example, *Caesar* and *genius*, but *Cornelius* and *Gustavus*). This rule applies to almost all derivatives from Latin and Greek.

DIPHTHONGS—*ae* and *oe* are pronounced like the *ee* of *beet*, *au* as in *caught*, *eu* as in *Teuton*.

ACCENT—Same as in Classical Latin.

CHAPTER TWO

Latin Nouns and Adjectives

WHEN a word is borrowed by one language from another, its form, its meaning, or both form and meaning, may be changed. In the lessons which follow, the principal rules applying to the changes of *form* that take place when Latin and Greek words are borrowed by English will be given. We are able to formulate such rules because these changes are fairly precise.

Changes in *meaning*, however, present a more difficult problem. Semantics—the name given to the branch of learning that has to do with the study of meanings and the shifts in meaning of words—is not an exact science; it can provide only a few all-embracing principles.

We shall, then, in the case of a given word, study its form and meaning in Latin, the changes in form that took place when the word was borrowed by English, and the meanings that English has given to it. The changes in form will be studied under general principles, but the changes in meaning —semantic changes, as they are called—will, in general, have to be studied individually for each word. What general principles there are which can help us to understand shifts in the meanings of words will be considered at appropriate points.

The material for our etymological study has been arranged by parts of speech. We shall first treat Latin nouns and adjectives that have been borrowed by English without other elements attached, and then the prefixes and suffixes that can

15

go with nouns and adjectives. The same procedure will be followed with verbs.

There are two grammatical points which must be understood if the succeeding material is to be completely mastered. The first of these, the declension of Latin nouns, is not entirely unfamiliar to you, since we also have declension of nouns in English. You will recall that *he* is declined

	SINGULAR	PLURAL
NOMINATIVE CASE:	*he*	*they*
POSSESSIVE CASE:	*his*	*their*
OBJECTIVE CASE:	*him*	*them*

while *boy* is declined

NOMINATIVE CASE:	*boy*	*boys*
POSSESSIVE CASE:	*boy's*	*boys'*
OBJECTIVE CASE:	*boy*	*boys*

Thus we see that in English not only are nouns declined (that is, they change their forms to adapt themselves for use in sentences), but that there are different types of declension. The same is true of Latin nouns. There are five different types of declension in Latin, named, simply, First Declension, Second Declension, and so on. Unlike English, which has only three cases, Latin has six. Of these, two, the nominative and the genitive (corresponding to the English possessive), are all-important for our study of word-derivation and will be dealt with at length. The four other cases, the dative, accusative, ablative, and vocative, are of less importance, and will receive mention only when the occasion demands.

Another grammatical consideration is that of gender. In English, nouns referring to males are "masculine," those referring to females are "feminine," and those referring to things without life are "neuter," that is, they have no gender, or have what is sometimes called "natural gender." In Latin, however, as in the Romance languages, many nouns which refer to things without life and which in English would be neuter are grammatically masculine or feminine; they have what is sometimes called "grammatical gender."

LESSON 1

First-Declension Nouns

Three forms of the Latin noun are important for us in our study of Latin derivatives: (1) the nominative case singular, since it is the form under which Latin nouns are listed in dictionaries; (2) the nominative plural, because the plural forms of some Latin nouns appear in English unchanged; (3) the base, since it contains the fundamental meaning of the English derivative and to it prefixes and suffixes may be attached to modify this meaning.

For Latin First-Declension nouns, almost all of which are feminine, these three forms are

	EXAMPLE
NOMINATIVE SINGULAR: ends in **-a**	**antenna** 'sailyard'
BASE: formed by dropping **-a**	**antenn-**
NOMINATIVE PLURAL: base + **-ae**	**antennae** 'sailyards'

When Latin First-Declension nouns enter English, the singular form, in many cases, remains unchanged, whereas the plural is anglicized. For instance,

LATIN NOUN	ENGLISH LOAN WORD
SING.: **arēna** 'sand,' 'sandy place'	*arena*
PLURAL: **arēnae**	*arenas*

Occasionally, however, particularly in scientific terms, both singular and plural forms appear in English unchanged. So,

LATIN NOUN	ENGLISH LOAN WORD
SING.: **nebula** 'mist,' 'cloud'	*nebula*
PLURAL: **nebulae**	*nebulae*

The endings **-a** and **-ae,** however, are not congenial to English. Accordingly most Latin First-Declension nouns appear in English with their endings anglicized: the Latin ending has either dropped off to permit a consonant to end the word, or has been replaced by silent *-e*.

LATIN NOUN	ENGLISH LOAN WORD
matrōna 'married woman'	*matron*
figūra 'shape'	*figure*

Other, somewhat less important, changes may also take place. For example, the un-English **-pp** left when the **-a** of the noun **mappa** was dropped has been reduced to *-p*, to give *map*. Under French influence Latin nouns ending in **-ia** appear in English with this ending replaced by *-y*, as **furia,** which becomes *fury*. Nouns ending in **-tia** have this ending replaced by *-ce*, also under French influence, as **grātia,** which becomes *grace*.

This lesson contains only a few of the Latin First-Declension nouns borrowed by English. A complete list would include such rare or scientific words as *alga, cicada, curia*, which are somewhat outside our field. Furthermore there are many compound words that contain the bases of First-Declension nouns; compound words, however, we are reserving for consideration in later lessons. Still others—*aura* and *mania*, for example—were borrowed by Latin from Greek; accordingly, they will be discussed in Part Two.

ETYMOLOGICAL NOTES

How words change in meaning is a fascinating subject. The color of a cardinal's robes, the fact that Roman soldiers were at one time paid in salt, the bad grammar of a Greek city—such queer and diverse matters are responsible for the

meanings of our words today.   In order to give you a taste of
this romantic side of word-study, we propose at this point in
each lesson to pick out some of the more colorful etymologies
and describe them for you.

Take, for example, the word **camera,** which has given us
the English words *chamber, camera,* and *comrade.*   When you
know that its meaning in late Latin is 'room,' you easily see
how the meaning of each derivative arose.   The essential part
of a *camera* is the little dark room where the film is kept.   As
a matter of fact, the earliest photographic apparatus was
called *camera obscura* 'dark room.'   A *comrade* is, etymologically, a 'roommate.'   The Germans have their own derivative
Kamerad, made familiar to us in World War I through its
use as an appeal for quarter by German soldiers.   The word
means 'friend,' 'comrade.'

Or take **cappa** 'cloak with a hood.'   It has given us *cap,
cape, cope,* and *chaplet,* which are immediately understandable,
since they all have something to do with a body or head covering.   Even the meaning of *chaperon,* which also comes ultimately from **cappa,** is easy to trace.   *Chaperon* originally
meant 'large hat,' suggesting that such hats were a distinguishing mark of older ladies who accompanied young women in
public for the sake of appearance.   But **cappa** has two other
derivatives which, at first blush, seem to have strayed far
from its original meaning of 'head covering' or 'body covering,' namely, *chapel* and *chaplain.*   The explanation of how
their current meanings arose lies in a tale told about St. Martin
of Tours, who lived in the fourth century A.D.   The story
runs that one night while serving on military duty, St. Martin
shared his cloak (**capella**) with a beggar.   On the following
night he had a vision in which Christ informed His angels of
this act of mercy.   Because of this, the cloak became a sacred
relic and was placed in a holy sanctuary.   It wasn't long before the sanctuary, which was merely the place that housed
the cloak, was also called **capella,** and so we have the word
chapel today.   The guardians of the sanctuary of the cloak,
the **capellānī** 'cloak-men,' have become our *chaplains.*

EXERCISES

1. Memorize the following Latin nouns with their meanings. Indicate the base of each. Following the principles set forth in this lesson, find for each an English derivative. Where necessary, determine from the dictionary the current meaning of the derivative.

camera 'room'	**nota** 'mark'
causa 'motive'	**opera** 'work'
cūra 'care'	**persōna** 'mask,' 'role,'
fōrma 'shape'	'character'
līnea 'linen thread,' 'string'	**via** 'way,' 'road'

2. Using the General Vocabulary (pp. 157–72), find the Latin noun and its meaning from which each of the following is derived. Where necessary, determine from the dictionary the current meaning: *alumna, facetiae, fortune, lacuna, norm, scintilla, vertebra.*

3. Form plurals of the nouns listed in Question 2. Can you formulate a rule to guide you in deciding when to use the plural ending *-ae*? The pluralization of *antenna* offers the clue.

4. Using the General Vocabulary, find the Latin noun and its meaning from which each italicized word in the following sentences and expressions is derived. With the aid of the dictionary determine the meaning of each in the context.

A (a) One hundred lions in the *arena*, matched against Numidian archers; (b) The *arena* on which modern philosophy has won all her victories; (c) A large *arena* for the employment of an increasing capital.

B The statement had all the authority of a papal *bull*.

C To spread suspicion, to invent *calumnies*, to propagate scandal, requires neither labor nor courage.

—JOHNSON

D ANTONY. What's his strength
By land?

CAESAR.   Great and increasing; but by sea
He is an absolute master.

ANTONY.   So is the *fame*.—SHAKESPEARE

E   (a) Directing his telescope toward *nebulae* and clus-
ters of stars; (b) His future was only a chaotic *nebula*.

F   (a) *Penury* with love, I will not doubt it,
Is better far than palaces without it.

—W. M. PRAED

(b) I labored under a peculiar embarrassment and
penury of words.

G   (a) *Vsurie* is a gayne of any thing aboue the principal, or that which was lent, exacted onely in consideration of the loan, whether it be corne, meat, . . . or such
like, as money.—TERMES LAWS

(b) The criminality of *usury* . . . [consists] in exact-
ing more than the usual rate of the market.—FARMER'S
MAGAZINE

(c) I would have paid her kiss for kiss,
With *usury* thereto.—TENNYSON

5. Give the doublets of *bill, chamber, crown, forge, lagoon,
parson, stencil, tinsel.*

LESSON 2

Second-Declension Nouns

The Second Declension includes masculine and neuter nouns.
Since these differ in the nominative singular and in other cases,
we must take them up separately.

Second-Declension Masculine Nouns.   Most of these end in
-us in the nominative singular.   The base is found by dropping this ending.   The nominative plural is formed by adding
-ī to the base.

NOMINATIVE SINGULAR	BASE	NOMINATIVE PLURAL
alumnus 'foster son'	**alumn-**	**alumnī** 'foster sons'

A few masculines of the Second Declension end in **-er** or **-ir** in the nominative singular. To determine the base of such nouns, another case-form, the singular of the genitive (corresponding in sense to the English possessive case) must be known; accordingly, in this book it will always be given along with the nominative. The genitive ends in **-ī,** and the base is found by dropping this ending.

NOMINATIVE SINGULAR	GENITIVE SINGULAR	BASE	NOMINATIVE PLURAL
minister 'servant'	**ministrī**	**ministr-**	**ministrī** 'servants'

Second-Declension Neuter Nouns. These end in **-um** in the nominative singular. The base is found by dropping this ending. The nominative plural is formed by adding **-a** to the base.

NOMINATIVE SINGULAR	BASE	NOMINATIVE PLURAL
cerebrum 'brain'	**cerebr-**	**cerebra** 'brains'

Second-Declension Nouns in English. Nouns of this declension, like those of the First Declension, appear in English with their endings unchanged, or anglicized; that is, the Latin ending either drops off, or is replaced by silent *-e.*

ENDING	LATIN NOUN	ENGLISH LOAN WORD
UNCHANGED:	**alumnus** 'foster son'	*alumnus*
	minister 'servant'	*minister*
	cerebrum 'brain'	*cerebrum*
ENDING DROPPED:	**digitus** 'finger,' 'toe'	*digit*
	pulpitum 'scaffold,' 'stage'	*pulpit*
ENDING REPLACED BY SILENT *-e*:	**nervus** 'sinew,' 'tendon'	*nerve*
	fīlum 'thread'	*file*

As in the case of First-Declension nouns, certain other changes in the endings may take place. The neuter ending **-ium** may be replaced by *-y*, as in **lilium,** which becomes *lily.* The endings **-tium** and **-cium** may be replaced, under French influence, by *-ce*, as in **spatium,** which becomes *space.*

The Art of Definition. In every lesson in this book, you will be asked to define words. This is not always easy to do with accuracy. Students often say, "I know what the word means, but I can't express it." "An antenna is, well—like a radio antenna." "Facetiae is when someone tries to be funny."

Caution on two points will help you in expressing the meaning of troublesome words. First, in defining a *noun*, be careful to give the meaning of the word *as a noun*; in defining a verb, be careful to give the meaning of the word *as a verb*; and so on. For example, *usury*, a noun, means, not 'to charge exorbitant interest,' but 'exorbitant interest'; *oscillate*, a verb, means not 'something which sways to and fro,' but 'to sway to and fro'; *timorous*, an adjective, means, not 'someone who is afraid,' but 'full of fear.'

In the second place be sure to include in your definition that which peculiarly distinguishes the word you are defining. It is insufficient, for example, to call a *chair* 'something to sit on.' The same definition applies also to a bench, a throne, a stool, a sofa. *Chair* must be so defined as to be distinguished from all these others.

The Figurative Use of Words. In the Introduction to Chapter Two (see page 15) we mentioned that, although shifts in meaning for the most part are so varied as to necessitate individual study for each word, there are a few general principles that can be pointed out. One of the most important is the development by words of a figurative meaning which, in some cases, supplants the literal meaning.

When we use a word in a sense different from, but suggested by, the literal sense, we say that the word is used figuratively. When we say, "The farmers are threshing wheat," we are using *thresh* in its literal sense, 'to beat grain in order to separate it from the chaff.' But when we say, "We are threshing out an argument," we are using the word figuratively in a metaphor. What we are implying is, "We are going over an argument again and again searching for truth, like farmers when they separate the wheat from the chaff by threshing."

Thousands of words have by metaphorical use developed, like *thresh*, a figurative meaning alongside the literal. We speak of a 'prizefight *arena*' (literal), or of the '*arena* of politics' (figurative); of a 'king's *crown*' (literal), or a '*crown* of glory' (figurative); of 'writing on *paper*' (literal), or of '*paper*-thin slices' (figurative); and so on.

In the examples just cited both the literal and the figurative meaning have been preserved in current use. There are thousands of other cases in which a literal meaning, after producing a figurative meaning, has died out and only the figurative meaning is currently to be found. The Latin noun **radius,** for example, meant originally 'spoke of a wheel.' When we speak today of "the *radius* of a circle" we are using a metaphor. What we are saying is, "the line that extends from the center of a circle to the circumference like the spoke of a wheel." We use the word figuratively, the only way it may be used in current English. A **stimulus** in Latin was originally 'a whip.' Today *stimulus* is used only figuratively, of anything that, as it were, "whips you on." *Cancer* preserves its literal meaning only as the name of the sign of the zodiac, the 'Crab.' As the name of a disease it means a 'crablike' growth that crawls over and eats away the body.

In the case of *radius* and *stimulus* and hundreds of other words, the driving out of the literal meaning by the figurative took place so long ago that most of us do not realize that the current meaning is really figurative. We become aware of it only when we delve into the etymology, when we see that the first meaning of *radius* was 'spoke of a wheel,' that that of *stimulus* was 'a whip.' There are very many everyday words in English whose current meaning, on etymological study, is revealed to be the result of highly poetic and picturesque figurative usage.

ETYMOLOGICAL NOTES

Colorful derivatives from Second-Declension nouns are so numerous that all we can do is offer you a few examples. There is *rostrum*, the present meaning of which, 'speaker's platform,' seems to have little to do with its original Latin meaning of 'bird's beak.' The relationship becomes clear, however, when we learn that the Romans used to adorn the speaker's platform in the Forum at Rome with prows of captured enemy warships which, because of their resemblance to a bird's beak, were called **rostra.** The word *dominoes* suggests some connection with **dominus** 'master.' Canons or 'masters' of a church wore a black garment called a *domino*. The game *dominoes* may have been given its name from the fact that the "pieces" are black, like the church garment. **Dominus,** incidentally, has also given us the words *dominie*, used by the Scotch for a 'schoolmaster' and colloquially by us for 'minister,' and *don*, the title of a Spanish nobleman, while **domina** 'mistress,' a feminine form, is the source of *dame*, and *duenna* 'elderly chaperon.'

Plumbum 'lead' is responsible for an interesting group of words. A direct derivative of it is *plumb*, a lead weight which builders and surveyors attach to a line and use to indicate a vertical direction. An object which stands perfectly vertical is said, in French, to be *à plomb* 'according to plumb'; and so we say that a person who maintains his self-possession and poise in difficult situations has *aplomb*. One who works with lead, especially with lead pipes, is a *plumber*. When the leadsman on a ship wants to test the depth of the water in which his ship is traveling, he *plunges* (etymologically 'heaves the lead') a weight over the side which sinks like a *plummet* (etymologically 'little lead weight').

Here are some words of everyday speech that are derived from Second-Declension nouns. *Master* comes from **magister** 'leader.' When used before a proper name, the tendency was to slur its pronunciation in order to place the emphasis on the proper name. Because of this tendency, the form *Mister* arose. A French derivative, **maistresse,** has given us *mis-*

tress, of which *Miss* is merely a contracted form. The triplets *price*, *prize*, and *praise* come from **pretium** 'price.' Even *annoy* has concealed in it a Latin noun of the Second Declension. It comes from the phrase **in odiō** 'in hatred,' 'hateful,' in which **odiō** is the ablative case (see p. 16) of **odium** 'hatred.' The Latin phrase was, as a matter of fact, borrowed twice, once through Old French and once through modern French. The first borrowing gave us *annoy* 'be hateful to,' and the second, *ennui* 'mental weariness caused by something that has become hateful.' *Ennui* is a doublet, therefore, of *annoy*.

The meanings of *genius* deserve a note. Beside its commoner meanings of 'extraordinary power of invention,' 'peculiar nature,' 'peculiar bent,' *genius* is used, as it frequently was in Latin literature, as the name given to a kindly protecting spirit who is assigned to a given man from birth and who watches over him during his lifetime. This usage helps to explain the sense of the doublet *genie*, familiar to all readers of *The Arabian Nights*. Incidentally the plural form of *genie*, and of *genius* in the special sense described above, is *genii*; when *genius* is employed in its commoner meanings, it is pluralized in the English fashion, *geniuses*.

EXERCISES

1. Memorize the following Latin nouns with their meanings. Indicate the base of each. Following the principles set forth in this lesson, find for each an English derivative. Where necessary, determine from the dictionary the current meaning of the derivative.

animus 'mind,' 'feeling'
arma (nom. plu.) 'arms'
circus 'ring'
locus 'p'ace'
modus 'measure,' 'manner'
nuncius 'messenger'

pretium 'worth,' 'value'
radius 'staff,' 'rod,' 'spoke oî a wheel'
sīgnum 'mark,' 'token'
terminus 'boundary'
verbum 'word'

2. Using the General Vocabulary (pp. 157–72), find the Latin noun and its meaning from which each of the following words is derived. Where necessary, determine from the dictionary the current meaning: *amulet, arbiter, lucre, palace, raceme, tedium, virus.* Form the plural of *focus* and *stimulus.* What is the meaning of the expression *taedium vitae?*

3. Using the General Vocabulary, find the Latin noun with its meaning from which each italicized word in the following sentences and expressions is derived. With the aid of the dictionary, determine the meaning of each in the context.

A (a) The Lever is an inflexible rod, moveable upon a point which is called the *fulcrum* or center of motion.— JOHN WOOD (b) The consulship was the *fulcrum* from which the whole Roman world was to be moved.

—MERIVALE

B (a) A tradition of two *Genii* which attend every man, one good, the other evill.—SAMUEL PURCHAS (b) By the wonderful force of *genius* only, without the least assistance of learning.—FIELDING

(c) My better *genius*, thou art welcome as
A draught of water to a thirsty man.

C The piece . . . ran for eleven nights before descending into the *limbo* of oblivion.—JOSEPH KNIGHT

D (a) There is the young lady herself, encompassed with a *nimbus* of petticoat.—GEORGE SALA (b) A *nimbus* of golden hair about his forehead; (c) The *nimbus*, one of the least beautiful clouds.

E On him had fallen the *odium* of the proscription and the stain of the massacres.—FROUDE

4. Determine which of the italicized words come from Latin. Then, for each of these, give the Latin form with its meaning: 'single *file*,' 'nail *file*'; 'fencing with a light *foil*,' 'wrapped in tin *foil*'; 'the *limb* of her garment,' 'amputate a *limb*'; 'subjunctive *mood*,' 'angry *mood*.'

5. Give the doublets of *campus, canker, folio, genie, limbo, raisin, ray, term.*

6. What is the meaning of the expression *sock and buskin?*

7. Determine the meaning of **focus** in Latin. Show how its use today illustrates the change from literal to figurative.

LESSON 3

Adjectives of the First and Second Declensions

All Latin adjectives fall into two groups: First- and Second-Declension adjectives, and Third-Declension adjectives. We shall reserve the study of the second group for the next lesson.

Latin adjectives behave like those of the Romance languages: that is, by changing their endings they accommodate themselves to the gender of the nouns they modify. Accordingly they have, in general, three forms: one to modify masculine nouns, one for feminine nouns, and a third for neuter nouns.

Adjectives of the First and Second Declensions are so named because they utilize the endings of these two declensions. When modifying masculine nouns, they have the same endings as masculine nouns of the Second Declension (nominative singular **-us, -er**; plural, **-ī**); when modifying feminines, they have the same endings as First-Declension nouns (nominative singular **-a**; plural, **-ae**); and when modifying neuters, they have the endings of neuter nouns of the Second Declension (nominative singular, **-um**; plural, **-a**). For convenience we shall give only the masculine singular form of adjectives. The base of First- and Second-Declension adjectives, like the base of masculine nouns of the Second Declension, may usually be found by dropping the ending **-us**. When the nominative singular does not reveal the base, the genitive singular will also be given (for example, **miser** 'wretched'; genitive singular, **miserī**; base **miser-**).

	MASCULINE	FEMININE	NEUTER
NOMINATIVE SINGULAR:	**bonus** 'good'	**bona**	**bonum**
NOMINATIVE PLURAL:	**bonī**	**bonae**	**bona**
BASE:	**bon-**		

A relatively small number of First- and Second-Declension adjectives have been borrowed without change. Of these, very few have been borrowed in the masculine or feminine form; the great majority came over in the neuter form. Further, all of them have been borrowed as nouns. In English, adjectives are frequently used as nouns: a man is 'a Red'; the ocean may be called 'the deep'; and so on. The same is true of Latin, especially of the neuter form: for example, **albus** 'white,' **album** 'a white thing.' Keep this fact well in mind since the use of Latin adjectives as nouns, especially in the neuter form, will recur constantly in subsequent lessons.

LATIN ADJECTIVE	ENGLISH LOAN WORD
miser 'wretched'; as noun, 'wretched person'	*miser*
noster 'our'; as noun, **nostrum** 'our thing'	*nostrum*

Most of the adjectives of the First and Second Declension that appear in English have been anglicized in form. The anglicization consists, as before, either of dropping the ending or of replacing it by silent -*e*.

LATIN ADJECTIVE	ENGLISH LOAN WORD
crispus 'quivering,' 'curly'	*crisp*
amplus 'spacious'	*ample*

Etymological Notes

When words pass from Latin into the Romance languages and from there into English, changes in form and in meaning often take place which quite conceal the Latin origin. There are some excellent examples among the derivatives of First- and Second-Declension adjectives.

Take **bellus** 'fair,' for example. The feminine **bella** has given us *belle*, which is an obvious derivation; but it is not so obvious that *beau* comes from the masculine **bellus.** Both *belle* and *beau* came through French. French, too, is responsible for the form of *beldam* 'hag,' which comes from **bella domina** 'fair lady.' The meaning is the result of irony; compare the modern use of the nickname 'Tiny' for a two-hundred-pounder. *Belladonna* 'the deadly nightshade' is a doublet of *beldam*, through Italian. *Belladonna* is part of the 'fair lady's' cosmetic kit; women at one time commonly used the drug to dilate the pupils of the eyes in the belief that this enhanced their attractiveness. The drug is still occasionally so used. We may add at this point two other derivatives through Italian, *Madonna*, which is simply **mea domina** 'my lady,' and *prima donna*, which is **prīma domina** 'first lady.'

Or take **altus** 'high,' 'deep.' The musical terms *alto* 'the part sung by the lowest female voices' and *alt* 'high in pitch,' come immediately to mind. In French, *altus* was transformed into *haut,* and it's an easy step from *haut* to *haughty*. And there's *hautboy*, the high-pitched woodwind instrument, which is more familiar to us under the Italian form *oboe*. The two words are doublets; the first syllable in each goes back to **altus.**

Fīrmus means 'fixed,' and the land acquired by a 'fixed payment' of rent is a *farm*. French is responsible for the change in form. **Plānus** means 'flat,' 'level,' 'smooth,' and a *plain* (through French) is 'flat,' while music played *piano* (through Italian) is 'smooth.' **Sōlus** means 'alone,' and a song that is sung alone is a *solo* (through Italian).

Here is a derivative that came through Spanish: *salver*, which today means a flat tray for carrying dishes or for presenting letters or cards. This current meaning reflects not a trace of the fact that the word ultimately comes from the Latin **salvus** 'safe.' It is common knowledge that in days gone by, because of the fear of poisoning, the custom existed in noble households of having all food and drink tasted before being served to make sure that they were 'safe.' This tasting was called *salva* in Spanish, and originally a *salver* was the tray that was used in the process.

EXERCISES

1. Memorize the following Latin adjectives with their meanings. Indicate the feminine and neuter forms and the base of each. Following the principles set forth in this lesson, find for each an English derivative. Where necessary, determine from the dictionary the current meaning of the derivative.

curvus 'bent'
fīrmus 'steadfast,' 'fixed'
medius 'middle'
plānus 'flat'

sacer, sacrī 'sacred'
sānus 'sound,' 'healthy,' 'rational'
sōlus 'alone,' 'single'

2. Using the General Vocabulary, find the Latin adjective and its meaning from which each of the following is derived. Where necessary, determine from the dictionary the current meaning: *brute, curt, dire, gelid, null, prone, robust.*

3. Using the General Vocabulary, find the Latin word and its meaning from which each italicized word in the following sentences and expressions is derived. Determine the meaning of each in the context.

A From the heights of his *august* fame and his more than seventy years, Pindar preaches to this young fire-eater moderation and quiet.

B *Crass* minds . . . whose reflective scales could only weigh things in the lump.—GEORGE ELIOT

C So are those *crisped* snaky golden locks
Which make such wanton gambols with the wind.
—SHAKESPEARE

D If by prude be meant a secretly vicious person who affects an excessive *decorum*, by all means let the prude disappear, even at the cost of shamelessness.

E Mark . . . read through the sermon once more. It seemed more *jejune* than ever.—COMPTON MACKENZIE

F There followed no Carbuncle, nor purple or *livide* Spots.—BACON

G (a) The *lurid*, stormy eloquence of Edmund Burke.

—ROBERT DALE (b) The *lurid* reflection of immense fires hung in the sky.—IRVING

H The translators . . . have happily preserved for us the *pristine* simplicity of our Saxon-English.—ISAAC D'ISRAELI

I Lo, Mephistophilis, for love of thee,
I cut mine arm, and with my *proper* blood
Assure my soul to be great Lucifer's.—MARLOWE

J In those days, every morning paper kept an author who was bound to furnish a daily *quantum* of witty paragraphs.—LAMB

K And this the cranny is, right and *sinister*,
Through which the fearful lovers are to whisper.
—SHAKESPEARE

L (a) Now the Liquors, in which these are generated, do always . . . lose their Tast and Smell, and so become *Vapid.*—NEHEMIAH GREW (b) The news of the morning become stale and *vapid* by the dinner-hour.—HAZLITT

4. The following are Latin phrases which have been taken over by English. Using the General Vocabulary, find the meaning of each in Latin. With the aid of the dictionary, determine the pronunciation and meaning of each in English.

lingua franca—Used as a noun in English: (a) " 'What do you want?'—he asked in *lingua franca*, that undefined mixture of Italian, French, Greek, and Spanish, which is spoken throughout the Mediterranean."—FREDERICK BURNABY (b) "But these same authors were also familiar with Latin, which, though called a dead language, has always been the professional dialect of ecclesiastics and a *lingua franca* for educated men."—GREENOUGH AND KITTREDGE

persōna grāta—Used as a noun in English.

terra fīrma—Used as a noun in English.

tōtō caelō—Ablative case and to be translated using 'by.' Used in English only with the verb 'to differ,' as an adverb: "The dome [of the Pantheon] . . . differs *toto caelo* from the normal mode of construction."—SIR G. G. SCOTT

5. Give the doublets of *curb, entire, grease, round.*

6. Using the General Vocabulary, determine the meaning of the Christian names *Alma, Augusta, Clare, Paula.*

7. Give two expressions that will illustrate respectively the literal and the figurative use of *supine.*

LESSON 4

Nouns and Adjectives of the Third Declension

Third-Declension Nouns. These, unlike nouns of the First and Second Declensions, have a variety of endings in the nominative singular. The genitive, however, ends consistently in **-is,** and the base may always be found by dropping this ending. The genitive will, therefore, be given (except where it is identical with the nominative) and should be memorized along with the nominative.

Again, unlike the First and Second Declensions, the Third Declension includes nouns of all three genders. The nominative plural of masculine and feminine nouns ends in **-ēs,** that of neuters in **-a.** Neuter nouns will be indicated by the symbol "n." All not so marked are masculines or feminines.

NOMINATIVE SINGULAR	GENITIVE SINGULAR	BASE	NOMINATIVE PLURAL
crux 'gallows,' 'cross'	crucis	cruc-	crucēs 'crosses'
ars 'skill'	artis	art-	artēs 'skills'
genus (n) 'race,' 'kind'	generis	gener-	genera 'races,' 'kinds'
sermō 'discourse'	sermōnis	sermōn-	sermōnēs 'discourses'
ōmen (n) 'foreboding,' 'sign'	ōminis	ōmin-	ōmina 'forebodings,' 'signs'

A few Third-Declension nouns have alternative bases, one found, in the usual way, by dropping the ending -is of the genitive singular; the other, by dropping merely the -s.

NOMINATIVE SINGULAR	GENITIVE SINGULAR	BASE	NOMINATIVE PLURAL
fīnis 'end'	fīnis	fīn- (as in *fin-al*) fīni- (as in *fini-al*)	fīnēs 'ends'

Third-Declension Adjectives. Third-Declension adjectives often have different endings for modifying masculine, feminine, and neuter nouns. However, since the feminine and neuter forms are relatively unimportant so far as English loan words are concerned, we shall limit our study to the masculine form only.

Many Third-Declension adjectives end in -is; the base may be found either by dropping this ending, or by dropping simply the -s (for example, **gravis** 'heavy,' base **grav-** or **gravi-**). Where the nominative singular does not end in -is, the genitive singular will also be given. The base may be found by dropping the -is or the -s of the genitive (for example, **atrōx** 'cruel,' genitive **atrōcis,** base **atrōc-** or **atrōci-**).

Third-Declension Nouns and Adjectives in English. The nominative frequently appears in English without change:

LATIN NOUN OR ADJECTIVE	ENGLISH LOAN WORD
lēns, lentis 'lentil'	*lens*
pauper 'poor'	*pauper*

More often the nominative or the genitive is anglicized in the usual fashion:

LATIN NOUN OR ADJECTIVE	ENGLISH LOAN WORD
imāgō, imāginis 'likeness'	*image*
orīgō, orīginis 'beginning'	*origin*
grandis 'full-grown,' 'great'	*grand*
satelles, satellitis 'attendant,' 'follower'	*satellite*
rudis 'unwrought,' 'uncouth'	*rude*

Specialization and Generalization of Meaning. Two of the most common types of semantic change are *specialization of meaning* and *generalization of meaning.* Specialization is the change from a general to a specific meaning. For example, in Latin, **minister** usually refers to 'a servant of any sort'; in English, however, *minister* usually denotes only 'a servant of the State or Church.' Again, the Latin adjective **sānus** means 'sound,' whether in mind or body, while *sane* in English is limited to mental health. **Albus,** as we have seen, means 'white,' and **album** was originally any 'white thing.' **Fābula,** to a Roman, meant any kind of 'tale'; in English a *fable* is a 'fictitious tale.'

The reverse of this process—the change from a specific to a general meaning—is called *generalization.* For example, **poena** in Latin means 'fine,' 'penalty'; but *pain*, its derivative through French, embraces all kinds of suffering, whether caused by a penalty or not. **Injūria** in Latin originally meant 'injustice'; today, however, 'injustice' is merely one form of *injury.*

A word frequently undergoes both processes in the development of its various meanings. Thus the Latin noun **arēna,** meaning 'sand' primarily, was first specialized to mean 'a sand-strewn place of combat' and then generalized to mean 'any place of combat,' whether strewn with sand or not.

ETYMOLOGICAL NOTES

Cross, crisscross, and *cruise* belong to the class of words treated in this lesson, since they all come ultimately from **crux.** *Cross* preserves the original Latin meaning. *Crisscross* is partly a development of *Christ's cross* and partly a reduplication of *cross* (reduplication is not uncommon: compare such words as *knickknack, gewgaw, bonbon, murmur*). When you *cruise* you tend to zigzag and 'cross' your own course. *Gender* and *genre* belong here, too, since they are doublets from **genus** 'kind,' 'sort.' *Gender* refers to such 'kinds' of grammatical classification as masculine, feminine, and neuter, while *genre* is a 'kind' of painting. The doublets *corpse* and *corps* come from **corpus** 'body.' A *corpse* is a 'dead body'; a *corps*, a 'body' of men.

Several titles of nobility stem ultimately from Third-Declension nouns. Thus *prince* comes from **prīnceps** 'first man,' the official title of the early Roman emperors; *duke*, from **dux, ducis** 'leader.' **Dux** has also yielded *doge*, the chief magistrate in the former republics of Venice and Genoa, and *duce*, a comparatively recent borrowing. *Count* is derived from **comes, comitis** 'companion.' **Comes stabulī** 'count of the stable,' 'equerry,' later used as a high military title, has come into English, through Old French, as *constable*. *Czar*, *Tsar*, and *Kaiser* are merely corruptions of **Caesar.** The Latin noun **rēx** 'king' has been borrowed as the given names *Rex* and *Roy*.

A number of derivatives which came into English through French have strayed far from their original Latin form. *Brief* is from **brevis** 'short,' *grief* from **gravis** 'heavy.' *Poor* is the doublet of *pauper*. *Dandelion* means etymologically 'tooth of a lion.' It comes, through the French *dent de lion,* from **dēns, dentis** 'tooth,' **dē** 'of,' and **leō, leōnis** 'lion.' The flower is so called because of a fancied resemblance of the lobes of its leaves to the teeth of a lion. *Pavilion* comes from **pāpiliō, pāpiliōnis** 'butterfly.' There is a fancied resemblance underlying this shift of meaning also, this time between the flapping sides of a tent and the motion of a butterfly's wings.

Umpire has a curious history. It's a derivative of the Latin expression **nōn pār** 'not equal.' The Latin became *nomper* in Old French with the sense 'third man,' 'odd man' (in a group of equals). This became *nompere* in Middle English. Naturally, in conversation, the word was often used with the indefinite article, "a nompere." In rapid colloquial speech, the two words were often run together as "anompere," just as we today often hear "anapple" instead of "an apple" or "anelephant" instead of "an elephant." Then the word was incorrectly redivided. Its original form was forgotten, the *n*, actually the first letter of the word, was thought to be part of the indefinite article, and the redivision yielded *an ompere*,

which finally became *an umpire*.   There are other cases of
this misplacing of an initial *n*.   The original form of *apron*
in English was *naperon*; the word is closely related to *napery*
'table linen.'   Again, "an adder" was formerly "a nadder."
And, to give the reverse of the process, "a nickname" was
formerly "an ekename."   Incidentally, **pār** appears in disguised form in several other English derivatives.   It's the
source of *peer*, which retains the Latin meaning, while *pair*
comes from its neuter plural, **paria** 'equal things.'   **Pār** must
not be confused with **pars, partis,** a noun meaning 'portion.'
It is **pars** which is involved in the etymology of *part, partake,*
and similar words, as well as in that of *parse*, the grammatical
term meaning 'to resolve a sentence into its component parts
and to describe them.'   *Parse* comes from **pars** as used in the
Latin schoolroom question: **Quae pars ōrātiōnis (est)?**   "What
part of speech (is it)?"

EXERCISES

1. Memorize the following Latin words with their meaning.
Following the principles set forth in this lesson, find for each
an English derivative and, where necessary, determine its current meaning.

3 declension

ars, artis 'skill'
corpus, corporis (n) 'body'
crux, crucis 'cross'
fīnis 'end'
fortis 'strong'
genus, generis (n) 'race,'
   'kind,' 'sort'

grandis 'great'
gravis 'heavy'
labor, labōris 'work'
opus, operis (n) 'work'
pars, partis 'portion'
similis 'like' (neuter **simile**)
vestis 'garment'

2. Using the General Vocabulary, find the Latin word and
its meaning from which each of the following is derived.
Where necessary, determine the current meaning: *axis, client,
codex, inane, index, vertex.*

3. Using the General Vocabulary, find the Latin word and
its meaning from which each italicized word in the following

sentences and expressions is derived.   Determine the meaning of each in the context.

A   Oldtime vaudeville was a *farrago* of every sort of entertainment.

B   Is this the *fine* of his fines, and the recovery of his recoveries, to have his fine pate full of fine dirt?

—SHAKESPEARE

C   (a) A *host* of golden daffodils; (b) Our genial *host*, all smiles and politeness; (c) The solemn ceremony of the elevation of the *host*.

D   My uncle was prominent among the *lares* and *penates* worshipped in our own household.—SANTAYANA

E   If . . . the *onus* is to fall upon the British troops, their numbers must be doubled, or even trebled.— WELLINGTON

F   (a) *Vice*-President of the committee; (b) Gambling is a *vice*; (c) Gripped in the jaws of a *vise*.

G   It now devolved on her to act the part of a wife who played both the tyrant and *virago* at home.—JAMES GRANT

H   "Dissect them with scalpels," says Teufelsdröckh, "the same *viscera*, tissues, livers, lights, and other life-tackle, are there."—CARLYLE

I   The whirlwind of his eloquence nearly drew me into its *vortex*.—MME. D'ARBLAY

4. The following Latin phrases have been taken over by English.   Using the General Vocabulary, find the meaning of each in Latin.   With the aid of the dictionary, determine the pronunciation and meaning of each in English.

fool's fire   **ignis fatuus**—Used as a noun in English: "I knew that to paint, as I should have wished to paint, was an *ignis fatuus*."—SANTAYANA

magnum opus—Used as a noun in English: "My *magnum opus*, the 'Life of Dr. Johnson' . . . is to be published on Monday."—BOSWELL

rāra avis—Used as a noun in English: "A perfect day with us is somewhat of a *rara avis*."

suī generis—Used generally as a predicate adjective: "Among orchestra leaders, Toscanini is considered *sui generis.*"

5. Using the General Vocabulary, find the Latin word, with its meaning, from which each of the following is derived: *area, opera, opus, pulpit, sermon.* Compare the original Latin meaning with the current meaning. Which illustrate specialization and which generalization?

6. Determine the *mood, number, person, tense,* and *voice* of the verb *dissect* in sentence 3H and of *drew* in sentence 3I. What is the etymological meaning of each of these terms?

Lesson 5

Comparison of Adjectives.   The Fourth and Fifth Declensions.   Adverbs

Comparison of Adjectives.   Most English adjectives have three degrees of comparison: a positive, a comparative, and a superlative. The comparative is formed by attaching *-er,* and the superlative by attaching *-est,* to the positive. To form all the degrees of an adjective is to *compare* it. Thus *great* is compared as follows: positive, *great*; comparative, *greater*; superlative, *greatest.*

Similarly, Latin adjectives are compared by attaching certain endings to the base of the positive, the comparative by attaching **-ior,** the superlative by attaching **-issimus.** Whether the adjective in its positive degree belongs to the First and Second Declension or to the Third Declension, in the comparative degree it is declined according to the Third-Declension type and, in the superlative degree, according to the First- and Second-Declension type. Similarly, the comparative appears in English in the same ways as Third-Declension adjectives (see Lesson 4), and the superlative in the same ways as First- and Second-Declension adjectives (see Lesson 3).

	POSITIVE	COMPARATIVE	SUPERLATIVE
NOM. SING. MASC.:	excelsus 'high'	excelsior, Gen. **excelsiōris**	excelsissimus
BASE:	excels-	excelsiōr-	excelsissim-

In English such adjectives as *good* (comparative *better*, superlative *best*) or *bad* (comparative *worse*, superlative *worst*) are irregular. Latin has its share of such irregulars. The more important are:

POSITIVE	COMPARATIVE	SUPERLATIVE
bonus 'good'	**melior** 'better'	**optimus** 'best'
exterus 'outside'	**exterior** 'outer'	**extrēmus** 'outermost'
īnferus 'under'	**īnferior** 'lower'	**īnfimus** 'lowest'
magnus 'great'	**mājor** 'greater'	**māximus** 'greatest'
malus 'bad'	**pējor** 'worse'	**pessimus** 'worst'
multus 'much,' 'many'	**plūs**, Gen. **plūris** 'more'	**plūrimus** 'most'
parvus 'small'	**minor** 'smaller' Neuter: **minus**	**minimus** 'smallest'
posterus 'following'	**posterior** 'later'	**postumus** 'last'
superus 'upper'	**superior** 'higher'	**suprēmus, summus** 'highest'
———	**interior** 'inner'	**intimus** 'inmost'
———	**prior** 'former'	**prīmus** 'first'
———	**propior** 'nearer'	**proximus** 'nearest,' 'next'
———	**ulterior** 'farther'	**ultimus** 'farthest'

Nouns of the Fourth and Fifth Declensions. The nominative singular of Latin nouns of the Fourth Declension ends in **-us**. The base may be found by dropping this ending or, more commonly, by dropping merely the **-s**. In order to distinguish Fourth-Declension nouns from masculines of the Second Declension, which also end in **-us,** the base of the former will be given along with the nominative singular.

The nominative singular of Latin nouns of the Fifth Declension ends in **-ēs.** The base may be found by dropping this ending.

The few Fourth- and Fifth-Declension nouns that appear in English have been borrowed either without change, or anglicized by replacing the ending with silent *-e.*

LATIN NOUN	ENGLISH LOAN WORD
sinus (sinu-) 'bent surface,' 'curve'	*sinus*
speciēs 'appearance,' 'kind'	*species*
tribus (trib-) 'tribe'	*tribe*

Adverbs. A number of Latin adverbs appear in English without change in form. Although used only as adverbs in Latin, many of them have been borrowed as nouns or as adjectives.

LATIN ADVERB	ENGLISH LOAN WORD
alibī 'in another place'	*alibi*
grātīs 'without recompense'	*gratis*

Etymological Notes

The words for 'mister' in the Romance languages go back to a Latin comparative form. **Senex** 'old,' 'old man,' in the comparative is **senior.** This form is the source of **señor** in Spanish and **signor** in Italian. The French **monsieur** and **monseigneur** are simply **meus senior** 'my sir.' In English, **senior** became *sire,* which was later shortened to form the doublet *sir. Surly* is merely a combination of *sir* and the common native English suffix *-ly.* It was originally spelled *sirly* and meant 'masterful.'

Nonplus and *ne plus ultra* contain **plūs** 'more,' the comparative of **multus** 'much.' *Nonplus* comes from an old scholastic usage; you were *nonplussed* when you had 'no more' to say. *Ne plus ultra,* literally 'no more beyond' is even more picturesque. The 'Pillars of Hercules' is the name given by the ancients to two hills, one on either side of the Straits of Gibraltar. These marked the end of the Mediterranean; beyond lay the uncharted ocean on which few ancient mariners dared to sail. So, on these Pillars of Hercules, we are told, stood the inscription **nē plūs ultrā** '(let there) not (be) more (sailing) beyond.'

Dismal comes partly from a Fifth-Declension noun. It's the Latin **diēs malī** 'evil days,' which in its Old French form *dis mal* was applied to the two days of evil omen that in mediaeval times were believed to come around every month. The expression was later misunderstood and used, first as an adjective with the noun 'days' (*dismal* days), then with other nouns. *Sprightly*, despite its native English appearance, goes back to the Latin Fourth-Declension noun, **spīritus** 'breath.' **Spīritus** became *esprit* in Old French which English borrowed as *sprite*. *Sprightly* is simply *sprite* with the addition of our English suffix *-ly;* its spelling was probably changed under the influence of the numerous English words ending in *-ightly* (*nightly*, *lightly*, and so on). Later on English took **esprit** as well, in the phrase *esprit de corps* 'spirit of regard for the honor and interests of the group to which one belongs.'

Tandem, the Latin adverb meaning 'at length,'—that is, 'finally'—illustrates the deviousness of the ways in which words can enter English. Its borrowing was simply the result of a wisecrack. Some university student, obviously fresh from a Latin class, saw two horses hitched, one behind the other, and observed that they were harnessed **tandem** 'at length,' that is, 'one after the other.' The borrowing of *item* is more legitimate but no less interesting. **Item** in Latin is an adverb meaning 'also.' On a bill or inventory, the first entry was headed **imprīmīs** 'first,' and each succeeding entry was headed **item** 'also.' It was a simple step to refer to each entry as an *'item.'*

EXERCISES

1. (a) Form and translate the comparative and superlative of **fīrmus, fortis, grandis, gravis, longus, plānus.** Determine

the base of the comparative and superlative of each. Form
the feminine and neuter of the superlative of each.

(b) Determine the base of the comparative and superlative of the irregular adjectives listed in this lesson. Form the
feminine and neuter of the superlative of each.

(c) List all the English derivatives that have come from
the irregular adjectives listed in this lesson *according to the
principles you have studied so far*. Where necessary, determine the current meaning.

2. (a) Using the General Vocabulary, find the Latin word
and its meaning from which each of the following is derived.
Where necessary, determine the current meaning: *alias, arc,
circa, fortissimo, grade, quondam, rabies, series, sinus*.

(b) Compare the Latin meaning of *arc, rabies, sinus* with
the current meaning. What type of semantic change does
each illustrate?

3. Using the General Vocabulary, find the Latin word and
its meaning from which each italicized word in the following
sentences and expressions is derived. Determine the meaning of each in the context.

A   Though the upper part of Durnover was mainly composed of a curious *congeries* of barns and farmsteads,
there was a less picturesque side to the parish.—HARDY

B   (a) Set up an *interim* committee; (b) Arrange to
meet in the *interim*.

C   One puzzled over the Latin inscriptions on the grave-
stones of old theologians and presidents of the college,
. . . the graves of ancient scholars, with virtues ending
in *issimus*.—VAN WYCK BROOKS

D   I will take up the judge's interrogatories as I find
them printed in the Chicago *Times* and answer them
seriatim.

E   I shall give you my cousin's Letter *Verbatim*, without altering a syllable.—STEELE

4. The following Latin phrases have been taken over by
English. Using the General Vocabulary where necessary, find
the meaning of each in Latin. With the aid of the dictionary,
determine the pronunciation and current meaning of each.

ā fortiōrī—ā is a preposition meaning 'from' and fortiōrī is the ablative case of fortior, the comparative of fortis 'firm,' 'strong.' This phrase is used as an adverb and adjective in English to introduce a fact which, if one already accepted is true, must also, and still more obviously, be true. Thus, in the sentence which follows, the speaker is reasoning *a fortiori*: "Three men couldn't finish that job in three days. You can't expect me to do it alone in one." The use of the phrase itself in a sentence is seen in the following: "It is . . . the duty of the State to consider, in the imposition of taxes, what commodities the consumers can best spare; and *a fortiori* to select in preference those of which it deems the use, beyond a very moderate quantity, to be positively injurious."

—MILL

ā priōrī—ā 'from' and priōrī, the ablative case of prior 'earlier'; used as an adjective or adverb in English. The phrase is employed when one reasons from definitions or principles that are regarded as self-evident, that is, deductively: "An action is good not because it has good results, or because it is wise, but because it is done in obedience to this inner sense of duty, this moral law that does not come from our personal experience, but legislates imperiously and *a priori* for all our behavior." —WILL DURANT Or: "Reason commands us, in matters of experience, to be guided by observational evidence, and not by *a priori* principles."—JAMES MCCOSH

ā posteriōrī—posteriōrī is the ablative case of posterior, the comparative of posterus 'coming after'; used as an adjective or adverb in English. The phrase refers to working back from effects to causes, that is, working inductively: "Knowledge *a posteriori* is a synonym for knowledge empirical, or from experience.—SIR WILLIAM HAMILTON

ipsissima verba—Used as a noun in English: "I learned the lessons that laid the foundation of my philosophy from Spinoza himself, from his *ipsissima verba*."

—SANTAYANA

nē plūs ultrā—Used as a noun in English: "I have often decided since, that being a conductor of a great orchestra is the *ne plus ultra* in glory and power."

—IRWIN EDMAN

prīmā faciē—Ablative case, to be translated 'at.' Used as an adjective or adverb in English, for example: "If a people . . . prostrated by character and circumstance could obtain representative institutions, they would inevitably choose their tyrants as their representatives, and the yoke would be made heavier on them by the contrivance which *prima facie* might be expected to lighten it."—MILL

summum bonum—Used as a noun in English: "Hobbes . . . considered absolute tranquillity and implicit obedience as the *summum bonum* of a state."—COLERIDGE

LESSON 6

Review

1. (a) Give the base of each of the following nouns and adjectives:

arbiter, arbitrī 'judge'
campus 'plain'
cliēns, clientis 'follower'
equus 'horse'
fortūna 'fate,' 'fortune'
grātus 'pleasing'

hospes, hospitis 'guest,' 'host'
inānis 'empty'
saeculum 'generation,' 'the world'
sēmen, sēminis (n) 'seed'

(b) To which declension does each of the above belong?

2. You are not, as yet, prepared to analyze compound words, that is, words containing bases with prefixes and suffixes attached; but you should by now be able to recognize bases when you see them in compound words. The following list of words contains bases of Latin words which you have

studied. Indicate (a) the base; (b) the Latin word, with its meaning, that contains this base (for example, *allocation*: (a) base *loc-;* (b) Latin noun: **locus** 'place'): *aggravation, ameliorate, definitive, depreciate, disintegration, evacuation, impartiality, incorporate, insinuate, intermediate, optimist, pejorative, reformation.*

3. For each italicized word, give (a) the Latin word from which it comes, (b) the meaning of the expression in which it appears: his *august* presence, *circa* A.D. 1800, one's better *genius*, a forced and *jejune* devotion, political *nostrums*, a *quondam* friend, not a *scintilla* of evidence, natures that differ *toto caelo.*

4. Give the etymological meaning of *chaplain, comrade, cruise, dandelion, dismal, item, piano, plummet, prima donna, umpire.*

CHAPTER THREE

Compound Nouns and Adjectives

W ORD FORMATION is a process in which prefixes or suffixes or both are attached to certain words or to their bases to form other words. We call such words *compounds*, since they are composed of more than one element. From the English noun *boy*, for example, by adding the native suffix *-ish*, the compound adjective *boyish* is formed.

The present chapter introduces the study of word formation in Latin and in English. In it are discussed the suffixes and prefixes that may be attached to Latin nouns and adjectives, the changes in meaning they effect, and the forms they take in English.[1]

Prefixes and suffixes modify the meaning of the word or the base to which they are attached. The *etymological meaning* of a compound word may be found by combining the meaning of the prefix and suffix with that of its base. This meaning in most cases differs, often rather widely, from the *current meaning*, which may be found only by consulting the dictionary. The etymological meaning, however, has a close and direct connection with the current meaning: not only does it contain the seed from which the latter has sprung, but the peculiar flavor of any compound may be ascertained only from it. Thus *vital*, composed of *vit-* (the base of the Latin noun **vīta** 'life') and the suffix *-al* (from **-ālis** 'pertaining to'),

---

[1] Word formation also includes multiple-base compounds—i.e., words formed from two bases. The discussion of these is reserved until the end of the chapter.

means etymologically 'pertaining to life.'   In certain contexts this is also the current meaning, as in the expression "a *vital* wound"—that is, "a wound which endangers life."   But *vital* is commonly used today in the sense of 'essential.'   This meaning is simply the outgrowth of the etymological meaning 'pertaining to life,' for anything that 'pertains to life' is *ipso facto* 'essential.'   Furthermore the current meaning of *vital* is not simply 'essential.'   A trace of its etymological sense survives, for it means 'as essential as the things that govern existence.'

Suffixes are of three kinds: adjective-forming, noun-forming, and verb-forming.   In the present chapter, only the first two kinds concern us.   It is important to remember that, in Latin, suffixes are almost always attached to the bases of words, never to complete words.   In some instances the combination of the elements was made, not in Latin, but in English or in French.   Such compounds will be indicated by an asterisk (*).

In the succeeding lessons we shall frequently use the term *simple derivative*.   By this we mean the derivative from a given Latin word without any prefixes or suffixes attached. Derivatives containing prefixes or suffixes or both, as mentioned above, are *compound derivatives* or simply *compounds*.

Lesson 7

Compound Adjectives

Lessons 7 to 10 are concerned with eight suffixes that form compound adjectives.   Most of these are attached to noun bases, where their function is to turn the noun which has supplied the base into an adjective.   In a relatively few cases the suffixes are attached to adjective bases.   In these instances they serve to produce an adjective somewhat different in meaning from the one that supplied the base.

1. Noun or adjective base plus the Latin suffix -ālis >[1]
English -al 'of,' 'belonging to,' 'pertaining to,' 'having the
character of,' 'appropriate to.'

LATIN NOUN OR ADJECTIVE	BASE	LATIN COMPOUND ADJECTIVE	ENGLISH LOAN WORD
margō 'edge,' 'border'	margin-	marginālis	*marginal*
digitus 'finger,' 'toe'	digit-	digitālis	*digital*
brūtus 'irrational'	brūt-	brūtālis	*brutal*

When a noun or adjective base has the consonant *l* in either
of its last two syllables, the Latin suffix -āris is generally used,
instead of -ālis, appearing in English in the form -ar and, in
a few cases, in the form -ary. Keep in mind that -āris will
be found attached to bases containing *l*.

LATIN NOUN OR ADJECTIVE	BASE	LATIN COMPOUND ADJECTIVE	ENGLISH LOAN WORD
populus 'people'	popul-	populāris	*popular*
similis 'like'	simil-	similāris	*similar*
mīles 'soldier'	mīlit-	mīlitāris	*military*

How to Analyze Words. A complete analysis of any English compound must provide the following: (1) The Latin
word from which the English word is directly derived. (2)
The base of the English word, and the Latin word with its
meaning that has supplied this base. Normally the nominative singular of the Latin word will be sufficient. Where,
however, the nominative does not reveal the base, the genitive
must also be given. (3) The English and Latin form and
meaning of all prefixes and suffixes. (4) The etymological
meaning of the English word. (5) The current meaning of
the English word. A complete analysis of the adjective *aboriginal*, for example, would be:

---

[1] The symbol (>) signifies *giving rise to.* When reversed (<), it signifies *derived
from.*

1. *aborīginālis
2. *-origin-* base of **orīgō, orīginis** 'beginning'
3. *ab-* Latin prefix **ab-** 'away from'
   -al Latin suffix **-ālis** 'having the character of'
4. Etymological Meaning: 'having the character of (existing) from the beginning'
5. Current Meaning: 'first,' 'indigenous'

In preparing an analysis it is not necessary to reach immediately for the dictionary. On the contrary, the best procedure is to see how far you can go without any aid from the dictionary. In analyzing the word *modal*, for example, you will immediately recognize that *-al* comes from **-ālis**. Some of you, at least, will then see that *mod-* is the base of **modus** 'manner,' since **modus** is a word you were specifically asked to memorize in Exercise 1 of Lesson 2. The etymological meaning is now apparent, namely, 'pertaining to a manner.' At this point—but only at this point—do you have to go to the dictionary to determine the current meaning.

Many of the words you will be called upon to analyze will, of course, contain bases coming from Latin words other than those you have memorized. You will be able to find the Latin words that have supplied these bases in the General Vocabulary.

ETYMOLOGICAL NOTES

Capitālis 'pertaining to the head (**caput, capitis**),' 'chief,' in its neuter form **capitāle,** was used in mediaeval times as a noun meaning 'principal source of income,' 'chief property.' It entered English first through Norman-French as *cattle*, reflecting the importance of livestock as a form of property in the Middle Ages. A later derivative was *chattel*, which today generally means 'movable property.' And, of course, the latest borrowing is *capital*, which is closest to the mediaeval meaning 'chief property.'

Another derivative having to do with property is *peculiar*. The base involved here comes from **pecūlium,** the word used by the Romans for 'private property.' The **pecu-** that ap-

pears here is a Latin root meaning 'cattle'; obviously, livestock in those days must have been the commonest form of
private property.   The important point, etymologically, is
that a man's **peculium** was 'property that was his very own.' = cattle
Peculiar thus means, basically, 'pertaining to that which is
exclusively one's own,' a meaning found, for example, in the
expression 'characteristics *peculiar* to a people.'   *Peculiar* in
the sense 'strange' results from the fact that what is 'exclusively one's own' may seem 'strange' to others.

Fuel goes back to a Late Latin compound adjective in **-ālis**;
it comes, through French, from **focālia** 'things that have to
do with the hearth,' the neuter plural of **focālis** 'pertaining
to the hearth (**focus**).'

Another derivative that contains **-ālis** in a disguised form
is *noel*, the word taken from the French as an expression of
joy at Christmas.   *Noel* goes back to **nātālis** 'pertaining to
birth (**nātus**).'

EXERCISES

1. To which declension do compound adjectives ending in
-ālis belong?   How can their base be found? — generally 3 declen?

2. Memorize the following Latin nouns with their meanings.
Indicate the base of each.   Using the suffix *-al*, form a compound adjective from each and, with the aid of the dictionary,
determine its current meaning.

annus 'year'	**nōmen, nōminis** (n) 'name'
caput, capitis (n) 'head'	**oculus** 'eye'
carō, carnis 'flesh'	**ōrdō, ōrdinis** 'order,' 'regular succession'
cor, cordis (n) 'heart'	
flōs, flōris 'flower'	**ōs, ōris** (n) 'mouth'
gradus (gradu-) 'step,' 'degree'	**pēs, pedis** 'foot'
lingua 'tongue,' 'language'	**socius** 'associate,' 'ally'
lītera 'letter'	**speciēs** 'appearance'
manus (manu-) 'hand'	**tempus, temporis** (n) 'time'
mors, mortis 'death'	**vōx, vōcis** 'voice'
mōs, mōris 'habit,' 'custom'	**vulgus** 'the masses,' 'the crowd'

3. Analyze the words *causal, fiscal, formal, generalissimo, glacial, local, plural, verbal.*

4. Analyze each of the italicized words and determine the meaning of the expression in which it appears: *carnal* temptation, *corporal* punishment, *crucial* situation, *exemplary* conduct, *festal* occasion, *integral* part, *lateral* motion, *medial* position, *nominal* fee, *radial* design, *radical* change.

5. Analyze each italicized word and determine its meaning in the context.

A It is beneath the dignity of the king's courts to be merely *ancillary* to other jurisdictions.—BLACKSTONE

B They were a race *insular* in temper as well as in geographical position.—MACAULAY

C He had abolished the distinction between the sacred and the *secular*, transferring to the credit of human genius all that had been ascribed to the divine.—VAN WYCK BROOKS

D What did he care for *temporal* interests? It was his vocation to discover God.—VAN WYCK BROOKS

E I'd play incessantly upon these jades,
Even till unfenced desolation
Leave them as naked as the *vulgar* air.

—SHAKESPEARE

6. Analyze *brute* and *brutal.* Distinguish between '*brute* force' and '*brutal* force.' Analyze *venial* and *venal.* Distinguish between a '*venial* coward' and a '*venal* coward.'

7. (a) *Cardinal* means, among other things, 'small scarlet bird,' and 'church dignitary.' How did these two meanings arise?

(b) Analyze the adjective *ordinal.* Give an example of a *cardinal* number and of an *ordinal* number.

8. **Rēgālia** and **marginālia** are neuter plurals which have been borrowed without change. Determine the etymological meaning of each. Show how it is reflected in the current meanings.

9. Give the doublets of *finale, hotel, loyal, personnel, royal.*

LESSON 8

Compound Adjectives (*Cont'd*)

In addition to **-ālis** and **-āris,** the following suffixes may also be attached to noun or adjective bases to form compound adjectives.

2. Noun or adjective base plus **-īlis** > *-ile,* rarely *-il,* characteristic 'of,' 'belonging to,' 'pertaining to,' 'having the character of,' 'appropriate to.' Equivalent in general to the native English suffixes *-ish, -ly, -like.*

LATIN NOUN	BASE	LATIN COMPOUND ADJECTIVE	ENGLISH LOAN WORD
hostis 'enemy'	host-	hostīlis	*hostile*

3. Noun or adjective base plus **-ānus** > *-an, -ane,* characteristic 'of,' 'belonging to,' 'pertaining to,' and so on.

LATIN NOUN	BASE	LATIN COMPOUND ADJECTIVE	ENGLISH LOAN WORD
urbs 'city'	urb-	urbānus	*urban, urbane*

Occasionally the vowel **-i-** is inserted as a connective between the base and **-ānus.**

LATIN NOUN	BASE	LATIN COMPOUND ADJECTIVE	ENGLISH LOAN WORD
Stentor, a herald, in the *Iliad,* with a powerful voice	Stentor-	*Stentoriānus	*stentorian*

Note the irregularly formed adjectives **hūmānus** 'pertaining to man (**homō, hominis**),' and **germānus** 'pertaining to a sprout, offshoot (**germen, germinis**).'

Learned Words and Popular Words. One of the exercises below contains the word *anile.* *Anile,* the dictionary will tell you, means 'old-womanish.' Yet, if you were to exclaim to someone, in a burst of temper, "Oh, stop being anile!" you would sound ridiculous. The reason is that *anile* is not a part of the popular vocabulary. It belongs rather to the stock of words that we learn more formally from books. Such words are called *learned* words. This does not mean that they are used only by savants, but merely that they do not belong to the group of words everybody knows and uses daily.

No one will doubt which column below should be marked 'Popular' and which 'Learned':

bit	modicum
book	volume
end	terminus
fat	corpulent
queer	eccentric

All the words in the 'Learned' column are derived from Latin or Greek. If you think back upon the words studied so far, you will note that most of them belong to the 'learned' group. There are, however, many that do not. *Camera* is hardly a learned word these days, nor is *circus* or *cause* or numerous others. The distinction is not one of etymology, but of usage: when a word is widely enough used it ceases to be 'learned' and becomes 'popular.'

It must be remembered that the distinction between learned and popular words, depending as it does upon usage, is variable and subjective. A word which seems popular to you may appear learned to one whose education has been inferior. Perhaps you now use quite naturally some words which a few years ago you regarded as learned. For you, at least, they have become popular.

It is important to distinguish between learned and popular

words for a very practical purpose—to insure a choice of language that will be appropriate to the circumstances. A word or expression too formal or too informal for its context distracts the reader's attention and interferes with the main objective, the communication of thought. The reader may express his annoyance by saying that the language is 'incongruous,' 'ludicrous,' or 'in bad taste.' The words we are studying are, for the most part, learned; be careful to use them only in appropriate contexts.

ETYMOLOGICAL NOTES

Gentīlis 'of the (same) clan (gēns, gentis),' later 'of one of the great Roman families,' has given us *gentile, genteel, gentle,* and *jaunty.* Gentīlis became **gentil** in French, and *jaunty* is just a phonetic spelling of the French form. All the derivatives reflect the Latin meaning to a certain degree. *Gentle,* for example, meant 'well-born' when it was first borrowed by English, a meaning still preserved in the expression "of *gentle* blood." A *gentle*man was, originally, a 'man of good family.' The current meaning of *gentle* derives from its application to the characteristics that supposedly accompany high birth.

The suffix **-ānus** is frequently disguised in English. *Sullen,* for example, is the result of combining the Latin **sōlus** 'lone' and **-ānus.** You may become *sullen,* apparently, when you spend too much time by yourself. A less completely disguised form of **-ānus** is *-ain,* the form the suffix takes when it passes through French. *Mountain* comes from **montānus** (**mōns, montis** 'mountain'), *certain* from **certānus** (**certus** 'determined'), *villain* from the popular Latin form **vīllānus** (**vīlla** 'farm'). A *villain* was originally a 'farm laborer.'

In the doublets *chieftain* and *captain,* the base as well as the suffix has been disguised. The suffix in each is, of course, **-ānus**; the base goes back to **caput, capitis** 'head.' The same altering of the base seen in *chieftain* appears in *kerchief,* the cloth you use to cover (**cooperīre;** *covrir* in Old French) the 'head,' and in *mischief,* where your 'head' may suffer a loss (**minus**; *mes-* in Old French).   Modern French has given us *chef*, the 'head' of a kitchen.

The adjectives *urban* and *urbane* show an interesting development.   The first is always used in a literal, the second in a figurative sense.   In Latin, **urbānus** means 'of a city.'   The literal meaning is preserved in *urban*, as in '*urban* dwellings,' which are 'dwellings of a city.'   *Urbane*, however, is used figuratively only: it means 'courteous,' 'polite,' 'polished in manner,' since courteousness and politeness are qualities, figuratively speaking, of the city-dweller.

EXERCISES

1. To which declensions do compound adjectives ending in **-īlis** and **-ānus** respectively belong?   How can their bases be found?

2. Analyze each of the italicized words and determine the meaning of the expression in which it appears: *anile* tantrums, *civil* marriage, cousin-*german*, *germane* to the case, *genteel* society, a verray parfit *gentil* knight, *juvenile* attempts, *puerile* ostentation, *senile* anger, *servile* flattery, *veteran* performer, *virile* view of human life.

3. The italicized words have in common the fact that they are derived from the names of Roman deities.   Analyze each and determine the meaning of the expression in which it appears: *cereal* seeds, *Jovian* features, *martial* music, *jovial* remarks, *mercurial* temperament.   Note that the meanings of the last two have been affected by astrology.

4. Analyze each italicized word (except, of course, those that have appeared earlier in the lesson) and determine, where necessary, its meaning in the context.

A   He had an itch for such transcendental *arcana* as spiritualism, crystal gazing, numerology, and the Freudian rumble-bumble.—MENCKEN

B   With *Jovian* recklessness he played with the artificial lightning which he generated.—LONDON TIMES

C   The average age of the population of the United States . . . is twenty-five years; the *median* age is twenty-one years.   The latter means the point at which there are as many people above as below.—BOSTON TRANSCRIPT

D   As Webster spoke for the outer life of the town, its property-sense and a kind of patriotism that largely represented its *mundane* pride, Channing spoke for the inner life of Boston.—VAN WYCK BROOKS

E   The only sounds disturbing the stillness were steady munchings of many mouths, and *stentorian* breathings from all but invisible noses.—HARDY

5. Consider the phrases 'a book full of *Shakespeariana*,' 'a collection of *Americana*.'   What form of **-ānus** appears in the italicized words?   What does it mean?

6. (a) List any five Latin-derived words from those studied in Lessons 1 to 7 which you consider definitely 'popular.'

(b) Separate the following into 'learned' and 'popular' words: *album, alumni, brute, codex, digital, febrile, germane, marginalia, medium, miser, nostrum, optimum.*

LESSON 9

Compound Adjectives (*Cont'd*)

In addition to the three previously discussed, the following suffixes may also be used to form compound adjectives.

4. Noun or adjective base plus **-īnus** > *-ine, -in* characteristic 'of,' 'pertaining to,' 'like,' 'characterized by'; equivalent to the native English suffixes *-ish, -like, -y, -ly.* Also used, especially in the form *-in,* to form names of chemical substances (*aspirin, insulin*).

LATIN NOUN	BASE	LATIN COMPOUND ADJECTIVE	ENGLISH LOAN WORD
sal 'salt'	sal-	salīnus	*saline*

The suffix -**īnus** is frequently used to form adjectives from the names of animals.

LATIN NOUN	BASE	LATIN COMPOUND ADJECTIVE	ENGLISH LOAN WORD
fēles 'cat'	**fēl-**	**fēlīnus**	*feline*

5. Noun or adjective base plus -**ārius** > -*ary* 'of,' 'pertaining to,' 'connected with.'

LATIN NOUN	BASE	LATIN COMPOUND ADJECTIVE	ENGLISH LOAN WORD
auxilium 'help,' 'aid'	**auxili-**	**auxiliārius**	*auxiliary*

Many Latin adjectives formed with -**ārius** were used as nouns in which the suffix denotes 'person belonging to,' 'person engaged in' or 'concerned with.'

LATIN NOUN	BASE	LATIN COMPOUND ADJECTIVE	ENGLISH LOAN WORD
lapis 'stone'	**lapid-**	**lapidārius**, originally 'pertaining to stone'; later 'one who works with stones'	*lapidary*

The suffix -**ārium,** neuter singular of -**ārius,** was used to form nouns in which it has the meaning 'place for.' It appears in English sometimes without change, more commonly in the form -*ary*.

LATIN NOUN	BASE	LATIN COMPOUND NOUN	ENGLISH LOAN WORD
aqua 'water'	**aqu-**	**aquārium** 'place for water'	*aquarium*
avis 'bird'	**avi-**	**aviārium** 'place for birds'	*aviary*

ETYMOLOGICAL NOTES

When you receive a *salary*, you are literally earning your 'salt,' for *salary* goes back to **salārius** 'pertaining to salt (**sal**).'

The connection between this and the current meaning lies in the fact that Roman soldiers used to get an allowance with which to buy salt, and this they called their **salārium.**

While we're talking about *salary,* we may as well take up the word *money.* *Money* goes back to a Latin root **mon-** which really means 'warn' and basically has nothing whatsoever to do with money. There was a temple in Rome in honor of the goddess **Jūnō Monēta,** Juno the 'Warner.' The temple got its name, according to one story, because Juno's voice was heard from it during an earthquake, warning the Romans to offer an expiatory sacrifice. It so happened that the Romans used the temple as a place to coin money; the **Monēta** (temple) became their mint. In Anglo-Saxon, **Monēta** became **mynet,** whence *mint;* while in Old French, it became *moneie,* whence *money,* with a shift of meaning from the place to the product of the place. And **monētārius,** of course, has given us *monetary.*

When **-ārius** passed through Old French it often took the forms *-er, -ier,* or *-eer* in English. Thus *carpenter* is from **carpentārius** 'person concerned with wagons (**carpentum**).' *Terrier* is from **terrārius** 'concerned with the earth (**terra**)'; terriers were once used by hunters to pursue foxes, badgers, and the like into their burrows in the earth. A *coroner* (***corōnārius**) is literally 'one who has to do with the crown (**corōna**)'; he was, originally, the officer charged with maintaining the rights of private property belonging to the crown. A *mariner* (**marīnārius**) is 'one concerned with the sea (**marīnus,** from **mare** 'sea')'. The *larder* (**lardārium**) is the 'place for the bacon (**lardum**).' A *privateer* (***prīvātārius**) is a private (**prīvātus**) vessel authorized for use against the commerce or navy of an enemy. The distinguishing mark of *chevaliers* and *cavaliers,* etymologically, is that they were 'horsemen' (**caballārius,** from **caballus** 'horse'); *chevalier* came through French, *cavalier* through Italian.

The *-er* in *usher* and *tiller* goes back to **-ārius.** An *usher* is really a 'doorman' (**ōstiārius,** from **ōstium** 'door'). *Tiller,* the steering lever attached to the rudder of a ship, takes its base from **tēla** 'web.'   In Old French *telier* (from *****tēlārius** 'pertaining to a web') meant originally 'weaver's beam,' and then came to mean, presumably because of its resemblance to a weaver's beam, 'stock of a crossbow.'   From meaning the part by which a crossbow is handled to meaning the similar part by which a rudder is handled is not too hard a step.

Sometimes the form that **-ārius** takes under French influence is so altered as to be almost unrecognizable.   **Calidus** means 'hot,' and a **calidārium** was a 'place for a hot bath.'   This has become *cauldron.*   The feminine **calidāria** became *chaudière* in Old French, meaning 'pot'; in English it's no longer the pot but one of the things that may go into it—*chowder.*   **Scūtum** means shield and a **scūtārius** was a 'shield-bearer'; his English descendants, *esquire* and *squire,* have taken on many new duties since they first served as shield-bearers for knights.   The form *esquire,* incidentally, is older than *squire.*   In Vulgar Latin the letter **e** was often placed before a word beginning with **s** followed by a consonant.   Thus **scūtārius** became in Vulgar Latin **'escūtārius,'** which ultimately was transformed into *esquire.*   This fact explains why we have *especial* alongside *special, estate* alongside *state, esprit* alongside *spirit.*

EXERCISES

1. To which declension do compound adjectives ending in **-īnus** and **-ārius** belong?   How can their base be found?

2. Memorize the following Latin nouns.   Indicate the base of each.   Using the suffixes you have studied hitherto, form an English word from each and determine its current meaning.

grānum 'grain,' 'seed'	**rota** 'wheel'
lūmen, lūminis (n) 'light'	**terra** 'earth'

3. (a) The following adjectives have in common the fact that they are derived from names of animals.   Analyze each: *aquiline, asinine, bovine, canine, equine, hircine, leonine, ovine, porcine, taurine, ursine, viperine, vulpine.*

(b) Give 'popular' synonyms for *equine, porcine,* and *vulpine.*

4. Analyze the following words: *diary, itinerary, library, literary, notary, summary, temporary, vaccine.*

5. Analyze each of the italicized words and determine the meaning of the expression in which it appears: *agrarian* reform, *arbitrary* ruler, *culinary* art, navigate an *estuary, ferine* cruelty, *funerary* urn, *matutinal* ablutions, *plenary* session, *rotary* motion, *tutelary* deity.

6. Analyze each italicized word (except those that have appeared previously) and determine its meaning in the context.

A "A work," concludes the well-nigh enthusiastic Reviewer, "interesting alike to the *antiquary,* the historian, and the philosophic thinker."—CARLYLE

B An Offer to paint them a Helen, as a Model and *Exemplar* of the most exquisite Beauty . . .

—JAMES HARRIS

C Like the other great *luminaries* of philosophy and science, Locke has shone on with tolerably uniform lustre.—HENRY ROGERS

D My conversation is slow and dull, my humor *saturnine* and reserved.—DRYDEN

E Sometimes a fox came near to my window, attracted by the light, barked a *vulpine* curse at me and then retreated.—THOREAU

7. Compare the etymological meanings of *carpenter, plumber, salary, seminary, usher* with their current meanings. What semantic change is revealed by each?

8. What is the meaning of the Christian names *Augustine, Justin, Pauline, Regina?*

9. Give the doublets of *coroner, premier, terrier, volunteer.*

LESSON 10

Compound Adjectives (*Concl'd*)

In addition to the five previously discussed, the following suffixes may also be used to form compound adjectives.

6. Noun or adjective base plus **-ōsus** > *-ous, -ose* 'full of,' 'abounding in.'

LATIN NOUN	BASE	LATIN COMPOUND ADJECTIVE	ENGLISH LOAN WORD
cōpia 'plenty'	**cōpi-**	**cōpiōsus**	*copious*
verbum 'word'	**verb-**	**verbōsus**	*verbose*

The suffix **-ōsus** is frequently used to anglicize Latin adjectives, that is, it serves simply to bring the adjective into English without affecting the meaning.

LATIN ADJECTIVE	BASE	LATIN COMPOUND ADJECTIVE	ENGLISH LOAN WORD
aemulus 'rivaling,' 'ambitious to equal'	**aemul-**	***aemulōsus**	*emulous* 'ambitious to equal'

7. Noun or adjective base plus **-lentus** > *-lent* 'full of,' 'given to,' 'like.' It should be noted that **-lentus,** unlike the suffixes previously studied, begins with a consonant. In order to attach a suffix beginning with a consonant to a base ending in a consonant, a *connecting vowel* is frequently inserted between the two. In words containing **-lentus** the connecting vowel may be **-u-, -o-,** or **-i-.**

LATIN NOUN	BASE	LATIN COMPOUND ADJECTIVE	ENGLISH LOAN WORD
vīrus 'poison'	vīr-	vīrulentus	*virulent*
somnus 'sleep'	somn-	somnolentus	*somnolent*

8. Noun or adjective base plus **-icus** > *-ic* 'of,' 'pertaining to.'

LATIN NOUN	BASE	LATIN COMPOUND ADJECTIVE	ENGLISH LOAN WORD
classis 'class,' 'rank'	class-	classicus	*classic*

There are two suffixes spelled **-icus** in Latin: a native suffix, as in **classicus** cited above, and the Latinized form of a borrowed Greek adjective-forming suffix (*see* Part Two, Lesson 2).

ETYMOLOGICAL NOTES

Humorous means etymologically 'full of liquid,' yet its current meaning seems to have little to do with liquids. *Bilious* today means 'irascible,' but its etymological meaning is 'full of bile'; on the surface, at least, there seems to be little connection between the two. If, however, we turn to the history of ancient medicine, we quickly discover that *humorous* has a good deal to do with liquids, and *bilious* with bile.

In ancient times doctors believed that in the body there existed four fluids or "humors" (**hūmor** 'liquid') namely blood, phlegm, choler (yellow bile), and melancholy (black bile). Three of these fluids are actually to be found in the body; 'black bile,' however, was purely imaginary. A good disposition, it was believed, depended upon a proper 'mixture' (**temperāmentum,** whence *temperament*) of the four fluids, while an excess of any one of the four caused changes in behavior. Thus if a man was chronically irascible, he was said to be *bilious*—that is, he had an excess of bile (**bīlis**) rather than an equal proportion of the four humors. If he was bright and cheerful, he was said to be *sanguine*, since brightness of temper and cheerfulness were believed to result from a surplus of blood (**sanguis, sanguinis**).   One who was moody and had a temperament that shifted readily was thought to have unequal amounts of the four humors and was consequently called *humorous*.   Since an excess of any of the four humors could cause a person to be eccentric in speech or in conduct, *humorous* assumed the meaning 'eccentric'; and since people who are eccentric are frequently the butt of jokes and ridicule, *humorous* finally took on its current meaning.

Italics is really 'Italian (type),' from **Ītalicus** 'of Italy (**Ītalia**).'   Italic type was designed and first used in Italy, specifically Venice, about 1500.

EXERCISES

1. To which declension do adjectives ending in **-ōsus, -lentus,** and **-icus** belong?   How can their bases be found?

2. Memorize the following Latin words with their meanings.   Indicate the base of each.   Using the suffixes you have studied hitherto, form an English word from each and determine, where necessary, its current meaning.

aqua 'water' (adj. **aqueus** 'watery')

grex, gregis 'flock'

mōnstrum 'wonder,' 'miracle'

numerus 'number'

varius 'varied'

3. Analyze the words *bellicose, nefarious, riparian, sinuous, turbulent, verbose, violent, precarious.*

4. Analyze each of the italicized words and determine the meaning of the expression in which it appears: *ceremonial* rites, *ceremonious* rites, *generic* differences, *grandiose* display, *histrionic* talents, *lachrymose* tale, *nebulous* faith, *noxious* influence, *onerous* duties, *opulent* fittings, *specious* words, *tenuous* attachment, *truculent* nature, *virulent* writings.

5. Analyze each italicized word and determine its meaning in the context.

A   Some of the sketches are full of *curious* beauty, that remote beauty which may be apprehended only by those who have sought it carefully.—PATER

B Your dinner and the *generous* islanders
By you invited, do attend your presence.

—SHAKESPEARE

C (a) Come, he hath hid himself among these trees,
To be consorted with the *humorous* night.

—SHAKESPEARE

(b) Yet such is now the duke's condition
That he misconstrues all that you have done.
The duke is *humorous*.—SHAKESPEARE

D (a) A youthful face,
Imperious, and of haughtiest lineaments.

—TENNYSON

(b) Only the *imperious* difficulties of distance and supplies delayed an indefinite British advance to the west.—CHURCHILL

E He caught the sound of *jocose* talk and ringing laughter from behind the hedges.—GEORGE ELIOT

F "All this is very well conceived, no doubt," said he, "and well executed. But it happens to be *otiose*."

—BEERBOHM

G I accepted . . . this choice of nightmares forced upon me in the *tenebrous* land invaded by these mean and greedy phantoms.—CONRAD

H The increasing laxity of the Mussulman world, and the practice of *vicarious* pilgrimage, have greatly diminished the numbers of the sacred caravans.—EDINBURGH REVIEW

6. What Latin word has supplied the base in each of the following pairs? Show how the meaning of the base is reflected in the current meaning of each word: *imperial* and *imperious*, *moral* and *morose*, *special* and *specious*.

Lesson 11

Prefixes

In addition to suffixes, which are attached to the bases of words to form compounds, certain elements called *prefixes* may be placed before words or bases.   A word with a prefix may contain a suffix as well.   Thus *subnormal* 'below the normal' is composed of the prefix *sub-*, meaning 'below,' 'under'; *norm-*, base of the Latin noun **nōrma** 'standard'; and the adjective-forming suffix *-al* < **-ālis.**

Latin prefixes are used principally with verbs, as will appear later.   We shall here limit ourselves to a study of those prefixes which may be attached to nouns and adjectives.

Prefixes

[The basic form of each prefix is given first.   The other forms are used before certain consonants for the sake of euphony, for example, **illēgālis** instead of **'inlēgālis.'**]

ab- 'from,' 'away from,' 'off'

ad- 'to,' 'toward,' 'for'

ante- 'before'

con-, com-, co-, cor- (prepositional form **cum**) 'with,' 'together,' 'together with,'; also used intensively ('very')

contrā- 'against,' 'in opposition'

dē- 'down,' 'off,' 'away,' 'from'

ex-, ē- 'out,' 'out of'

extrā- 'outside,' 'outside of'

in-, il-, im-, 'in,' 'on'; 'not'

inter- 'between'

intrā- 'within'

ob- 'to,' 'against,' 'meeting'

per- 'through,' 'by,' 'to the bad'; also used intensively ('very')

prae- 'before,' 'previous'

prō- 'in front of,' 'forth,' 'for,' 'instead of'

sē- 'apart,' 'without'

sub- 'under'

super- 'above,' 'over'

ultrā- 'beyond'

In a few cases the base of a noun or adjective is altered slightly when compounded with a prefix. Thus **aptus** 'fit,' when compounded with **in-** 'not' becomes **-eptus**, as in *inept*. Note also *inert* from **in-** 'not' and **ars, artis.**

Almost all the prefixes listed above are used in Latin as prepositions and appear as such in Latin phrases which have been adopted by English without change. The nouns and adjectives that follow these prepositions in such phrases will almost always show endings unfamiliar to you. The reason is that you have studied only the nominative and genitive cases, whereas Latin prepositions govern the accusative and ablative. Of those listed above, **ab, cum, dē, ex (ē), prae, prō** are followed by the ablative; **in** ('in,' 'on'), **sub,** and **super** by the ablative or accusative; the rest by the accusative.

ETYMOLOGICAL NOTES

Consider the words *sewer* and *scamper*. They seem to have, at first sight, a rather un-Latin form. Not only are they Latin, but they both contain the common Latin prefix **ex-** 'out of.' We have already seen that an *aquarium* is etymologically a 'place for water.' Through Old French ***aquāria,** the feminine form, became *ewer* 'pitcher.' And ***exaquāria** 'place for (carrying) water out' became *sewer*. To *scamper* means etymologically 'to get out of the field.' It goes back to **ex-** and **campus** 'field.' Earlier, *scamper* meant 'to flee,' and was used of armies leaving the field of battle in flight. The same prefix is responsible for the first syllable of *escape*. To *escape* is 'to take off (**ex-**) your cloak (**cappa**).'

A *companion* is etymologically 'one who breaks bread (**pānis**) with (**com-**) you.' *Enemy* contains the prefix **in-** 'not.' It is related to *inimical* and really means 'one who is unfriendly (**in-** + **amīcus** 'friendly').' An *antler* is a branch that, etymologically, stands 'before your eyes.' It goes back to a Late Latin form **antoculāris** 'in front of the eyes,' a combination of **ante** and **oculus.** A thing was *preposterous* originally when it, although naturally coming 'after (**posterus**)' was reversed and placed 'before (**prae-**).'

Sovereign comes from a preposition plus a suffix. Its ancestor is **superānus** (**super** + **-ānus**). The *g* etymologically does not belong in the word and only crept in by a false association of *sovereign* with *reign*.

EXERCISES

1. Analyze the words *adrenaline, adverbial, confines, congenial, contemporary, contrary, extraordinary, immoral, immortal, impersonal, impervious, infirmary, inglorious, ingrate, obnoxious, obvious, perennial, preliminary, premature, pronominal, subpoena, supercilious, ultramarine.*

2. Analyze each of the italicized words and determine the meaning of the expression in which it appears: *ante-bellum* America, *coeval* with the rise of individualism, *condign* punishment, *devious* methods, *egregious* blunders, *extempore* speech, *impecunious* old maid, *interstellar* space, *intravenous* injection, *supranormal* force.

3. Analyze each italicized word and determine its meaning in the context.

A The English are not *aboriginal*, that is, they are not identical with the race that occupied their home at the dawn of history.—WILLIAM STUBBS

B They serve as *intermediaries* between the labourers, who want instruments of labour, and the possessors of those instruments.—SOUTHEY

C They were at the moment enjoying a sort of *interregnum* from Roman authority.—FREDERICK FARRAR

D To warp our choice by assuming as proved the general conclusion for which we are collecting materials is, in the full sense of the term, *preposterous*.—HOUSMAN

E (a) Not of the Bible only, but of those precious remains of *profane* literature.—FREDERICK SCRIVENER.
(b) No one *profane* to the profession of artist ever acquired a just notion of any picture by reading.—HOWELLS
(c) It is ordered that *profane* swearing shall be a sufficient crime to dismiss any labourer.—SIR CHRISTOPHER WREN

F   And pretty child, sleep doubtless and *secure,*
That Hubert for the wealth of all the world
Will not offend thee.—SHAKESPEARE

G   Patiently to earn a spare bare living, and quietly to
die . . . —this was her highest *sublunary* hope.

—DICKENS

H   But he was far from attractive to a woman's eye,
ruled as that is so largely by the *superficies* of things.

—HARDY

I   Perhaps, in that *super-mundane* region, we may be
amused with seeing the fallacy of our own guesses.

—JEFFERSON

J   (a) Such of our horses as had not been tired out . . .
were taken with us as pack-horses, or *supernumeraries.*

—IRVING

(b) I . . . sunk to be a *supernumerary* for 1*s.* a night
at one of the theatres.—HENRY MAYHEW

4. (a) Distinguish between *intramural* and *intermural* athletics.

(b) The Latin words **ingenium** 'inborn quality' and **ingenuus** 'freeborn' are derived from **in-** 'in' and **gen,** a Latin root meaning 'beget.' With the addition of **-ōsus,** the former has given us *ingenious,* the latter *ingenuous.* Distinguish between the two.

(c) Etymologically speaking, what does a *consort* do?

5. The following Latin phrases appear in English. Using the General Vocabulary where necessary, find the meaning of each in Latin. With the aid of the dictionary, determine the pronunciation and meaning of each in English:

ad hoc—Used as an adjective in English: "If there was an isolated fact which he could in no wise fit into his theory, he would dismiss it with some farfetched *ad hoc* explanation."

ex parte—Used as adjective or adverb in English, for example: "*Ex parte* statements to which the accused had no opportunity of replying."—JOHN LINGARD

pro forma—Used as adjective or adverb in English, for example: "When a document is drawn up . . . with the special object of complying with some legal requirement it is said to be done *pro forma.*"

LESSON 12

Compound Nouns

Certain suffixes may be used to form compound nouns. Of these suffixes some may be attached to noun bases, some to adjective bases, some to either.

1. The following suffixes may be attached to noun bases to form diminutive nouns:

		MASCULINE	FEMININE	NEUTER
Noun Base	+	-culus	-cula	-culum
" "	+	-ellus	-ella	-ellum
" "	+	-illus	-illa	-illum
" "	+	-olus	-ola	-olum
" "	+	-ulus	-ula	-ulum

You will note that each diminutive suffix has three endings, one for each of the three genders. With a few exceptions, masculine forms of the suffixes are attached to masculine nouns, feminine forms to feminine nouns, and neuter forms to neuter nouns. When the suffix **-culus** is attached to a base ending in a consonant, a connecting vowel, usually **-i-,** is generally used.

You will notice from their endings that masculine and neuter diminutives belong to the Second Declension, and feminine diminutives to the First Declension. The ways in which nouns of these declensions appear in English have been described in Lessons 1 and 2.

LATIN NOUN	BASE	LATIN DIMINUTIVE NOUN	ENGLISH LOAN WORD
rēte 'net'	rēt-	rēticulum	reticule, reticle
pannus 'cloth,' 'rag'	pann-	pannellus	panel
cōdex 'book,' 'code'	cōdic-	cōdicillus	codicil
gladius 'sword'	gladi-	gladiolus	gladiolus _gladiola_
nōdus 'knot'	nōd-	nōdulus	nodule

If you observe the popular pronunciation of _veteran_ and _interesting_, you will find that they are often pronounced "vetran" and "intresting" with a complete suppression of the vowel following the accented syllable. Such suppression of vowels may be found in the derivatives of diminutives formed with -culus or -ulus.

LATIN NOUN	BASE	LATIN DIMINUTIVE NOUN	ENGLISH LOAN WORD
artus 'joint'	art-	articulus	article
scrūpus 'sharp stone'	scrūp-	scrūpulus	scruple

In a few cases the diminutive suffix -culus is attached directly to the nominative, and not to the base.

LATIN NOUN	BASE	LATIN DIMINUTIVE NOUN	ENGLISH LOAN WORD
corpus, corporis (n) 'body'	corpor-	corpusculum	corpuscle

If a base ends in a consonant plus -r-, the -r- is usually dropped before the diminutive suffix -ellus is attached.

LATIN	BASE	LATIN DIMINUTIVE NOUN	ENGLISH LOAN WORD
scalprum 'scalpel,' 'knife'	scalpr-	scalpellum	scalpel

The diminutive ending -et (or -ette), borrowed from Old French, is as important as the Latin diminutive suffixes listed above. It is widely used in English, being attached to the bases of Latin nouns and almost always retaining its full diminutive force—for example, coronet 'little crown (**corōna**),' turret 'little tower (**turris**).'

2. Noun base plus **-ātus** > -ate 'office of,' 'period of office of,' 'holder of office of,' 'group engaged in some common action,' 'group characterized by some common quality.'

LATIN NOUN	BASE	LATIN COMPOUND NOUN	ENGLISH LOAN WORD
prīnceps 'chief'	**prīncip-**	**prīncipātus**	*principate*

ETYMOLOGICAL NOTES

Some of the most picturesque etymologies in English have been furnished by Latin diminutives. These turn up in so many unexpected places and in such a wide variety of forms that all we can do is offer a few examples.

Etymologically, a *pill* is a 'little ball' (**pilula,** from **pila**), a *panel* a 'little rag' (**pannellus,** from **pannus**), a *satchel* a 'little sack' (**sacellus,** from **saccus**). A *lintel*, the timber or stone that bounds the top of a doorway, is a 'little boundary' (***līmitellum,** from **līmes, līmitis**). *Shambles* used to mean the stalls on which butchers displayed their meats. It's the plural of *shamble* 'butcher's bench,' from **scamellum,** diminutive of **scamnum** 'bench.' A huge modern railroad *trestle* hardly reflects its etymology; a *trestle* was originally a 'little cross-beam' (***trānsitellum,** from **trānstrum,** whence *transom*). *Nucleus*, etymologically 'small nut,' 'kernel,' is related to **nucula,** diminutive of **nux, nucis** 'nut.' **Pūpillus** 'little boy (**pūpus**)' has given us *pupil* 'schoolboy.' *Pupil* 'center of the eye' has a slightly different etymology. **Pūpa,** the feminine of **pūpus,** in Latin means not only 'girl' but 'doll.' The *pupil* of the eye comes from **pūpilla** 'little doll,' perhaps because of the doll-like images that appear there. The little dolls manoeuvred by strings are *puppets* (**pūpa** + *-et*). *Puppy* and *pup*, incidentally, go back to **pūpa**.

Pommel, the rounded knob, as on the hilt of a sword, means 'little apple,' etymologically; it comes from **pōmellum*, diminutive of **pōmum** 'apple.' The verb 'to pommel' comes from the fact that the *pommel* of a sword in bygone days played at times the same role that the butt of a gun occasionally does today.

A *butler* is, strictly speaking, a 'bottler.' **Buttis** 'cask' is the source of *butt*, **butticula** 'little cask' of *bottle*, and **butticulārius* 'one who has to do with bottles' of *butler*. One of a butler's chief duties is to look after the wine-cellar. Dishes and utensils of all sorts are kept in a *scullery*, although a *scullery* was originally a place for 'little trays,' 'little dishes' (**scutella**, from **scutra** 'tray,' 'platter'). **Scutella** itself has given us *-scuttle* in coal-*scuttle*. The verbs 'scuttle (a ship)' and 'scuttle (away)' are not related in any way to **scutella**: the first may come from Dutch, and the second is connected with *scud*.

Jail comes from a Latin diminutive. Its ancestor is **caveola*, the diminutive of **cavea** 'cage.' A jail is etymologically, therefore, a 'little cage.' **Cavea**, incidentally, has produced other derivatives in English. *Cage* comes from it, as does the *-coy* in *decoy*. A *decoy*, originally, was a sort of net 'cage' with which ducks were snared. No certain explanation has been offered for the first syllable of the word. The verbs *soil* and *sully* are doublets and may come from a Latin diminutive. They certainly are derived from the Old French verb **soillier** 'to defile.' The attractive possibility exists that **soillier** comes from **suculus** 'little pig (**sūs**),' but it is only a possibility and has not been definitely proved.

Bugle is short for *bugle*-horn. In Old French, a *bugle* was a 'young bull,' from **būculus**, the diminutive of **bōs** 'bull.' *Buckle* means etymologically 'little cheek' (**buccula** from **bucca** 'cheek'). The shift in its meaning is easy to follow. **Buccula** was applied to the part of a helmet that shielded the cheek.

From this meaning to 'shield,' from 'shield' to 'boss on a shield,' and from there to *buckle* were easy steps.

EXERCISES

1. Give the etymological meaning of *calculus, castle, formula, glandular, globule, jocular, magistrate, muscle, particular, senate, vacuole.*

2. Analyze the words *auricle, cerebellum, funicular, novel, ventricle.*

3. Analyze each of the italicized words and determine the meaning of the expression in which it appears: roofs surmounted by *cupolas*, control the *curvets* of his horse, published in twelve *fascicles, meticulous* discipline, an *opuscule* of fifty pages.

4. Analyze each italicized word and determine its meaning in the context.

A   (a) The basest of created *animalcules*, the Spider itself, has a spinning-jenny . . . within its head.

—CARLYLE

(b) He had that lively quicksilver world of the *animalcule* passions, the huge pretensions, the placid absurdities, under his eyes in full activity.—MEREDITH

B   An itching ear, delighting in the *libellous* defamation of other men . . . —DONNE

C   (a) Some of these *Tabernacles* [of the Tartars] may quickely be taken asunder, and set together againe.

—HAKLUYT

(b) How undesirable it is to build the *tabernacle* of our brief lifetime out of permanent materials.

—HAWTHORNE

5. From what Latin word is each of the following groups ultimately derived?   Identify all the prefixes and suffixes used: (1) *cell, cellar, cellulose, intercellular*; (2) *grain, granary, granule, granular*; (3) *mode, modal, model, commode.*

6. Determine the etymological meanings of *pill* and *pupil* ('schoolboy').   What semantic change does the current meaning of each reveal?

LESSON 13

Compound Nouns (*Cont'd*)

There are three suffixes which may be attached to adjective bases.

1. Adjective or noun base plus **-itās** > *-ity*, forming abstract nouns meaning 'quality of,' 'state of.'

LATIN ADJECTIVE	BASE	LATIN COMPOUND NOUN	ENGLISH LOAN WORD
brevis 'short'	**brev-**	**brevitās**	*brevity*
vēnālis (**vēnum** 'sale' + **-ālis**)	**vēnāl-**	**vēnālitās**	*venality*

Adjectives ending in **-ius** take **-ētās** instead of **-itās**.

LATIN ADJECTIVE	BASE	LATIN COMPOUND NOUN	ENGLISH LOAN WORD
varius 'different'	**vari-**	**variētās**	*variety*

When suffixes are added to nouns ending in **-itās**, the **-ās** is dropped. *Hereditary* (from **hērēditārius**) consists of:

hered-	base of **hērēs, hērēdis** 'heir'
-it-	from **-itās** 'state of'
-ary	from **-ārius** 'pertaining to'

2. Adjective base plus **-itūdō** (genitive **-itūdinis**) > *-itude*, forming abstract nouns.

LATIN ADJECTIVE	BASE	LATIN COMPOUND NOUN	ENGLISH LOAN WORD
sōlus 'lone,' 'single'	**sōl-**	**sōlitūdō**	*solitude*

3. Adjective base plus **-itia** > *-ice*, forming abstract nouns.

LATIN ADJECTIVE	BASE	LATIN COMPOUND NOUN	ENGLISH LOAN WORD
jūstus 'righteous'	**jūst-**	**jūstitia**	*justice*

In later Latin, **-itia** was frequently spelled **-icia**.

Abstract Nouns. You will note that the suffixes listed above form *abstract nouns.* Such nouns name (a) a quality, as in *magnitude* 'quality of being great' (synonymous, element for element, with the native English *greatness*); (b) a state, as in *solitude* 'state of being alone,' (synonymous, element for element, with *loneliness*); (c) an act, as in *motion* 'act of moving.' The last type of abstract noun involves verb bases; examples of it will not appear until we come to the study of verbs.

On the other hand, nouns that name a thing or a class of things, as opposed to naming a quality or state, are called *concrete nouns.* *Chair, table, book, fascicle, amulet, cerebrum* are all concrete nouns.

Abstract to Concrete. A noun which was originally abstract in meaning may take on a concrete meaning. The abstract noun *justice,* for example, when used in such phrases as 'the chief justice,' 'justice of the peace,' has the concrete meaning 'person who administers justice.' The Latin noun **cīvitās** means basically 'citizenship' (**cīvis** 'citizen' + **-itās**). In later Latin it took on the concrete meaning 'city' and is, in fact the word from which *city* is derived. *Charity* (etymologically 'dearness,' from **cārus** 'dear' + **-itās**) was originally an abstract noun, but we use it in a concrete sense in such a phrase as 'a donation to a favorite *charity.*'

ETYMOLOGICAL NOTES

Old French transformed **-itia** into **-esse**, which was adopted as **-ess** by English. Thus *duress* goes back to **dūritia** (**dūrus** 'hard'), *largess* to **largitia** (**largus** 'copious'), *caress* to ***cāritia** (**cārus** 'dear'). A curious case is offered by *riches,* which really should be spelled 'richess.' It is not a plural of *rich* at all: the ending -es goes back to **-itia,** as its Middle English spelling *richesse* reveals.

EXERCISES

1. To what declensions do nouns formed with **-itās, -itūdō,** and **-itia** belong respectively? How may their bases be found?

2. Memorize the following Latin words with their meanings. Using the suffixes and prefixes studied hitherto, form as many derivatives as you can from each. Determine, where necessary, the current meaning of these derivatives.

aequus 'equal'
clārus 'clear'
deus or **dīvus** 'god'
levis, 'light (in weight),'
　'light-minded'

probus 'good'
rēctus 'upright,' 'straight'
vērus 'true'

3. Form a Latin-derived word synonymous, element for element, with each of the following native English words (example: *highness—altitude* [**altus** 'high' + **-itūdō** '-ness']): *healthiness, heartiness, heaviness, wordiness.*

4. Analyze the words *animosity, aptitude, avaricious, extremity, fortitude, generosity, impartiality, humanitarian, incivility, jocularity, longitude, majority, malicious, morality, priority, proprietary, solitary.*

5. Analyze each of the italicized words and determine the meaning of the expression in which it appears: *affinity* of languages, *comity* of nations, related by *consanguinity*, steep *declivity*, a visiting *dignitary*, *felicitous* choice of words, overcome by *lassitude*, *paucity* of supplies, *proclivity* towards laziness, point of *satiety*, *sobriety* of judgment, *vacuity* of a foolish conversation.

6. Analyze each italicized word and determine its meaning in the context.

　A　(a) The *amenities* of diplomacy; (b) The *amenity* of the climate.

　B　'Gore' is quite as taurine [a name] as [Redvers]

'Buller.' What hint of *ovinity* would there have been for us if Sir Redvers' surname had happened to be that of him who wrote the *Essays of Elia?*—BEERBOHM

C   (a) This *precious* stone set in the silver sea; (b) The worthless strictures of *precious* critics; (c) The *preciosity* of Pater and Stevenson.

D   In fine *vicissitude*, Beauty alternates with Grandeur.
—CARLYLE

7. Give the doublets of *dainty, property, solitaire.*

8. (a) Explain the change of meaning illustrated by *acerbity* in the phrase 'the *acerbity* of Dean Swift.'

(b) Determine the etymological meaning of *caress, levity, monstrosity.* What semantic change is revealed by the current meaning of each?

9. What is the linguistic relationship between *multitudinous* and *plural?*

LESSON 14

Compound Nouns (*Concl'd*)

The last noun-forming suffixes to be considered are those which may be attached either to noun or adjective bases.

1. Noun or adjective base plus **-mōnia** or **-mōnium** > *-mony*, forming abstract nouns.

LATIN NOUN OR ADJECTIVE	BASE	LATIN COMPOUND NOUN	ENGLISH LOAN WORD
pater 'father'	**patr-**	**patrimōnium**	*patrimony*
ācer 'sharp'	**ācr-**	**ācrimōnia**	*acrimony*

2. Noun or adjective base plus **-ia** > *-y*, rarely *-ia*, forming abstract nouns.

LATIN NOUN OR		LATIN COMPOUND	ENGLISH
ADJECTIVE	BASE	NOUN	LOAN WORD
mīles 'soldier'	mīlit-	mīlitia	*militia*
custōs 'guard'	custōd-	custōdia	*custody*
memor 'mindful'	memor-	memoria	*memory*

In a few cases, **-ia** has been completely dropped. Thus *discord* comes from **discordia**, *concord* from **concordia**, *vigil* from **vigilia** (**vigil** 'awake').

3. Noun or adjective base plus **-ium** > *-y*, forming either abstract nouns or nouns of place.

LATIN NOUN OR		LATIN COMPOUND	ENGLISH
ADJECTIVE	BASE	NOUN	LOAN WORD
augur 'soothsayer'	augur-	augurium	*augury*

4. Noun or adjective base plus **-ismus** > *-ism*, forming abstract nouns in which the suffix has the meaning 'state of,' 'attachment to,' 'adherence to,' 'belief in,' 'doctrine of,' 'practice of,' 'conduct characteristic of.'

		LATIN COMPOUND	ENGLISH
LATIN NOUN	BASE	NOUN	LOAN WORD
ego 'I'	ego-	*egoismus	*egoism*

5. Noun or adjective base plus **-ista** > *-ist*, forming agent nouns in which the suffix has the meaning 'one who believes in,' 'one who is an adherent of,' 'one who advocates to an extreme,' 'one concerned with.'

		LATIN COMPOUND	ENGLISH
LATIN NOUN	BASE	NOUN	LOAN WORD
ego 'I'	ego-	*egoista	*egoist*

The suffixes **-ismus** and **-ista** are not native Latin, although they are often attached to the bases of Latin words. As we shall see later, they are ultimately derived from Greek.

Degeneration of Meaning. Consider the word *saloon*. It is the doublet of *salon*, and originally meant simply 'large room.'

On ships, passengers eat in the dining *saloon*, which is usually the most pretentious room aboard. In the United States, *saloon* was specialized to mean 'place where intoxicating liquors are sold and drunk.' As such places fell into disfavor, the word started to lose its respectability, and by the beginning of World War I it had come into complete disrepute. As a matter of fact, so low had its meaning fallen that, after the repeal of prohibition, the New York state legislature officially forbade its use, in favor of the term *bar*. Even *bar* is traveling downhill, for, these days, the more fashionable *bars* prefer to call themselves 'clubs.' The process whereby a word, originally uncolored by social disapproval, degenerates to the point where it connotes contempt, reproach, or the like—acquires a *pejorative* meaning (**pējor** 'worse'), to use the technical phrase —is known as *degeneration of meaning*.

There are a number of words in English that have undergone this process. *Villain*, for example, means etymologically 'belonging to a farm' (**vīllānus**, from **vīlla** 'farm'). In Latin, **vīllānus** was specialized to mean 'a slave attached to a farm.' Then it shifted its meaning to 'farm laborer.' It was at this point that its degeneration started. From 'farm laborer' it came to be used of anyone who did not belong to the gentry, and finally of anyone who was guilty of rascality, a quality, supposedly, of the lower classes and not to be found in the gentry. *Fabulist* meant originally 'writer or inventor of stories (**fābula**)' or, with specialization of meaning, 'writer of fables.' Today *fabulist* can also mean 'liar'; the *fabulist* has degenerated from merely an inventor of fictitious stories to an inventor of deliberate fictions, of falsehoods.

Elevation of meaning. On the other hand, the meaning of a word can shift to one more elevated in character. *Minister*, for example, which first meant 'servant,' can today be used of the highest officials of a government. A *marshal*, etymologically a 'horse boy,' may today be the highest military officer in a nation. *Constable* has suffered both elevation and degeneration of meaning. From its original sense 'equerry' it rose, in mediaeval times, to the dignity of a high military title. From this highwater mark it has descended to its current respectable but far less dignified meaning.

EXERCISES

1. To which declension do nouns formed with each of the suffixes discussed in this lesson belong? How may their bases be found?

2. Memorize the following Latin words. Indicate the base of each. Using the prefixes and suffixes studied hitherto, form an English derivative from each. Determine, where necessary, its current meaning.

dūrus 'hard'
grātus 'pleasing,' 'agreeable,' 'grateful'

sonus 'sound'
testis 'witness'

3. Determine the etymological meaning of *dentist, florist, insomnia, jurist, linguist, militarist, misery, optimistic, pessimistic, vocalist.*

4. Give the meaning of the suffix in each of the following words: *commerce, hospice, interlude, ministry, prejudice.*

5. Analyze the words *inartistic, inertia, gracious, matrimony, sacristan, succulence.*

6. Analyze each of the italicized words and determine the meaning of the expression in which it appears: *atavistic* tendencies, *infamy* of his actions, *injudicious* choice, accused of *nepotism*, accused of *perfidy*, *supersonic* speed, *virulence* of his hatred.

7. Analyze each italicized word and determine its meaning in the context.

A The simplest phase . . . of *animism* is that in which a spirit or spirits are thought of as dwelling in some particular thing or some particular spot.—CYRIL BAILEY

B "I contacted him" . . . has become part . . . of general conversation, despite the . . . bared teeth of the *purists.*—NEW YORK TIMES

C   The river bears no empty bottles, sandwich
     papers, . . .
   Or other *testimony* of summer nights.—T. S. ELIOT
D   Yon foaming flood seems motionless as ice;
     Its dizzy *turbulence* eludes the eye.—WORDSWORTH

8. Determine the etymological meaning of *libertine* and
purist. What semantic change is revealed by the current
meaning of the first? by the meaning of the second as used in
sentence 7B?

LESSON 15

Multiple-Base Compounds.   Numerals

Up to this point we have studied only compounds in which
one base appears. *Multiple-base compounds* may also be
formed by uniting two or more bases.

Words so formed are divided into *descriptive* and *dependent*
compounds, according to the relationship between the bases.
If the first base modifies or describes the second, the word
belongs to the first category.   *Left-handed*, for example, is a
case in point, since its first base *left* describes the second base
hand. *Multilateral* is another, since the first base *mult-*
(**multus** 'many') modifies the second base *later-* (**latus, lateris**[n]
'side').

When the first base is the object of the second, we are deal-
ing with a *dependent compound*. A *fortune teller* is 'one who
tells fortunes'; the first base is here the object of the verb *tell*.
Since dependent compounds, as the example above shows,
involve verb bases, we shall postpone their study.

Latin Numerals. The following numerals are important
because of their derivatives in English (forms in parentheses
are combining forms used in multiple-base compounds):

CARDINALS

ūnus 1
duo (bi-) 2
trēs (tri-) 3
quattuor (quadri-) 4
quīnque 5
sex 6
septem 7
octō 8
novem 9
decem 10
centum 100
mīlle 1,000

ORDINALS

prīmus 'first'
secundus 'second'
tertius 'third'
quārtus 'fourth'
quīntus 'fifth'
sextus 'sixth'
septimus 'seventh'
octāvus 'eighth'
nōnus 'ninth'
decimus 'tenth'
centē(n)simus $\frac{1}{100}$
mīllē(n)simus $\frac{1}{1,000}$

DISTRIBUTIVES

singulī '1 each'
bīnī '2 each'
ternī or trīnī '3 each'
quaternī '4 each'
quīnī '5 each'
sēnī '6 each'
septēnī '7 each'
octōnī '8 each'

novēnī '9 each'
dēnī '10 each'
quīnquāgēnī '50 each'
sexāgēnī '60 each'
septuāgēnī '70 each'
octōgēnī '80 each'
nōnāgēnī '90 each'
centēnī '100 each'

mīllēnī '1,000 each'

NUMERAL ADVERBS

sēsqui 'one and a half times'
bis 'twice'
ter 'three times'

The combining form sēmi- 'half' appears in multiple-base compounds.

Although Latin numerals have provided more than a few simple derivatives and a large number of compound derivatives, perhaps their chief importance lies in forming multiple-base compounds. Thus *biped* is composed of *bi-* from the Latin combining form bi- '2,' and -*ped*, base of the Latin noun pēs, pedis 'foot.' Similarly, *quinquelateral* consists of *quinque,* the Latin cardinal **quīnque** '5'; *-later-,* base of tʜ Latin noun **latus, lateris** 'side'; and *-al* (**-ālis**).

The form **-ennium** 'year period,' derived from **annus** 'year,' is frequently found as the second element in multiple-base compounds: *triennium,* '3-year period,' *quinquennium* '5-year period.' Care should be taken in analyzing such words as *centennial* and *centenary.* *Centennial* is a multiple-base compound from **centum** '100' and **-ennium,** while *centenary* is simply **centen-,** base of the distributive **centēnī** 'hundred each,' 'hundred,' and **-ārius.**

ETYMOLOGICAL NOTES

Obviously *September* has something to do with **septem** '7,' *October* with **octō** '8,' and so on. Why, then, is September actually the *ninth* month of the year and October the *tenth*? The answer is that the Romans originally started their year on March 1—which would make September properly the seventh month, October the eighth, and so on. In 153 B.C., probably, the Romans put back the beginning of the year to January 1, but never bothered to change the names of the months to make them correspond with the new arrangement.

The names of most of our coins come from Latin numerals. *Cent* is from **centum,** the number of cents in a dollar. *Dime,* the tenth part of a dollar, goes back, through Old French, to **decimus.** *Quarter* comes, through Old French, from **quārtārius** 'a fourth part' (**quārtus** + **-ārius**). *Dollar* is of Germanic origin.

Deuce, the two at cards and at dice, is from **duo.** As an exclamation of annoyance ("The deuce!") it probably was first used when the two, which is a losing throw, turned up on the dice. *Trey,* the three at cards and dice, comes from **trēs.** *Dozen* goes back, through Old French, to **duodecim** '12' (**duo** + **decem**). A *carillon* was originally a set of four bells; its ancestor is **quadriliō,** a compound whose base comes from **quadri-,** or from **quadrus** 'square.' The same base appears in *quadrille* 'square dance.'

Among multiple-base derivatives in which Latin numerals

appear, probably the most familiar is *travel*.   This word goes
back to **trepālium,** the Late Latin name for a certain instrument of torture probably made with three beams (**trēs** + **pālus**
'beam').   **Trepālium** entered English first as *ṭravail* 'toil,'
'labor' and then as *travel,* because of the great difficulties involved therein in bygone days.   *Drill* 'heavy fabric of cotton
or linen,' despite its form, comes in part from a Latin numeral.
Its ancestor is **trilīx,** a combination of **tri-** and **līcium** 'thread.'
In a mediaeval university you could choose either the curriculum known as the **trivium,** or the one called the **quadrivium.**
The 'three roads' of the former were grammar, rhetoric, and
logic; the 'four roads' of the latter were arithmetic, geometry,
astronomy, and music.

Here are some multiple-base compounds involving Latin
words other than numerals.   The *porpoise* is etymologically
a 'pig-fish' (**porcus** + **piscis**), named from the extremely useful function it performs as a scavenger.   **Porcus** also appears
as the first element of *porcupine*; the second base comes from
spīna 'thorn.'   The *grampus,* the large blowing, spouting fish,
is etymologically a 'fat fish' (**crassus** + **piscis**).

EXERCISES

1. Divide the following into descriptive and dependent compounds: *bootblack, bankteller, curveball, dropkick, housecleaner,
overcoat, prizefight, proofreader.*

2. Give the etymological meaning of the following multiple-
base compounds: *aquaplane, bicameral, binocular, manicure,
magnanimous, multiform, peninsula, rectangle, rectilinear, trivial, unanimity, uniform, velocipede.*

3. Analyze each of the italicized multiple-base compounds
and determine the meaning of the expression in which it appears: *aquamarine* sky, *atrabilious* temperament, *bilateral*
agreement, *bilingual* inscription, *cuneiform* writing, maintain
one's *equilibrium, equivocal* reply, *longevity* of Biblical characters, await the *millennium,* the forest *primeval, unilateral* denunciation of a treaty, recite in *unison, verisimilitude* of his
portrayal.

4. Which words in the following list are multiple-base compounds: *bicentennial, centenarian, millenary, millennium, quadrilateral, secondary, tercentenary*? Explain your answer. Determine the current meaning of each word.

5. Analyze each italicized word and determine its meaning in the context.

> A   A blank was as good as a prize, if one had the *equanimity* to take it without whimpering or discontent
>
> —VAN WYCK BROOKS
>
> B   The future Golden Age of *Millenarianism* is as impossible a notion as the past Golden Age of Mythology.
>
> —JULIAN HUXLEY
>
> C   He fancied that he had felt himself in the *penumbra* of a very deep sadness.—HARDY
>
> D   I lived in a continual, indefinite, pining fear; tremulous, *pusillanimous*, apprehensive of I knew not what.
>
> —CARLYLE
>
> E   He was a sort of scandalous chronicle for the *quidnuncs* of Granada.—IRVING

6. (a) Which is larger, a *folio* volume, or a *quarto* volume? Show how the etymology of the words provides the answer.

(b) Why is the *centigrade* system for measuring heat so called?

(c) How long was the period of *quarantine* originally?

(d) What is the *Septuagint*? Why was it so named?

(e) Pétain was an *octogenarian* when World War II began. Approximately when was he born?

(f) How long is a *sesquipedalian* word?

(g) How many *biennial* celebrations could have been held between 1940 and 1944? How many *biannual* celebrations?

Lesson 16

Review

1. Define and illustrate:

(a) specialization and generalization of meaning, change from literal to figurative meaning, degeneration of meaning, learned word and popular word.

(b) abstract noun, concrete noun, simple derivative, compound derivative, descriptive compound, dependent compound.

2. Arrange all the suffixes you have studied so far into six lists, as follows, indicating alongside each suffix whether it may be attached to a noun or to an adjective base or to either:

(a) All meaning 'of' or 'pertaining to.'

(b) All meaning 'full of' or 'given to.'

(c) All that form diminutive nouns.

(d) All that form nouns of office.

(e) All that form abstract nouns.

(f) All that form agent nouns.

3. Give the Latin-derived words that are synonymous, element for element, with the following native English words: *godliness, goodness, greatness, heaviness, lightness.*

4. Give the Latin word (and its meaning), the base of which appears in each of the following: *alleviation, amanuensis, approbation, congregation, connotation, consignment, contemporaneous, convocation, declaratory, elongated, excruciating, inexorable.*

5. Analyze *commodious, enormity, equilibrium, gratitude, humanitarianism, pedicure, puritanical, quinquagenarian, sacristan, society, vulgarity.*

6. Give the etymology of all italicized words:

(a) A work in two *cornulent quarto* volumes.—ILLUS-TRATED LONDON NEWS

(b) The *literary* Tories, George Ticknor's *circle*, for *example*, called it the *Hospital* for Incapables.—VAN WYCK BROOKS

(c) I'm very good at *integral* and differential *calculus*,
    I know the scientific names of beings *animalculous*;
    In short, in *matters* vegetable, *animal*, and *mineral*,
    I am the very *model* of a modern *Major-General*.

—W. S. GILBERT

(d) And yet a little story of a shipwrecked sailor, . . . exploring none of the *arcana* of *humanity* and deprived of the *perennial* interest of love, goes on . . . while CLARISSA lies upon the shelves unread.—STEVENSON

7. Compare the etymological meaning of each of the following with its current meaning. What semantic change does each reveal? *cancer, chevalier, militia, morose, nostrum, pauper, special, squire.*

8. Give the etymological meaning of *butler, cattle, chef, dime, gentle, humorous, porpoise, salary, usher.*

CHAPTER FOUR

Latin Verbs

VERBS are *conjugated*, that is, they have a present, past, and future tense, an active and passive voice, an indicative and subjunctive mood, and so forth. We have seen that Latin nouns fall into five declensions; Latin verbs fall into four conjugations.

The most important form of a Latin verb for our purposes is the present active infinitive. This form tells to which of the four conjugations a verb belongs. If its present infinitive active ends in **-āre,** a verb belongs to the First Conjugation; if in **-ēre,** to the Second Conjugation; if in **-ere,** to the Third; if in **-īre,** to the Fourth (note that the only distinction between verbs of the Second and those of the Third Conjugation is the presence or absence of a long mark over *e*).

Another useful verb-form is the first person singular present indicative active (corresponding in English to, for example, "I say," "I do," "I go," and so on). The endings of this form for the four conjugations are: First Conjugation, **-ō,** Second Conjugation, **-eō,** Third Conjugation, **-ō** and **-iō,** Fourth Conjugation, **-iō.** You will note that there are two types of Third-Conjugation verbs: (a) those ending in **-ō,** and (b) those ending in **-iō.** These must be carefully distinguished for reasons that will appear later.

The following chart shows examples of the four conjugations:

CONJUGATION	PRESENT INDICATIVE ACTIVE	PRESENT INFINITIVE ACTIVE
I	laudō 'I praise'	laudāre 'to praise'
II	moneō 'I warn'	monēre 'to warn'
III (a)	dūcō 'I lead'	dūcere 'to lead'
(b)	capiō 'I take'	capere 'to take'
IV	audiō 'I hear'	audīre 'to hear'

There is also a class of verbs in Latin known as *deponent* verbs. Deponent verbs are *passive* in *form* but *active* in *meaning*. They are easily recognizable by their present infinitive endings, which are: First Conjugation, -ārī; Second Conjugation, -ērī; Third Conjugation, -ī; Fourth Conjugation, -īrī. So far as we are concerned, the only difference between deponents and regular verbs is that perfect participles of the former are translated as active and not passive (see below, page 91).

Nouns, as we have seen, have only one base. Verbs usually have four bases: the present-infinitive base, the perfect-participial base, the present-participial base, the gerundive base. Never speak merely of "the verb base": always specify one of the four just mentioned.

LESSON 17

The Present Infinitive and the Perfect Participle

The Present Infinitive. The endings of the present infinitive for the four conjugations have already been mentioned. The present-infinitive base is found by dropping these endings.

CONJUGATION	PRESENT INFINITIVE ACTIVE	PRESENT INFINITIVE BASE
I	laudāre 'to praise'	laud-
	mīrārī 'to wonder at'	mīr-
II	monēre 'to warn'	mon-
	verērī 'to fear'	ver-
III (a)	dūcere 'to lead'	dūc-
	lābī 'to fall'	lāb-
(b)	capere 'to take'	cap-
	patī 'to suffer'	pat-
IV	audīre 'to hear'	aud-
	partīrī 'to share'	part-

The Perfect Participle. The perfect participle (when regular) is formed by adding certain endings to the base of the present infinitive. In the First Conjugation -ātus is added; in the Second, -itus; in the Third, -tus; in the Fourth, -ītus. The First Conjugation is usually regular, but the others offer numerous exceptions. Whether the perfect participle is regularly or irregularly formed, its last two letters are -us, and the perfect-participial base is found by dropping these letters.

The perfect participle is declined like an adjective of the First-Second Declension (see Lesson 3). The -us is replaced by -a when the participle modifies a feminine singular noun, by -um when it modifies a neuter singular noun, and so on.

Except in the case of deponent verbs, the perfect participle is passive in meaning; laudātus, for example, perfect participle of laudāre 'to praise,' is translated 'having *been* praised,' or simply 'praised.' The perfect participle of deponent verbs is active: ūsus, for example, perfect participle of ūtī 'to use,' is translated 'having used.'

CONJU-GATION	PRESENT INFINITIVE	PRESENT-INFINITIVE BASE	PERFECT PARTICIPLE	PERFECT-PARTICIPIAL BASE
I	laudāre 'to praise'	laud-	laudātus 'having been praised,' 'praised'	laudāt-

CONJUGATION	PRESENT INFINITIVE	PRESENT-INFINITIVE BASE	PERFECT PARTICIPLE	PERFECT-PARTICIPIAL BASE
	mīrārī 'to wonder at'	mīr-	mīrātus 'having wondered at'	mīrāt-
II	monēre 'to warn'	mon-	monitus 'having been warned,' 'warned'	monit-
	verērī 'to fear'	ver-	veritus 'having feared'	verit-
III (a)	dūcere 'to lead'	dūc-	ductus 'having been led,' 'led'	duct-
	lābī 'to fall'	lāb-	lapsus 'having fallen'	laps-
(b)	capere 'to take'	cap-	captus 'having been taken,' 'taken'	capt-
	patī 'to suffer'	pat-	passus 'having suffered'	pass-
IV	audīre 'to hear'	aud-	audītus 'having been heard,' 'heard'	audīt-
	partīrī 'to share'	part-	partītus 'having shared'	partīt-

Vocabulary Listing of Verbs. All verbs are listed under the present infinitive. In order to distinguish Third-Conjugation verbs of type (a) from those of type (b), -iō (-ior for deponents) is placed in parentheses after the latter: **facere (-iō)** 'to do'; **patī (-ior)** 'to suffer.' Except in the case of First-Conjugation verbs, almost all of which are regular, the perfect participle will be given after the present infinitive: **mergere, mersus** 'to dip.' Occasionally, a verb has no perfect participle; this fact will be indicated by a dash: **urgēre, ———** 'to press.'

Latin Verb-Forms in English. Some Latin verb-forms have been taken over by English without change. A group of third-person singular active forms, for example, has been borrowed as nouns. Thus *caret*, the symbol (∧) we use to indicate that something is missing, literally means 'it lacks'; *exit*, the stage direction, means 'he goes out'; *deficit* means 'it is wanting'; *tenet*, a doctrine one holds, means 'he holds.' *Veto*, as the *-o* indicates, is a first person singular which in Latin means 'I forbid.' *Credo*, one's system of belief, is the Latin for 'I believe.' *Video*, the popular term for television, is etymologically 'I see.' *Memento* is an imperative meaning 'remember!' Sometimes the verb-form is part of a phrase which English has taken over. *Habeas corpus* literally means (that) 'you have the body'; it is the name of a writ which requires that a person be brought before a judge or court, especially one who has been thrown into prison for reasons that smack of illegality.

EXERCISES

1. (a) Memorize all the forms and the meaning of the following verbs.

dūcere, ductus 'to lead'
ferre (base **fer-**), **lātus** 'to bring,' 'to bear' (irregular verb of the Third Conjugation)
fundere, fūsus 'to pour'
mittere, missus 'to let go,' 'to send'
mūtāre 'to change'

plicāre, plicātus or **plicitus** 'to fold'
rogāre 'to ask,' 'to propose a law'
servāre 'to save'
sequī, secūtus 'to follow'
trahere, tractus 'to draw'
vidēre, vīsus 'to see'

(b) To which conjugation does each verb belong?

(c) Form the perfect participle (where it is not given). Translate the perfect participle.

(d) Form the present-infinitive and perfect-participial base.

(e) Translate **dūcō, fundō, mūtō, torqueō, teneō.**

(f) Identify the following forms: **ductum, fūsae, missa, mūtātī.**

2. (a) Determine the etymological meaning of *affidavit, ignoramus, interest, posse, recipe*.

(b) Determine the etymological and current meaning of *caveat, fiat, floruit, habitat, stet*.

3. The following are Latin phrases which English has taken over. Determine the pronunciation and current meaning of each.

ipse dīxit 'he himself said it'—Used as a noun in English: "The campaign speech of today is not a recital of facts, but a series of *ipse dixits*: you are to take the speaker's word that everything bad, from high prices to lack of rain, is directly traceable to his political opponents."

nōn sequitur 'it does not follow'—Used as a noun in English: "Without really understanding the point under discussion, he blurted out some remark—a *non sequitur*, as a glance at the bewildered expressions around him immediately revealed."

tabula rāsa 'erased tablet'—Used as a noun in English: "The very fact of being on a holiday . . . makes you keen. . . . Your mind has become a *tabula rasa*—wax to be inscribed anyhow by any one."—BEERBOHM

vade mēcum 'go with me'—Used as a noun in English:
Aristotle's rules,
The *vade mecum* of the true sublime,
Which makes so many poets, and some fools.—BYRON

4. Determine the current meaning of the following abbreviations: *cf.* (= **confer** 'compare'), *q.v.* (= **quod vide** 'which see'), *sc.* (= **scīlicet** 'it is permitted to know'), *viz.* (= **vidēlicet** 'it is permitted to see'), *i.e.* (= **id est** 'that is').

LESSON 18

The Present Infinitive and the Perfect Participle in English. Denominative Verbs

The Present Infinitive. This form, with its ending dropped or replaced by silent -*e*, may be borrowed as a verb.

PRESENT INFINITIVE	ENGLISH VERB
errāre 'to wander'	*err*
urgēre 'to press'	*urge*
tendere 'to stretch,' 'to hold a course'	*tend*

Such verbs may be made over into nouns in English. Thus we have *an urge* alongside *to urge*.

The Perfect Participle. This form has produced English adjectives, verbs, and nouns.

(a) *Adjectives.*—The perfect participle is used in Latin as an adjective and appears, therefore, in English as such. The changes in form are the same as occur in the borrowing of First-Second Declension adjectives (see Lesson 3).

PRESENT INFINITIVE	PERFECT PARTICIPLE	ENGLISH ADJECTIVE
sēdāre 'to calm'	sēdātus 'calmed'	*sedate*
rapere 'to seize'	raptus 'seized'	*rapt*
spargere 'to scatter'	sparsus 'scattered'	*sparse*

Since perfect participles are used as adjectives, the suffixes previously mentioned as attachable to adjective bases (see Lessons 7–10, 13, 14) may be attached to perfect-participial bases as well. Thus, in *prenatal,* -*al* has been attached to *nāt-*, base of nātus, the perfect participle of nāscī. A complete analysis of this word would be:

(1) *praenātālis

(2) *-nat-* base of **nātus,** perfect participle of **nāscī** 'to be born'

(3) *pre-* Latin prefix **prae** 'before'

    -al   Latin suffix **-ālis** 'of,' 'pertaining to'

(4) Etymological Meaning: 'before birth'

(5) Current Meaning: same as etymological meaning

(b) *Verbs.*—The perfect participle may give rise to verbs as well as adjectives. This is especially true of *denominative* verbs (see below).

PRESENT INFINITIVE	PERFECT PARTICIPLE	ENGLISH VERB
penetrāre 'to pierce'	**penetrātus** 'pierced'	*penetrate*

(c) *Nouns.*—Nouns are derived from perfect participles in either of two ways:

1. The perfect participle is in form a First-Second Declension adjective. We have already pointed out that the neuter of any Latin adjective may be used as a noun (see Lesson 3, page 29).

PRESENT INFINITIVE	PERFECT PARTICIPLE	LATIN NOUN	ENGLISH NOUN
sternere 'to spread'	**strātus** 'spread'	**strātum** 'something spread'	*stratum*
facere 'to do'	**factus** 'done'	**factum** 'something done'	*fact*

2. The perfect participle, in its masculine form, may be made into a noun of the Fourth Declension. Such nouns are *abstract* in meaning and usually come over into English as such. The changes in form are the same as those described for Fourth-Declension nouns (see Lesson 5).

Since these Fourth-Declension nouns are identical in form with the masculine of the perfect participles from which they come, in order to distinguish the two we have included their bases in parentheses in the following table of examples.

PRESENT INFINITIVE	PERFECT PARTICIPLE	LATIN ABSTRACT NOUN	ENGLISH NOUN
cēnsēre 'to assess'	cēnsus (cēns-)	cēnsus (cēnsu-) 'assessment'	census
agere 'to do'	actus (act-)	actus (actu-) 'a doing'	act
ūtī 'to employ,' 'to use'	ūsus (ūs-)	ūsus (ūsu-) 'a using,' 'employ-ment'	use
lābī 'to fall'	lapsus (laps-)	lapsus (lapsu-) 'a falling'	lapse

The bases of these Fourth-Declension nouns are found by merely dropping the final -s, as shown in the table above. To them, the suffixes described in Lessons 7–10, 13, and 14 may be attached; for example, *visual* =

(1) **vīsuālis**
(2) **vīsu-** base of **vīsus** 'sight,' Fourth-Declension abstract noun from **vīsus,** perfect participle of **vidēre** 'to see'
(3) *-al* Latin suffix **-ālis** 'pertaining to'
(4) Etymological Meaning: 'pertaining to sight'
(5) Current Meaning: same as etymological meaning

Denominative Verbs. A denominative verb is one that has been formed from a noun or adjective. Latin denominatives are, with some exceptions, formed by adding **-āre**, the First-Conjugation ending, to a noun or adjective base. They appear in English in the same ways as other verbs.

LATIN NOUN OR ADJECTIVE	DENOMINATIVE VERB	ENGLISH LOAN WORD
arma 'weapons'	**armāre** 'to equip with weapons,' **armātus**	*arm* (verb)
aequus 'equal'	**aequāre** 'to make equal,' **aequātus**	*equate*
locus 'place'	**locāre** 'to place,' **locātus**	*locate*

A few denominatives are deponent. A few belong to other than the First Conjugation.

		ENGLISH
LATIN NOUN	DENOMINATIVE VERB	LOAN WORD
cavilla 'mockery'	cavillārī 'to mock,'	*cavil*
	cavillātus	
testis 'witness'	testārī 'to witness,'	*testate*
	testātus	
fīnis 'limit,' 'end'	fīnīre 'to limit,' fīnītus	*finite*

The following analysis of *granulate* will show the pattern to be used in analyzing derivatives of denominative verbs:

(1) *grānulātus, perfect participle of *grānulāre,
     denominative verb from   grānulum 'little grain',
         a compound of   grānum 'grain'
             and   -ulum diminutive suffix
(2) Etymological Meaning: 'to make into little grains'
(3) Current Meaning: same as etymological meaning

ETYMOLOGICAL NOTES

Cantata, borrowed through Italian like so many of our musical terms, offers no etymological difficulty. **Cantāre**, a First-Conjugation verb, means in Latin 'to sing,' its perfect participle is **cantātus**, and the feminine form of that is **cantāta**. *Armada*, a borrowing through Spanish this time, is also clear: it comes from **armāta**, feminine of **armātus** 'armed' (**armāre** 'to arm'). Now, we can take a further step to such words as *arcade* and *tirade* which have come to us through French. The French ending *-ade* only partially disguises the fact that, like *cantata* and *armada*, these words come from Latin perfect participles. An *arcade* is something 'made into (the shape of) an arch' from **arcāta**, perfect participle of **arcāre** 'to arch' (denominative of **arcus**). A *tirade* is a 'long-drawn-out' speech from *tīrāta, perfect participle of *tīrāre 'to draw.' The ending *-ad*, which is even commoner than *-ade*, has the same origin. **Sal** means 'salt' in Latin, and the verb meaning 'to salt' would theoretically be *salāre, *salātus; the most important thing about a *salad*, etymologically, therefore, is that it is 'salted.' Similarly, the *ballad* in origin must have had a good deal to do with dancing (**ballāre** 'to dance').

Sometimes the perfect-participial ending of First-Conjugation verbs received much more drastic treatment. Under certain circumstances it was changed in French to *-ée* or *-é*, both of which became *-y* in English. Thus **armāta,** which we saw produce *armada* through Spanish, in French became *armée,* whence *army*; **jūrāta** 'sworn' became *jurée* and finally *jury*; **volāta 'flown' (volāre 'to fly') became *volée* 'flight' and finally *volley*. *Jelly* comes from the French *gelée* 'frost,' from **gelāta** 'frozen' (**gelāre** 'to freeze'; the Italian word for 'ices' is *gelati*).

Some everyday words go back to Latin denominative verbs. When you *pay* a bill you etymologically 'make peace,' since *pay* comes ultimately from **pācāre** (**pāx, pācis** 'peace'). To *search* is 'to go in circles'; the verb is from **circāre** (**circus** 'circle'). When you *peel* an orange you etymologically 'strip it of its hair'; **pilus** means 'hair' in Latin, **pilāre** 'to remove hair,' and *peel* probably comes from the latter. *Lease* and the *laissez* of *laissez faire* are closely connected; both come from **laxāre** 'to loosen,' 'to release,' denominative of **laxus** 'loose.' Then there is *solder*, ultimately from **solidāre** 'to make solid (**solidus**).' **Solidus** is an interesting word. Under the Roman emperors it was the name given to a gold coin, a use which is preserved today among the British in their abbreviation 's.' Although we translate this as 'shilling,' it really stands for **solidus** (the 'd.,' translated as 'pence,' stands for **dēnārius,** a Roman silver coin of low denomination). A *soldier* (**solidārius) is etymologically 'one who works for **solidī** ('money'),' a reflection of the days when mercenary armies were the rule.

A pair of words which come from Latin denominative verbs and which, though identical in form in English, are totally different in origin are *quarry* 'prey' and *quarry* 'excavation for building stone.' The latter is literally a 'place for squaring.' It goes back, through French, to the Late Latin **quadrāria,** from **quadrāre** 'to square,' denominative of **quadrus.** Stone is still quarried in squares today. Incidentally, **quadrāta,** the perfect participle of **quadrāre,** became *carré* in Old French, and is preserved in the name of the famous district in New

Orleans, the Vieux Carré, literally 'old quarter.' The other
quarry has to do with skins or hides and not stones. Today
it means the object of a hunt while still very much alive, but
centuries ago it referred to an animal only after it had been
hunted down, killed, and skinned. The *quarry* in those days
was the animal's entrails which, wrapped in the hide, were
given to the hounds. The significant point, etymologically,
is that the entrails were put in the slain animal's hide, for
quarry goes back, through the Old French **curée**, to *coriāta
'skinned' (*coriāre 'to skin,' from **corium** 'hide').

EXERCISES

1. Memorize all the forms and the meaning of the following
verbs. Form a simple derivative from each.

clāmāre 'to cry out'

fārī, fātus 'to speak'

movēre, mōtus 'to move'

solvere, solūtus 'to loose,' 'to free'

stāre 'to stand'

stringere, strictus 'to draw tight'

tendere, tēnsus or **tentus** 'to stretch,' 'to hold a course'

terere, trītus 'to rub,' 'to wear'

torquēre, tortus 'to twist'

2. Form Latin denominative verbs meaning the following
(all are First Conjugation): 'to (make) good,' 'to middle,' 'to
mouth,' 'to number,' 'to (produce) a race,' 'to (set a) boundary,' 'to step,' 'to wheel,' 'to work.' Form a simple derivative from each.

3. Analyze the following words:

   (a) *clang, err, purge*

   (b) *fatalism, notice, sanctity, sectarian, tributary*

   (c) *animate, articulate, calculate, capitulate, circulate, radiate*

   (d) *actual, actuate, casualty, flatulent, habituate, punctual, punctuate.*

4. Analyze each of the italicized words and determine the
meaning of the expression in which it appears: *carping* critic,

cavil about details, *coruscating* wit, to *fulminate* criticisms, a *hiatus* in his chain of evidence, *importune* for improvement of conditions, *militate* against success, *mulct* a person of what is his due, *postulate* the existence of a supreme deity, *strata* of society, *sumptuary* laws, *tacit* understanding, *verging* on manhood, *vitiates* his conclusions, a copy of the *Vulgate*.

5. Analyze each italicized word and determine its meaning in the context.

A When he broke too many resolutions, he introduced into his reckoning sets of fixed exceptions, amendments on amendments. . . . By this means, and others, he made himself a *casuist*.—VAN WYCK BROOKS

B A fouler *fact*
Did never traitor in the land commit.—SHAKESPEARE

C To *insulate* ourselves, to retire from all aid, and to wrap ourselves in the mantle of self-sufficiency. . . .
—JEFFERSON

D Manifold are the tastes and dispositions of the enlightened *literati*, who turn over the pages of history.
—IRVING

E (a) A pendulum *oscillates;* (b) *oscillate* between good and evil; (c) *vacillate* between two courses of action.

F In all the *polite* Nations of the World, this part of the Drama has met with publick Encouragement.
—ADDISON

G Thou concludest like the *sanctimonious* pirate, that went to sea with the Ten Commandments, but scraped one out of the table.—SHAKESPEARE

H Time has *tessellated* the surface of the canvas.
—BEERBOHM

6. Give the doublets of *coy, ditto, feat, isolate, privy, strait.*

7. Determine the etymological meaning of *actuary* and *levee* (of a river). What semantic change does the current meaning of each reveal?

8. The following are Latin phrases which have been taken over by English. Determine the pronunciation and meaning of each in English.

ad infīnītum 'to infinity'—Used as an adverb in English:
So, naturalists observe, a flea
Hath smaller fleas that on him prey;
And these have smaller still to bite 'em;
And so proceed *ad infinitum.*—SWIFT

dē jūre and dē factō 'according to law,' 'according to the
facts'—Used as adjectives or adverbs in English, for example: "In most large corporations, stockholders exercise *de jure* control, while *de facto* control remains in the
hands of the board of directors."

ipsō factō 'by that very fact'—Used as an adverb in English: "The best possible critic of the Iliad would be, *ipso
facto,* . . . incapable of being the author of it."

—SIR PHILIP FRANCIS

LESSON 19

Prefixes

Although prefixes are occasionally used with nouns (cf. Lesson 11), their chief importance is in the formation of compound verbs.

PRESENT INFINITIVE	PREFIX	LATIN COMPOUND VERB	ENGLISH LOAN WORD
solvere 'to loosen,' 'to free'	ab- 'from'	absolvere	*absolve*
PERFECT PARTICIPLE			
solūtus 'having been freed'	ab-	absolūtus	*absolute*

When compounded with prefixes, verbs frequently depart slightly from their normal form. In such cases the form to be used in compounds will be placed in parentheses, immediately following the regular form—for example, **caedere, caesus (-cīdere, -cīsus)** 'to cut.'

PRESENT INFINITIVE	PREFIX	LATIN COMPOUND VERB	ENGLISH LOAN WORD
caedere 'to cut'	**ex-** 'out'	**excīdere**	*excide*
PERFECT PARTICIPLE			
caesus 'having been cut'	**ex-**	**excīsus**	*excise* (verb)

Such changes are found in denominative verbs as well: **sacrāre, sacrātus** (denominative of **sacer, sacrī** 'sacred') becomes, in compounds, **-secrāre, -secrātus; causāre, causātus** (from **causa** 'cause') becomes **-cūsāre, -cūsātus.**

The basic form and meaning of each prefix are given first in the list below and in subsequent lists. The other forms are used before certain consonants for the sake of euphony—for example, **attendere** instead of **'adtendere,' differre** instead of **'disferre,'** and so on.

After some prefixes we have added the note: "also used intensively." A prefix so marked in certain words may give up its basic meaning and be used merely to intensify the meaning of the base to which it is attached. For example, **con-** means basically 'with,' but in the word *convince* (**vincere** 'to conquer') it is used intensively: *convince* means 'to conquer completely (in a discussion).' Prefixes so used may be translated 'very,' 'thoroughly,' 'completely,' or the like.

ab-, abs-, ā- 'from,' 'away from,' 'off,' 'to the bad'
ad-, a-, ac-, af-, ag-, al-, an-, ap-, ar-, as-, at- 'to,' 'toward' (denotes adherence, addition, or proximity); also used intensively
ante- 'before'
circum- 'around,' 'about,' 'on all sides'

con-, com-, col-, cor-, co- (prepositional form **cum**) 'with,' 'together,' 'together with'; also used intensively

contrā- 'against,' 'contrary,' 'in opposition'

dē- 'down,' 'off,' 'away' (denotes reversal, undoing, deprival, or ridding of); also used intensively

dis-, dī-, dif- 'asunder,' 'apart,' 'separately,' 'not,' 'un-'

ETYMOLOGICAL NOTES

Note that the prefix **a-** is ambiguous: it may be a form either of **ab-** 'away' or **ad-** 'toward.' Thus the *a-* of *aver* goes back to **ad-** (**advērāre* 'to assert as true,' from **vērus** 'true'), but the *a-* of *averse* (**āversus** 'turned away') is from **ab-**. The word meaning etymologically 'turned toward' is *adverse*. This word, incidentally, reflects the fact that its ancestor **adversus** was once a sailor's term. The ancients could sail efficiently only with a following wind, so a wind that came from head on, that was 'turned toward them,' was, naturally, an *adverse* wind.

The prefix **contrā-**, when borrowed through French, appears in English as *counter-*. Thus we have *counteract* (**contrā-** + **actus,** perfect participle of **agere**), *countersign* (**contrā-** + **sīgnāre**), and the like.

The verbs listed below in Question 1 of the Exercises have numerous derivatives through French. *Conceive* and *conceit* go back to **capere.** *Conceive* comes from **concipere** 'to seize thoroughly (with the mind),' a compound of **con-** and **capere.** The perfect participle **conceptus** has given us *conceit.* Similarly, **dēcipere** has produced *deceive*, and **dēceptus**, its perfect participle, *deceit.* **Jungere** has yielded *join*, **adjungere** *adjoin*, and so on, and **jūnctus,** the perfect participle, is the source of *joint.* **Stringere** has given *strain*, **constringere**, *constrain*, and **strictus,** the perfect participle, *strait.* The *-tain* that appears in *contain, detain,* and so forth, is from **-tinēre,** the form **tenēre** takes in compounds. **Factum,** perfect participle of **facere,** is the source not only of *fact,* but of *feat* and *fait.* Correspondingly, **dēfectus,** the perfect participle of **dēficere** (**dē-** + **facere**) has produced *defect* and *defeat. Counterfeit* and *dis-*

comfit belong to this group too. The first comes from the mediaeval Latin **contrāfactus,** the second from **discōnfectus.**

In other derivatives, the original source is even more disguised. *Point* is from **punctum,** neuter of **punctus** 'pricked,' perfect participle of **pungere.** *Paint* is from **pictus,** the perfect participle of **pingere** 'to paint'; its doublet is *pinto,* used of horses that are so colored as to give the appearance of being 'painted.' Then there are *route* and *rout* from **ruptus** 'broken,' the perfect participle of **rumpere.** A road that is 'broken' through is a *route,* and an army when 'broken' breaks into a *rout.* *Couch* and *allow,* unlikely as it appears, are related. *Couch* comes from **collocāre,** the denominative of **locus** plus the prefix **con-;** to *couch,* after all, involves 'placing' of a sort. The denominative formed from **locus** with **ad-** is **allocāre** and this word is the source of *allow* in some of its sense. 'To *allow* (him a share)' is etymologically 'to place (a share) at (his side).'

EXERCISES

1. Memorize all the forms and meanings of the following verbs. Using the prefixes listed in this lesson, form a derivative from each.

agere, actus (-igere, -actus) 'to do,' 'to act,' 'to drive'

capere (-iō), captus (-cipere, -ceptus) 'to take,' 'to grasp,' 'to hold'

cernere, crētus 'to sift,' 'to distinguish'

facere (-iō), factus (-ficere, -fectus) 'to make,' 'to do'

flectere, flexus 'to bend'

gerere, gestus 'to bear,' 'to carry on'

jacere (-iō), jactus (-jicere, -jectus) 'to throw'

jungere, jūnctus 'to join'

jūrāre 'to swear'

lūdere, lūsus 'to play'

-plēre, -plētus 'to fill'

putāre 'to reckon,' 'to think'

regere, rēctus (-rigere, -rēctus) 'to straighten,' 'to rule'

rumpere, ruptus 'to break'

scrībere, scrīptus 'to write'

struere, strūctus 'to build'

tenēre, tentus (-tinēre, -tentus) 'to hold'

vertere, versus 'to turn'

vincere, victus 'to conquer'

volvere, volūtus 'to roll'

2. Analyze the following words:

(a) *abstain, collide, commute, conjoint, defunct, destitute, diffuse, disappoint, disconsolate, dissolute, distort, distrain*

(b) *accommodate, adore, aggravate, alleviate, approximate, combine, consecrate, convoke, decapitate, declare, degenerate, designate, deviate, dislocate, divulge*

(c) *advent, appetite, commentary, conquest, consensus, context, contract, detritus, dispensary, district, victuals*

3. What is the meaning of the prefix in *adhere, associate, concise, concoct, contort, contrite, convulse, distend*?

4. (a) Form Latin compound verbs having the following etymological meanings and give an English derivative from each: 'to cry out to,' 'to pour together,' 'to move down,' 'to stand against,' 'to bring together.'

(b) Form Latin denominative compound verbs having the following etymological meanings and give an English derivative from each: 'to place to,' 'to price down,' 'to (make) very steadfast,' 'to liken to,' 'to work together,' 'to flock together.'

5. Analyze each italicized word and determine the meaning of the expression in which it appears: an *adjunct* of the verb, to *ameliorate* conditions, *antepenultimate* syllable, an *apposite* remark, to *arrogate* unconstitutional powers to oneself, to *asperse* an enemy's character, *composite* as well as simple units, to *confute* a theory, to provide a *conspectus*, a sentence difficult to *construe*, *consummate* skill, *contrapuntal* treatment of a theme, to *corrugate* one's brow, jailed for *defalcating*, to *deprecate* his anger, *disaffected* members of the government, to *divagate* from the topic.

6. Analyze each italicized word and determine its meaning in the context.

A   The fact is I was completely unnerved by a sheer blank fright, pure *abstract* terror, unconnected with any *distinct* shape of physical danger.—CONRAD

B   (a) Kneeling at the bedside, his nose *adumbrating* the coverlid of my bed.—MARRYAT   (b) Its duties were very ill defined, or rather not defined at all, but only *adumbrated.*—JAMES MILL

C   Through *attenuated* tones of violins
    Mingled with remote cornets.—T. S. ELIOT

D   His two chamberlains
    Will I with wine and wassail so *convince*
    That memory, the warder of the brain,
    Shall be a fume.—SHAKESPEARE

E   So, by a roaring tempest on the flood,
    A whole armado of *convicted* sail
    Is scatter'd and disjoin'd from fellowship.
                      —SHAKESPEARE

F   The left-hand path, *declining* fearfully,
    Was ready downfall to the deepest hell.—KYD

G   What deadlier than that square jaw, with the bone
so sharply *delineated* under the taut skin?—BEERBOHM

H   Tell me what state, what dignity, what honour,
    Canst thou *demise* to any child of mine?
                      —SHAKESPEARE

I   He wisely refrained from *deputing* the task of tending his sheep at this season to a hireling.—HARDY

J   A great number of people in every age, do want morality without religion: it is a great *desideratum*.
                  —JAMES BOWLING MOZLEY

K   Sham'st thou not, knowing whence thou art
      extraught,
    To let thy tongue *detect* thy base-born heart?
                      —SHAKESPEARE

L   There are few words in the English language which
are employed in a more loose and *uncircumscribed* sense
than those of the Fancy and the Imagination.—ADDISON

7. The following phrases contain words that are sometimes
confused. Determine the etymological meaning of each pair
and show how it provides the clue for distinguishing between
them.

    A   *abjure* drink; *adjure* him to keep his vow

    B   *cónjure* up ghosts of the past; *conjúre* him to help

    C   *abrogate* a law; *contravene* a law

    D   *adduce* instances; *conduce* to a better understanding

    E   "Father" *denotes* one that has begotten; "father"

connotes male sex, greater experience, affection, guidance, and so forth.

8. Precisely how are *defer* ('postpone'), *defer* ('submit'), and *differ* linguistically related?

LESSON 20

Prefixes (*Cont'd*). Frequentative Verbs

ex-, ē-, ef- 'out,' 'out of,' 'from,' 'off,' 'forth,' 'without'; also used intensively

in-, il-, im-, ir- 'in,' 'on,' 'upon,' 'into,' 'toward,' 'against'

in-, il-, im-, ir- 'not,' 'un-'

inter-, intel- 'between'

intrō- 'within'

ob-, oc-, of-, op- 'to,' 'toward,' 'for,' 'against,' 'meeting,' 'in the way,' 'hindering,' 'veiling'; also used intensively

per-, pel- 'through,' 'to the bad'; also used intensively

post- 'after'

Frequentative Verbs. The Romans formed certain verbs by attaching the ending **-āre**—that is, the present infinitive ending of the First Conjugation—to the bases of perfect participles. Verbs so formed serve to express repeated or intensive action and are, therefore, called *frequentative verbs.* Even in Latin, however, these verbs often lose their frequentative or intensive force and it consequently rarely appears in English.

	LATIN VERB	FREQUENTATIVE VERB	ENGLISH LOAN WORD
PRESENT INFINITIVE:	**premere** 'to press'	**pressāre** 'to keep on pressing'	*press* (verb)
PERFECT PARTICIPLE:	**pressus**	**pressātus**	——

	LATIN VERB	FREQUENTATIVE VERB	ENGLISH LOAN WORD
PRESENT INFINITIVE:	**dīcere** 'to say'	**dictāre** 'to keep on saying'	——
PERFECT PARTICIPLE:	**dictus**	**dictātus**	*dictate*

You will note that, so far as its form is concerned, the verb *press* could be derived from the perfect participle **pressus** as well as from the frequentative verb **pressāre**. In ambiguous cases such as this only the dictionary can provide the answer.

ETYMOLOGICAL NOTES

Words that contain the element *-pose* (*expose, compose,* and so forth) are related to both **pausāre** 'to cease,' and **pōnere** 'to set.' They take their form from **pausāre** which in French became *poser; pose,* thus, is the doublet of *pause.* But their meaning comes from **pōnere**: *compose* is not 'to cease together,' but 'to set together,' *expose* is 'to set out,' and so forth.

When combined with prefixes, **caedere** 'to cut' becomes **-cīdere**, and **cadere** 'to fall' becomes **-cidere**, making it difficult to distinguish between their English derivatives without recourse to the dictionary. *Excide* 'to cut out' derives from **caedere** but *coincide* 'to fall in together' from **cadere**. Incidentally, *excise*, the tax term, is not from **excīdere** 'to cut out.' It probably comes, through Dutch, from *accēnsus, a Late Latin compound of **cēnsēre**, **cēnsus** 'to reckon.' Another pair of Latin verbs to be distinguished is **pendēre** 'to hang' (with a perfect participle **-pēnsus,** found in compounds only), and **pendere, pēnsus** 'to weigh,' 'to pay.' *Append* 'to hang to,' *depend* 'to hang from,' and so forth are from the former, but *expend* 'to pay out' is from the latter. Another pair easily confused is **pangere** 'to drive in,' 'to fasten' and **pacīscī** 'to make an agreement,' since the perfect participle of both is **pactus.** *Cómpact,* 'an agreement' is, of course, from the second. *Compáct*, the adjective meaning 'well fastened together,' comes from the first.

When borrowed through French, **in-** (**im-**) often turns up in English as *en-* (*em-*). *Endorse*, for example, is from **indorsāre** 'to note on the back (**dorsum**),' *enchant* from **incantāre**, *employ* from **implicāre**. French has handled the prefix **ex-** even more roughly, for in some derivatives it is now represented only by an initial *s-*. *Scour* 'to cleanse,' for example, is from **excūrāre** 'to take good care of,' *scourge* from **excoriāre** 'to flay,' *scarce* from **excerptus** 'plucked out.' *Sluice*, the gate that controls the level of a body of water by shutting out the inflow, is from **exclūsa**, the feminine perfect participle of **exclūdere** 'to shut out.' *Svelte* 'lissom,' 'supple,' a rather elegant word, comes from a rather prosaic ancestor, **exvellitus** 'pulled out,' the perfect participle in Vulgar Latin of **exvellere**.

We mentioned above that *employ* comes from **implicāre**, a compound of **plicāre** 'to fold.' So do *imply, implicate*, and *implicit*. When you *imply* something, it is 'folded in' what you say; when something gets you 'in its folds' you are *implicated*; when something is not obvious but buried 'within the folds' of a statement, it is *implicit*. **Displicāre**, 'to spread the folds out,' 'to scatter,' is another compound of **plicāre**. From it we have gotten, through French, *deploy* and *display*; you *deploy* an army when you, as it were, 'spread its folds,' and you *display* an object when you 'spread the folds' apart so that it can be seen. **Explicāre** has given us *explicate, explicit*, and the noun *explóit*. The verb *explóit*, although closely related does not make a fourth, since it comes from the frequentative verb *****explicitāre**.

Here are a few more derivatives from frequentative verbs. *Jet* and *jut* are doublets from **jactāre**, the frequentative of **jacere**. *Jetty* 'that which juts out (into the sea)' is from **jactātus** (cf. *jury, jelly, volley* in Etymological Notes, Lesson 18). **Quassāre**, the frequentative of **quatere**, **quassus** 'to break,' 'to smash' is responsible for *quash* and for the *-cas* of *fracas*. The latter, which we took from the Italian *fracasso* is literally an 'under smashing' (**īnfrā** 'below' + **quassāre**).

Chant is from **cantāre,** the frequentative of **canere, cantus** 'to sing.'

EXERCISES

1. Memorize all the forms and meanings of the following verbs. Using the prefixes listed in this and the previous lesson, form two derivatives from each.

caedere, caesus (**-cīdere, -cīsus**) 'to cut'

habēre, habitus (**-hibēre, -hibitus**) 'to have,' 'to hold'

legere, lēctus (**-ligere, -lēctus**) 'to gather,' 'to read,' 'to choose'

pausāre 'to cease' (see Etymological Notes)

pendēre, -pēnsus 'to hang'

pōnere, positus 'to place,' 'to set' (see Etymological Notes)

portāre 'to carry'

premere, pressus (**-primere, -pressus**) 'to press'

pungere, punctus 'to prick'

quaerere, quaesītus (**-quīrere, -quīsītus**) 'to seek'

salīre, saltus (**-silīre, -sultus**) 'to leap'

secāre, sectus 'to cut'

sedēre, sessus (**-sidēre, -sessus**) 'to sit'

sistere, status (**-sistere, -stitus**) 'to stand,' 'to cause to stand'

statuere, statūtus (**-stituere, -stitūtus**) 'to set up'

trūdere, trūsus 'to push'

2. (*a*) Memorize all the forms and meanings of the following verbs. Using the prefixes listed in this and the previous lesson, form two derivatives from each.

(*b*) Form a frequentative verb from each and translate it. With or without the use of prefixes, form a derivative from each frequentative verb.

dīcere, dictus 'to say'

pellere, pulsus 'to drive'

pendere, pēnsus 'to weigh,' 'to pay'

sentīre, sēnsus 'to feel'

3. (*a*) Form Latin compound verbs having the following etymological meanings and give an English derivative from each: 'to lead within,' 'to bring in,' 'to follow out,' 'to twist

out,' 'to turn to the bad,' 'to pour in,' 'to let go through,' 'to draw out,' 'to stretch in,' 'to drive out,' 'to take between,' 'to throw in the way,' 'to set after,' 'to build in the way,' 'to write after,' 'to swear to the bad.'

(*b*) Form Latin denominative compound verbs having the following etymological meanings and give an English derivative from each: 'to work out,' 'to (put) care to,' 'to (play) middle (man) between,' 'to lengthen out,' 'to (put into) flesh.'

(*c*) What words, derived from Latin compound denominative verbs are equivalent, element for element, to *embody, unended, unlettered, unwitnessed.*

4. Analyze the words *decompose, emissary, enunciate, eventual, impersonate, ineffectual, ingratiate, inquest, obituary.*

5. The following list contains eight pairs of words that are linguistically related. Select the pairs and show in each case what the relationship is (for example, *conduce* and *induct* are related. *Conduce* contains **dūc-** present-infinitive base of **dūcere** 'to lead,' and *induct* contains **duct-,** perfect-participial base of the same verb): *coincide, collate, concise, conjoint, consult, content, convert, defer, disappoint, excide, excoriate, expunge, exult, inoculate, inquire, insult, interfere, obverse, oculist, pertain, quarry, score.*

6. Analyze each italicized word and determine the meaning of the expression in which it appears: *engender* a new spirit, *enjoin* silence, *eviscerate* a sacrificial victim, *excoriate* with a tongue-lashing, *exculpated* and released, *execrate* one's lot in life, *expatiate* on a subject, *extirpate* crime, *immured* for years, *imprecate* evil upon, *innate* modesty, *inordinate* lack of discipline, an *inveterate* smoker, an *obdurate* father, *obfuscate* the issue, *obsess* his interest, *oppugn* his honesty, salary plus *perquisites.*

7. Analyze each italicized word and determine its meaning in the context.

A　(a) It may seriously *affect* his health.　(b) We hope to *effect* an improvement.

B   Yet has he,
In his immortal spirit, been as free
As the sky-searching lark, and as *elate.*—KEATS
C   Spare not the babe,
Whose dimpled smiles from fools *exhaust* their
        mercy.—SHAKESPEARE
D   As if . . . Teufelsdröckh had not already *expecto-rated* his antipedagogic spleen.—CARLYLE
E   Proves, not only by great authorities brought to-gether, but by *exquisite* reasons and theorems almost mathematically demonstrative . . . —MILTON
F   The whole house, inclusive of the complaining flag-staff on the roof, *impended* over the water.—DICKENS
G   Letters, more or fewer, from all the four winds, *im-pinge* against thy Glass walls, but have to drop unread.
                                —CARLYLE
H   He *implied* that I was wrong and I *inferred* this im-plication from his tone.
I   My eyes began to fail me and be in pain . . . which I *impute* to sitting up late writing and reading by candle-light.—PEPYS
J   The serpent sly
Insinuating wove with Gordian twine
His braided train, and of his fatal guile
Gave proof unheeded.—MILTON
K   And the sense of *occult* rivalry in suitorship was so much superadded to the palpable rivalry of their busi-ness lives.—HARDY
L   You are to fight: who is your *opposite?*
    What is the quarrel?—WEBSTER

8. (a) "The bouncer eliminated any chance of trouble by eliminating the three drunks." Which use of *eliminate* is nearer the etymological meaning of the word?

(b) Etymologically speaking, what sort of punishment produced *excruciating* pain?

(c) An *excursus* is etymologically a 'running away.' As used currently, a 'running away' from what?

(d) To *exonerate* is etymologically 'to unburden.' As used currently, to unburden from what?

(e) What is the meaning of the prefix in *obliterate*?

(f) Determine the etymological meaning of *impede* and *expedite*. What semantic change does their current meaning reveal?

(g) Which use of *explode* is earlier, '*explode* a theory,' or 'bombs *explode*'? Explain your answer.

Lesson 21

Prefixes (*Concl'd*)

prae- 'before,' 'ahead,' 'in advance,' 'previous(ly),' 'surpassing(ly)'

prō- 'before,' 'in front of,' 'forth,' 'for'

re- (**red-** before vowels) 'back,' especially 'back to an original or former state or position'; 'backward,' 'again'; used chiefly to form words denoting repetition of the action of the verb or restoration to a previous state; also used intensively

retrō- 'backward,' 'back,' 'situated behind'

sē- (**sēd-** before vowels) 'aside,' 'apart'

sub-, suc-, suf-, sug-, sup-, sus- 'under,' 'below,' 'from below,' 'lower,' 'in secret,' 'to help,' 'in addition,' 'instead'

super- 'above,' 'over'

trāns-, trā- 'across,' 'over,' 'beyond,' 'through', 'on or to the other side of,' 'into a different state or place'

Etymological Notes

Prō- when borrowed through French appears in English as *pur-*. **Prōportāre,** for example, has given through French *purport*; **prōsequī** has given *pursue*, **prōvidēre,** *purvey* (*purvey* is thus the doublet of *provide*).

Super- through French appears as *sur-*. Thus **supervīvere** 'to live over' has produced *survive* and **supervidēre** *survey*. *Surfeit*, the result of 'overdoing,' goes back to **super-** and **factus**, perfect participle of **facere**. The *sur-* of *surround* comes from **super-**, but its second element etymologically has nothing whatever to do with *round*. *Surround* in English earlier meant 'to overflow,' which accurately represents its Latin source, a combination of **super-** and **undāre**, the denominative verb of **unda** 'wave.' Its form in Old French was *suronder*. This, in English, on purely fanciful grounds, was associated with *round*, and the current spelling was the result. The process whereby the meaning or form of a word is affected by such haphazard associations is known as *folk-etymology*.

Here are some words in which the original form of the prefix has been rather thoroughly covered over by French. The *ral-* of *rally* covers up **re-** and **ad-**. *Rally* is from **re-adligāre*; when troops *rally* round their leader they are binding (**ligāre**) themselves to (**ad-**) him again (**re-**). The *res-* of *rescue* conceals **re-** and **ex-**. The word comes from the Old French *rescoure*, which is derived from **re-**, **ex-**, and **-cutere**, the form **quatere** 'to shake' takes in compounds. In *source* and *souvenir* the hidden prefix is **sub-**. The first goes back to **surgere** 'to rise,' a compound of **sub-** and **regere**; the second is from **subvenīre** 'to come to the mind.' **Sub-** is also concealed in *sudden*. This word comes from **subitāneus**, which is an extension of **subitus** 'that which has come in secret,' a Fourth-Declension abstract noun from **subitus**, perfect participle of **subīre** 'to come or go in secret.'

Prose and *verse* come from the same base, **versus** 'turned,' perfect participle of **vertere** 'to turn.' A line of poetry, a *verse*, is 'a turning'; you 'turn' to it from the end of the previous line, and 'turn' away from it to the beginning of the next. **Prōversus** 'turned forward,' 'straightforward' was contracted to **prorsus** and then to **prōsus**. **Prōsa** (**ōrātiō**) 'straightforward speech' is the source of *prose*, speech with no 'turnings' in it.

EXERCISES

1. Memorize all the forms and meanings of the following verbs. Using any prefixes, form two derivatives from each.

cēdere, cessus 'to go,' 'to yield'

claudere, clausus (-clūdere, -clūsus) 'to shut'

currere, cursus 'to run'

fīgere, fīxus 'to fix,' 'to fasten'

fluere, fluxus 'to flow'

frangere, frāctus (-fringere, -frāctus) 'to break'

gradī (-ior), gressus (-gredī, -gressus) 'to step'

prehendere, prehensus 'to grasp'

specere (-iō), spectus (-spicere, -spectus) 'to look'

spīrāre 'to breathe'

sūmere, sūmptus 'to take'

venīre, ventum 'to come,' 'to go'

2. (a) Form Latin compound verbs having the following etymological meanings and give an English derivative from each: 'to lead apart,' 'to save ahead,' 'to stand back,' 'to follow forth,' 'to draw from under,' 'to bring back,' 'to do across,' 'to hold in front of,' 'to pour forth,' 'to bend back,' 'to set in a different place,' 'to gather apart,' 'to leap back,' 'to push forth,' 'to move back.'

(b) What words, derived from Latin compound verbs, are equivalent, element for element, to *forecast, oversee, understand, underwrite, unforeseen?*

3. Give the meaning of the prefix in *recede, repute, revere, revolve, suborn, substitute, succor, suffix, support, transgress, translate.*

4. Analyze the words *derelict, compromise, propensity, prospectus, recital, recompense, response, resuscitate, reverberate, subordinate, substratum, secretary, segregate, transept.*

5. The following list contains eight pairs of words that are linguistically related. Select the pairs and show in each case what the relationship is (see Exercises to Lesson 20, Question 5, for example): *commit, concrete, demote, deposit, discern, dissolve, expense, explicit, impend, infringe, postpone, refract, remis remove, reply, resolute, response, secrete, supply, suspense.*

6. Analyze each italicized word and determine the meaning of the expression in which it appears: the *precepts* of Plato, *prelates* and some others of lesser rank, to *prorogue* parliament, *proscribed* his enemies, *recondite* words, *replete* with clichés, *superannuated* senators, *transmute* lead into gold.

7. Analyze each italicized word and determine its meaning in the context.

A   Joey was now *preferred* from the stable to attend on his lady, to go on her errands, stand behind her chair.
—FIELDING

B   He had just reached the time of life at which 'young' is ceasing to be the *prefix* of 'man' in speaking of one.
—HARDY

C   O! let the vile world end,
And the *premised* flames of the last day
Knit heaven and earth together.—SHAKESPEARE

D   The English, though in conversation often tongue-tied, when they take a pen in their hands are inclined to *prolixity*.—MAUGHAM

E   Abate the edge of traitors, gracious Lord,
That would *reduce* these bloody days again,
And make poor England weep in streams of blood!
—SHAKESPEARE

F   A street piano, mechanical and tired,
Reiterates some worn-out common song.
—T. S. ELIOT

G   Such a man excels in general principles, but fails in the particular application.   He is knowing in *retrospect*, and ignorant in foresight.—JOHNSON

H   I shall *review* Sicilia, for whose sight
I have a woman's longing.—SHAKESPEARE

I   To feel at least a patriot's shame,
Even as I sing, *suffuse* my face . . . —BYRON

J   Certain of the early provincial poets . . . have fabled that, like Romulus, he was *translated* to the skies and forms a very fiery little star, somewhere on the left claw of the crab.—IRVING

K   In this brief *transit* where the dreams cross
    The dreamcrossed twilight between birth and
        dying . . . —T. S. ELIOT
L   We have been, let us say, to hear the latest Pole
    Transmit the Preludes through his hair and finger-
        tips.—T. S. ELIOT

8. (a) Which of the following uses of *resolve* is nearer the etymological meaning: "resolve a problem," "resolve to go"?

(b) Determine the etymological meaning of *retort*. What semantic change is illustrated by the word in the expression "chemical *retort*"? in "angry *retort*"?

(c) What is the difference between *translating* Hebrew into English and *transliterating* Hebrew into English?

(d) Which side of a coin is the *obverse* and which the *reverse*?

(e) What is the doublet of *propose*?

(f) From the sentences in Question 7, select an example of a *predicate* noun and of a *predicate* adjective.

LESSON 22

The Present Participle

Formation. In addition to the present infinitive and the perfect participle, there is a third form of the Latin verb, the present active participle, which has yielded a large number of words in English. The present participle is formed by attaching certain endings (see column 4 below) to the base of the present infinitive. It functions in Latin as an adjective and is declined as an adjective of the Third Declension (see Lesson 4). Its base, like that of adjectives of the Third Declension, is found by dropping the genitive ending **-is.**

CONJU-GATION	PRESENT INFINITIVE	BASE	PRESENT PARTICIPLE		
			Nominative	*Genitive*	*Base*
I	laudāre 'to praise'	laud-	laud-āns 'praising'	laud-antis	laudant-
II	monēre 'to warn'	mon-	mon-ēns 'warning'	mon-entis	monent-
III (*a*)	agere 'to do,' 'to drive,' 'to direct'	ag-	ag-ēns 'doing'	ag-entis	agent-
(*b*)	capere (-iō) 'to take'	cap-	cap-iēns 'taking'	cap-ientis	capient-
IV	audīre 'to hear'	aud-	aud-iēns 'hearing'	aud-ientis	audient-

Note the difference in the formation of the present participle of the two types of Third-Conjugation verbs.

The Present Participle in English. The bases of Latin present participles, simple and compound, appear in English most frequently as adjectives, occasionally as nouns.

PRESENT INFINITIVE	PRESENT PARTICIPLE	ENGLISH LOAN WORD
urgēre 'to press'	urgēns, urgentis 'pressing'	*urgent*
ēloquī 'to speak out'	ēloquēns, ēloquentis 'speaking out'	*eloquent*
agere 'to do,' 'to drive'	agēns, agentis 'doing'	*agent*

Suffixes previously mentioned as attachable to adjective bases (see Lessons 7–10, 13, 14) may be used with present participial bases. Thus, in *accidental*, -ālis has been attached to accident-, base of the present participle of accidere (ad- + cadere 'to fall').

In Old French all present-participial endings were leveled to *-ant.* Those present participles, therefore, which were borrowed through Old French often show this ending in English instead of their regular endings.

PRESENT INFINITIVE	PRESENT PARTICIPLE	ENGLISH LOAN WORD
mordēre 'to bite'	**mordēns, mordentis** 'biting'	*mordant*

ETYMOLOGICAL NOTES

We shall start with *infants*, go through *infantrymen*, and end up with *fairies*.

To make a proper start we must begin with **fārī, fātus** 'to speak' and go from there to the present participle **fāns, fantis** 'speaking.' This combined with **in-** 'not' gives **īnfāns, īnfantis,** whence *infant*. Apparently, so far as the Romans were concerned, the most salient characteristic of a baby was its inability to speak. Now let us try *infantry*. There seems, at first sight, little in common between the hard-bitten *infantry*man and the tender *infant*, but we have clues which furnish the solution of the problem. The first is the fact that the Italians applied **infante,** their derivative of **īnfāns,** not merely to babies but to young boys as well. The next clue is the knowledge we have that young boys often served in olden days as attendants upon knights. This they did, not mounted but—and this is the important point—on foot. So, **infanteria,** meaning in Italian first 'band of young men' then 'band of foot-attendants,' has produced *infantry* 'soldiers who fight on foot.'

But we promised to end up with *fairies*. To do that we must retrace our steps to **fātus,** the perfect participle of **fārī.** **Fātus** means 'spoken,' and **fātum,** its neuter, would therefore mean 'that which has been spoken,' whence the meaning of our derivative *fate*. The plural **fāta** was used of the three dread goddesses who controlled all human destinies, the *Fates* as we call them. In later Latin, **fāta** became singular 'goddess of fate,' and with this meaning entered Old French in the form **fae.** This became *fay* in English, no longer limited to the goddess of fate, but applicable to any goddess. Now, just as the mischief that a knave is capable of is called 'knavery' or the magic performed by witches, 'witchery,' in earlier

English the enchantment that a *fay* was capable of was called 'fay-ery' or, as it was spelled, *faerie*. Somewhere along the line of the subsequent development of the word, a mistake was made: *faerie*, now spelled *fairy*, came to be used no longer of the enchantment, but of the enchanter.

EXERCISES

1. Memorize all the forms and meanings of the following verbs. Form and translate the present participle of each. With or without prefixes, form an English derivative from the present participle of each.

cadere, cāsus (-cidere, -cāsus) 'to fall'
crēscere, crētus 'to grow'
haerēre, haesus 'to stick'
īre, itum (pres. part. base **ient-**) 'to go'
loquī, locūtus 'to speak'

nāscī, nātus 'to be born'
patī (-ior), passus 'to suffer'
petere, petītus 'to seek'
tangere, tāctus (-tingere, -tāctus) 'to touch'
valēre, —— ' 'to be strong,' 'to be worth'

2. Form English words that mean etymologically 'running back,' 'loosening,' 'coming together,' 'making thoroughly,' 'ruling,' 'holding together,' 'leaping back,' 'causing to stand back,' 'stepping in,' 'breathing toward.'

3. Analyze the words *discordant, dormant, invariant, radiant, resultant, scintillant, sedentary, superintendent, tenant, transcendental*.

4. Analyze each italicized word and determine the meaning of the expression in which it appears: *aberrant* verb-forms, *cogent* reasons, a *concomitant* of wartime life, *deterrent* weather, *exigent* needs, all *extant* copies, *inadvertent* remarks, *incipient* tuberculosis, *redolent* of bygone days.

5. Notice how Shakespeare uses the italicized words in the following passages. In each instance the etymological meaning provides the clue to the poet's usage.

    A Let it stamp wrinkles in her brow of youth,
       With *cadent* tears fret channels in her cheeks.

                                      (Lear)

B   The people love me, and the sea is mine;
     My powers are *crescent*, and my auguring hope
     Says it will come to the full.

                            (Antony and Cleopatra)

C   (*of the ghost of Hamlet's father*)
              And at his warning (*that is, cockcrow*),
     Whether in sea or fire, in earth or air,
     The *extravagant* and erring spirit hies
     To his confine.

D   His antique sword,
     Rebellious to his arm, lies where it falls,
     Repugnant to command.   (Hamlet)

6. Analyze each italicized word and determine its meaning in the context.

A   I find that I have always walked straight, serenely *imprescient*, into whatever trap Fate has laid for me.

                                   —BEERBOHM

B   (a) The gray roof of the sky soon broke with the *incumbent* weight of light, letting in sunshine through the narrow fracture to the sea.—TOMLINSON   (b) It is *incumbent* upon all men to come to the aid of their country.   (c) The present *incumbent* has had three years in office.

C   In free speech, earnest or gay, amid *lambent* glances . . . such was the element they now lived in.—CARLYLE

D   Yet he was not only the same man, but that man, with his sinister qualities, formerly *latent*, quickened into life by his buffetings.—HARDY

E   It's not instinct that makes Casanovas and Byrons and Lady Castlemaines; it's a *prurient* imagination artificially tickling up the appetite, tickling up desires that have no natural existence.—ALDOUS HUXLEY

F   (a) Forasmuch as God would that the faculties both *intelligent* and *sentient* should predominate in the head . . . —JOHN GUILLIM   (b) His mind was a mirror of the *sentient* universe.

G The exhibition of character may be made *subservient* to the purpose of the action.—NEWMAN

H The orator yields to the inspiration of a *transient* occasion.—THOREAU

7. (a) Determine the etymological meaning of *crescent*. Its Latin ancestor was specialized in mediaeval times to mean 'the waxing (or waning) moon.' What semantic change has subsequently taken place in English?

(b) What semantic change is illustrated by *diffident*?

(c) What semantic change is illustrated by *salient* in the expression 'a *salient* into enemy territory'? in the expression 'the *salient* facts'?

8. (a) What is the difference between an *imminent* danger and an *immanent* danger?

(b) What is the difference between a *proponent* of democracy and an *exponent* of democracy?

9. (a) What phenomenon of nature is responsible for the current meaning of *orient* and *occident*?

(b) Is it *consonant* with the phonetic facts to call *b, c, d, f, g, h* and so forth *consonants*?

(c) Etymologically speaking, what does *pungent* smoke do to the nostrils?

(d) What is the meaning of the proper names *Constantine* and *Vincent*?

(e) What is the *antecedent* of the word *that* in each of its two occurrences in sentence 6E?

LESSON 23

The Present Participle (*Concl'd*)

Abstract nouns may be formed in Latin by attaching the suffix **-ia** to the present-participial base. Since this base always ends in **-t,** the last three letters of such abstract nouns will be **-tia.** In English this ending is changed to *-ce* or *-cy*.

English derivatives of these nouns generally retain the abstract meaning.

PRESENT INFINITIVE	PRESENT PARTICIPLE	BASE	ABSTRACT NOUN	ENGLISH LOAN WORD
fīdere 'to trust'	**fīdēns**	**fīdent-**	**cōnfīdentia** 'the state of trusting thoroughly'	*confidence*
fluere 'to flow'	**fluēns**	**fluent-**	**fluentia** 'quality of flowing'	*fluency*

The adjective-forming suffixes studied in Lessons 7–10 are frequently attached to the base of these abstract nouns. In *confidential,* for example, *-al* (*-ālis*) has been added to **-fīdenti-,** base of **-fīdentia.**

Etymological Notes

Īnfluentia, the ancestor of *influence,* was at one time used as an astrological term, a fact that explains how its basic meaning, 'a flowing upon,' came to be altered to the sense that *influence* has today. Astrologists used to believe that the planets controlled the fortunes of mankind by means of a mysterious power that 'flowed' from them 'upon' mortals. Their technical term for this power was **influentia.** Furthermore, among the specific things that the planets controlled, it was believed, was the occurrence of a certain common throat and bronchial disease—hence the meaning of *influenza,* the doublet of *influence.* The form of *influenza* shows that the borrowing was done through Italian, since there the **-tia** ending of these abstract nouns from the present participle is altered to **-za.** Thus *cadenza* is the doublet of *cadence* and *extravaganza* of *extravagance.*

Romance, despite its form, does not come from a Latin abstract noun ending in **-tia.** Its ancestor, as a matter of fact,

is an adverb. **Lingua Rōmānica** 'the Roman tongue' was the
name given to Vulgar Latin, the vernacular from which, as
has already been pointed out, French, Italian, Spanish, and
so on are derived.   The adverb **rōmānicē** means 'in the Roman tongue,' and this is the word that has given us *romance*.
Thus the Romance languages are languages derived from 'the
Roman tongue.'   And *romances* are so called because originally they were tales told **rōmānicē**—that is, in this vernacular.

Trance and *enhance* are also somewhat deceptive in form:
present participles play no part in their etymology either.
The first is from the Old French *transe,* which goes back to
trānsīre 'to go across,' 'to die.'   *Enhance,* meaning literally
'to heighten,' is closely connected with *haughty;* it comes from
***inaltiāre,** a denominative from **altus** 'high.'

Here are a few more derivatives through French. *Obeisance*
is not only the symbol, but also the doublet, of *obedience;* the
two words come from **oboedientia** (**oboedīre** 'to obey,' composed of **ob-** and **audīre** 'to hear').   *Penance* and *penitence*
are from **paenitentia** (**paenitēre** 'to repent').   *Seance* is literally 'a sitting'; its ancestor is ***sedentia** from **sedēre**.   *Nui-
sance* has been softened in meaning in English. **Nocentia,**
the form from which it is derived, is the abstract noun from
nocēre 'to harm.'

EXERCISES

1. The three words *intend, pretense,* and *superintendent* come
from the present infinitive, perfect participle, and present participle, respectively, of **tendere, tēnsus** 'to stretch.'   Form
similar sets of three words from each of the following: **facere,
pōnere, sedēre, solvere, tenēre, vertere.**

2. What English words mean etymologically 'the state of
not sticking together,' 'result of bringing together,' 'the act
of following,' 'the state of not doing thoroughly,' 'the state
of leaping back,' 'the state of standing together'?

3. Which words in the following list are *not* derived from

Latin present participles: *consequence, difference, enhance, opulence, predominance, radiance, virulence*? Explain your answer.

4. The following list contains eight pairs of words that are linguistically related. Select the pairs and show in each case what the relationship is: *precise, immerse, contingency, concept, move, antecedent, strict, difference, ingress, tact, dilate, stringency, incipient, emergency, demote, recess, gradient, casual, tract, prelate.*

5. Analyze the words *circumstance, conscientious, correspondence, differentiate, expectancy, inconsequentiality, licentious, penitentiary, residential.*

6. Analyze each italicized word and determine the meaning of the expression in which it appears: the *cadences* of eighteenth-century prose, the *ebullience* of youth, the *incidence* of desertion in any army, words of a scientific *provenience*, ineffective *remonstrance*, concealed by his *reticence, sententious* phrases, the *tendentious* writings of some proletarian novelists, the *translucency* of the sky.

7. Analyze each italicized word and determine its meaning in the context.

A   Advise the prince; no doubt, an easy tool,
    Deferential, glad to be of use.—T. S. ELIOT

B   Then blest be heaven and guider of the heavens,
    From whose fair *influence* such justice flows.—KYD

C   It is hard to understand his *intransigence* in the light of all efforts to compromise with him.

D   It will be laid to us, whose *providence*
    Should have kept short, restrain'd, and out of haunt,
    This mad young man.—SHAKESPEARE

E   *Redundance* is more excusable in speech than in writing.

F   Some more or less aesthetic ladies and gentlemen . . . laid their cheerless heads together and decided that they would meet once every month and dance old-fashioned dances . . . Thus they would achieve a *renascence*—I am sure they called it a renascence—of 'Merrie England.'—BEERBOHM

G Who, though she could not *transubstantiate*
All states to gold, yet guilded every state.—DONNE

8. (a) What Latin word lies at the base of *relevance, allevi-ate,* and *Levantine?* Show how its meaning is reflected in the current meaning of each of these three words.

(b) Give an example of a *confluence.* Name a type of *excrescence* on the skin.

(c) What would you find in a *concordance* of Shakespeare?

(d) Determine the etymological meaning of *ambulance, currency, agency, fluency.* What semantic change is illustrated by the current meaning of the first two? by *agency* in the expression "work for an advertising *agency*"? by *fluency* in the expression "the speaker's *fluency*"?

(e) What is the doublet of *complaisance?*

(f) Which are more closely synonymous, the etymological meanings of *repugnance* and *reluctance,* or their current meanings? Explain your answer.

Lesson 24

Multiple-Base Compounds

In Lesson 15 we discussed multiple-base compounds formed by combining the bases of nouns and adjectives. Verbs and verbal elements are also so used.

Any verb base may be used as the second element in a multiple-base compound. The second element of *lucifer,* for example, is derived from a present infinitive (**ferre** 'to bear'), of *tripartite* from a perfect participle (**partītus,** perfect parti-ciple of **partīrī** 'to share'), of *liquefacient* from a present par-ticiple (**faciēns, facientis,** present participle of **facere** 'to make'). The first element comes most often from a noun or adjective, occasionally from an adverb or a verb.

Multiple-base compounds with a second element derived

from a verb may be either descriptive or dependent. Descriptive compounds, which may also be formed by combining adjectives and nouns, have already been discussed in Lesson 15. In dependent compounds the second member is regularly a verb or verbal element, and the first member depends upon or serves as object of the verbal idea contained therein. Of the three examples given above, *lucifer* ('bearer of light') and *liquefacient* ('making into water') are dependent compounds; *tripartite* ('three-shared') is descriptive.

The verbs **agere, capere,** and **facere** have special forms for use in multiple-base compounds, namely **-igāre, -cipāre,** and **-ficāre.** As the ending **-āre** shows, these forms belong to the First Conjugation. Thus *navigate* =

(1) **nāvigātus**

(2) *nav-,* base of **nāvis** 'ship'

   -igate, from **-igātus,** perfect participle of **-igāre,** form of **agere, actus** 'to drive' used in multiple-base compounds

(4) Etymological Meaning: 'to drive a ship'

(5) Current Meaning: same as etymological meaning. The form **-ficāre** appears in English as *-fy,* with the meaning 'to make,' 'to form into.' Thus *clarify* 'to make clear' comes from **clārificāre.** Related to **-ficāre** is **-ficus,** an adjective-forming element that means 'making,' 'causing.' It appears in English as *-fic.* Thus *pacific* means etymologically 'peace-making' (**pāx, pācis** 'peace').

Several combinations constantly recur as the second member of dependent compounds. These are:

1. *-ferous* 'bearing,' 'producing' composed of **-fer-,** base of **ferre,** and *-ous* from **-ōsus** (see Lesson 10). Thus *coniferous* means 'cone-bearing (**cōnus** 'cone').' *-fer,* without the suffix may be used to form nouns—for example, *conifer* '(a tree) that bears cones.'

2. *-vorous* 'eating' composed of **-vor-,** present infinitive base of **vorāre** 'to devour,' and *-ous.* Thus *carnivorous* means 'flesh-eating (**carō, carnis** 'flesh').' *-vora* indicates classes of animals according to the food they eat—for example, *carnivora*

'flesh-eating animals.' The singular of *-vora* is *-vore*, as in *carnivore* 'a flesh-eating animal.'

3. *-colous* 'inhabiting' composed of **-col-,** present-infinitive base of **colere** 'to inhabit,' and *-ous.* Thus *stagnicolous* means 'pool-inhabiting (**stāgnum** 'pool,' 'standing water').'

4. *-parous* 'giving birth to,' 'producing,' 'secreting' composed of **-par-,** present-infinitive base of **parere** 'to give birth,' 'to bear,' and *-ous.* Thus *viviparous* means 'producing live (**vīvus**) young.'

ETYMOLOGICAL NOTES

Quintessence, 'the most essential part of anything,' 'the purest manifestation of anything,' has a long etymological history. Empedocles, a Greek philosopher of the fifth century B.C., believed that the universe consisted of four material elements: earth, air, fire, and water. A century later Aristotle postulated a fifth immaterial element, which he believed was finer than and essential to the existence of the other four. This fifth element he called ***pémptē ousía,*** literally, 'fifth being.' ***Ousía*** is an abstract noun from the present participle of the Greek verb ***eînai*** 'to be.' The mediaeval philosophers found difficulty in translating this expression into Latin because Classical Latin had no present participle of the verb **esse** 'to be.' Consequently, they were forced to coin a participle **essēns, essentis** 'being,' from which they formed the abstract noun **essentia** 'essence,' thus providing an almost exact equivalent of the Greek ***ousía.*** The whole expression was translated **quīnta essentia** 'fifth essence.' It is from this Latin expression that *quintessence* is directly descended.

EXERCISES

1. Which words in the following groups are descriptive compounds and which dependent?

(a) *bankteller, bootblack, dogcatcher, firefighter, fortune-teller, shareholder, stronghold, vacuum-cleaner*

(b) *benevolent, deify, equivalent, jet-propelled, manuscript, participate, purify, rectify*

2. What part of speech is the first base in each of the following multiple-base compounds: *benefit, certify, glorify, gratify, horrify, justify, satisfy, specific, stupefy.*

3. Analyze the words *aqueduct, diversify, equidistant, fumigate, genuflect, intensify, maintenance, modify, mortify, participant, personify, significance, terrific, verdict, vivisect.*

4. Analyze each of the italicized words and determine the meaning of the expression in which it appears: arrowheads and other *artifacts, castigate* an offender, hardly *edified* by his answer, the *equivocating* of diplomats, *exemplify* the best in literature, *grandiloquent* oratory, *manumit* a slave, *mitigate* the bad effects, the *munificence* of private charity, *omnivorous* curiosity, send *plenipotentiary* delegates to a conference, *prolific* writers, *stultified* him in his friends' eyes, concerts offering a *variegated* program.

5. Analyze each italicized word and determine its meaning in the context.

A　This is your devoted friend, sir; the manifold linguist and the *armipotent* soldier.—SHAKESPEARE

B　My father began to dig into the depths, into the primary and *auriferous* rock of the Scriptures.

　　　　　　　　　　　　　　　　—DR. JOHN BROWN

C　As the old woman hobbled down the church steps, her face bore a *beatific* expression that would have gladdened the soul of a mediaeval painter.

D　So attaining the political effects of Nudity without its *frigorific* or other consequences . . .—CARLYLE

E　The English ear has been accustomed to the *mellifluence* of Pope's numbers.—JOHNSON

F　Their intercourse with other lands and peoples had *mollified* their mental habits; indeed, almost as much as their wide-flung commerce, a little good Madeira softened the old rigidities.—VAN WYCK BROOKS

G　Zeus, in the *Iliad*, is hot-tempered, amorous, and luxurious—by no means *omnipotent* or *omniscient*.

H   She looked about for the flowers and found them on the window sill, between two *pestiferous* sinks.

I   What is the most fundamental need of man? It would be interesting to conduct a *plebiscite* on such a question.—JULIAN HUXLEY

J   So clear was the stream that it seemed not water at all, but some invisible *quintessence* in which the happy minnows and the weeds were vibrating.—FORSTER

6. (a) What creatures are *penniferous? terricolous? arboricolous? herbivorous? insectivorous? frugivorous? luminiferous? oviparous?*

   (b) What trees are *bacciferous? coniferous? nuciferous?*

   (c) What may be *morbific? soporific?*

7. What variant form of **facere** is evident in the words *magnificent* and *beneficent?*

LESSON 25

Inceptive Verbs.   The Gerundive

Inceptive Verbs.   These are verbs that denote the beginning of an action or state. They are formed by adding **-scere** to the base of present infinitives, nouns, or adjectives. A connecting vowel, most often **-ē-**, precedes the **-scere.** Thus **valēscere** 'to begin to be well' is the inceptive verb formed from **valēre** 'to be well.' The present participles of inceptive verbs have given rise to a number of English derivatives, in some of which the inceptive force is retained—for example, *convalescent* 'beginning to get well.'

The Gerundive.   The last form of the Latin verb that is important for our purposes is the gerundive. This is formed by adding the endings **-andus, -endus, -endus** (**-iendus** in the case of **-iō** verbs), and **-iendus** to the present-infinitive base of verbs of the First, Second, Third, and Fourth Conjugations, respectively. It is declined like an adjective of the First and Second Declension (see Lesson 2): **-andus,** for example, would be used for agreement with masculine nouns, **-anda** for agreement with feminines, **-andum** with neuters.

The gerundive, like the perfect participle, is passive in meaning. Furthermore, it expresses necessity, fitness, or obligation. This force is usually retained in English. A *memorandum*, for example, is a 'to-be-remembered thing,' from **memorāre** 'to cause to remember.'

CONJU-GATION	PRESENT INFINITIVE	BASE	GERUNDIVE
I	**amāre** 'to love'	**am-**	**amandus** 'to-be-loved'
II	**verērī** 'to fear'	**ver-**	**verendus** 'to-be-feared'
III (a)	**agere** 'to do'	**ag-**	**agendus** 'to-be-done'
(b)	**capere** (**-iō**) 'to take'	**cap-**	**capiendus** 'to-be-taken'
IV	**audīre** 'to hear'	**aud-**	**audiendus** 'to-be-heard'

The gerundive sometimes appears in English in combination with the suffix *-ous* which, in these instances, does not affect the meaning (see Lesson 10).

ETYMOLOGICAL NOTES

In 1622 Pope Gregory XV organized a committee of cardinals to unify and supervise the work of foreign missions. This group was entitled *Congregatio de Propaganda Fide* 'Congregation for Propagation of the Faith.' *Propaganda* (the gerundive of **prōpāgāre** 'to multiply,' 'to spread') was brought into English through its use in this title.

Lavāre 'to wash' is the source of a number of derivatives. The present infinitive has yielded, through Italian, the noun *lava*, and is partly responsible for the verb *lave*. The first person singular future, **lavābō** 'I shall wash'—the first word in *Psalms* XXVI, 6—has been borrowed without change as a noun, meaning either the 'liturgical act' which this psalm accompanied, or the 'towel' or 'basin' used in this act. *Laundry* is derived ultimately from the gerundive **lavandus** 'to- be-washed.'

EXERCISES

1. Give the etymological meanings of the following words:
   (a) *adolescent, incandescent*
   (b) *dividend, legend, multiplicand, referendum, stupendous, subtrahend, tremendous*

2. Analyze each italicized word and determine the meaning of the expression in which it appears: the *agenda* are longer than usual, the first *efflorescence* of Greek culture, *horrendous* newspaper headlines, a *recrudescence* of civil strife.

3. Analyze each italicized word and determine its meaning in the context.

   A (a) The swell of a good organ produces a most perfect *crescendo.*—CHAMBERS' CYCL. (b) Its chief merit as a play is the *crescendo* of its interest.—SYMONDS

   B But while she spoke, there was a fragrance in the atmosphere around her, rich and delightful, though *evanescent.*—HAWTHORNE

   C The Mayor of the towne was come in his gowne and is a very *reverend* magistrate.—PEPYS

4. (a) What is the difference between an *obsolete* word and an *obsolescent* word?

   (b) "The last five pages of the book are devoted to a list of *corrigenda* and *addenda.*" What did the list contain?

   (c) What do the feminine given names *Amanda* and *Miranda* mean?

   (d) Determine the etymological meaning of *propaganda* and *concupiscence.* What semantic change is illustrated by the current meaning of each?

   (e) What is the difference between a *reverend* member of the clergy and a *reverent* member of the clergy?

5. The following are Latin phrases which English has taken over. Determine the current pronunciation and meaning of each.

   ad captandum (vulgus) 'for the sake of pleasing the crowd'—Used as an adjective or adverb in English; for example: "This *ad captandum* merit was, however, by no means a recommendation of it, according to the severe

principles of the new school, which reject rather than
court popular effect."—HAZLITT

quod erat dēmōnstrandum 'which was to be demon-
strated'—Abbreviated Q.E.D. in English

Lesson 26

Review

1. Define and illustrate: deponent verb, denominative verb,
frequentative verb, inceptive verb.

2. Form an English derivative from each of the four bases
of **ferre** and of **crēscere**.

3. Give the English words that mean etymologically: 'lead
back,' 'move in front,' 'gather out,' 'bring together,' 'turned
across,' 'draw back,' 'push in the way,' 'fold thoroughly,' 'let
go under,' 'draw very tight,' 'sift apart,' 'play with,' 'set forth,'
'sticking together,' 'not suffering,' 'stepping,' 'going before,'
'cutting,' 'placing together,' 'carrying out.'

4. Give the Latin-derived word that is synonymous, element for element, with each of the following: *outcry, understand, outstretch, foresee.*

5. Analyze the following words:

(a) *circumscribe, superinduce*

(b) *abstruse, anniversary, beatitude, exactitude, insensate,
intensity, Lucifer, portentous, reprobate, suggest, transversal*

(c) *formulate, modulate, remunerate, vaccinate*

(d) *commissary, intellectual, victuals*

(e) *contingent, effulgence*

(f) *legendary, reprimand*

6. Give the etymological meaning of *caret, infantry, influenza, pinto, prose, quintessence, rally, romance, salad, search,
veto.*

CHAPTER FIVE

Compound Nouns and Adjectives Formed from Verbs

CHAPTER THREE was devoted to compounds formed by combining various suffixes with the bases of nouns and adjectives. The present chapter is concerned with those suffixes that may be attached to present-infinitive and perfect-participial bases of Latin verbs to form compound nouns and adjectives. (For general remarks on the use and meaning of suffixes, see the introduction to Chapter Three.)

LESSON 27

Compound Nouns

(a) *Present-Infinitive or Perfect-Participial Base Plus Noun-Forming Suffix.* The suffix -iō (genitive -iōnis) may be attached either to the present-infinitive base or, as is much more common, to the perfect-participial base. This suffix, appearing in English in the form *-ion*, forms abstract nouns in which it has the meaning 'state of,' 'process of,' 'act of,' 'or result of the act of.'

135

			LATIN	
PRESENT	PERFECT		COMPOUND	ENGLISH
INFINITIVE	PARTICIPLE	BASE	NOUN	LOAN WORD
opīnārī 'to suppose,' 'to think'		opīn-	opīniō, opīniōnis	*opinion*
agere 'to do'	actus	act-	actiō, actiōnis	*action*

ETYMOLOGICAL NOTES

In a great number of cases, -iō, -iōnis is added to bases that end in -t-. The combination -tiō, -tiōnis produced this way, when borrowed through French, appears in English as -*son*, since -ti- came to be pronounced in French with some sort of *s*-sound (compare -tia > -*ce*, p. 124). Thus the doublet of *ration* (ratiō, ratiōnis; from ratus, perfect participle of rērī 'to think' + -iō) is *reason*. *Tradition* is the 'giving across' (trādere, trāditus, from trāns- + dare 'to give') of beliefs or customs to posterity. *Treason*, its doublet, is the 'giving across' of a city or army, and so on, to an enemy. Vēnārī means 'to hunt,' and vēnātiō, vēnātiōnis 'the result of the act of hunting'; apparently the commonest 'result of the act of hunting' used to be *venison*. In Latin the 'act of sowing' is satiō, satiōnis (from satus, perfect participle of serere 'to sow'). What we call the spring *season* was originally the time of the spring 'sowing.'

Station is etymologically 'the result of the act of standing' (status, perfect participle of stāre 'to stand' + -iō, -iōnis), and a *stationer* etymologically is 'one who has to do with a station' (stationārius). Its current meaning is the result of specialization. In mediaeval Latin, stationārius meant 'shopkeeper,' that is, someone who, unlike a peddler constantly moving about, sold goods in a fixed location. Then the word was again specialized to refer to booksellers, since they, in mediaeval times, commonly had their own stalls in the market place. The mediaeval bookseller not only sold books but also writing materials, or, as we would put it, *stationery*.

EXERCISES

1. In which of the following words has the present-infinitive base been used and in which the perfect-participial base? In each case give the present infinitive and the meaning of the verb that has supplied the base: *auction, aversion, conclusion, legion, pension, region, station, suspicion, vision.*

2. Give the etymological meaning of *absolution, confusion, injection, promotion, tension, traction.*

3. The following are derived from denominative verbs. Give for each the Latin noun or adjective (with its meaning) that has supplied the base: *affirmation, annihilation, approbation, assimilation, collaboration, coronation, declaration, determination, excavation, insubordination, mediation, prolongation, radiation, summation.*

4. Analyze the following words:
    (a) *cessation, capitulation, compassionate, dictionary, eviction, functionary, gesticulation, inflationary, ostentation, rationality, reactionary, sedition*
    (b) *locomotion, modification, stupefaction, vivisection*

5. Analyze each italicized word and determine the meaning of the expression in which it appears: Vergil's use of *alliteration, animadversions* prompted by prejudice, *defection* from the party, *delineation* of character, *deprivation* caused by *depredation*, a *dissertation* on American slang, *divination* by communication with the dead, the *elision* of vowels, prayers and *incantations*, an *intimation* of forthcoming evil, *redintegration* of national prosperity, chosen by *sortition.*

6. Analyze each italicized word and determine its meaning in the context.

    A Juvenal is perhaps the only ancient author who habitually substitutes *declamation* for poetry.—NEWMAN

    B His [Aristotle's] natural taste led him to delight in the *explication* of systems.—NEWMAN

    C I will not force your will, but leave you free
      To your own *election*.—MASSINGER

    D A sweet *profusion*
      Of soft *allusion*

This bold *intrusion*
Shall *justify.*—w. s. GILBERT
E Thou hast no *speculation* in those eyes
Which thou dost glare with.—SHAKESPEARE

7. Give the meaning of the prefix in each of the following words: *consecration, obstruction, perversion, requisition, subvention, transformation.*

8. Distinguish between:

(a) the *acceptance* of a new word and the *acceptation* of a new word.

(b) a man's *vocation* and a man's *avocation.*

(c) family *affection* and the *affectation* of family affection.

9. (a) Carlyle has said: "An unmetaphorical style [of writing] you shall in vain seek for: is not your very *Attention* a *Stretching-to*?" Explain this statement.

(b) Determine the etymological meaning of *election* and *conjunction.* What semantic change is illustrated by *election* in the sentence 'Who won the *election*?' by *conjunction* in the expression 'a *conjunction* and a relative pronoun?'

(c) Why is a *carnation* so called? a *preposition*?

Lesson 28

Compound Nouns (*Cont'd*)

(b) *Present-Infinitive Base Plus Noun-Forming Suffix.*

1. Present-infinitive base plus **-mentum** > -*ment* 'state of,' 'quality of,' 'act of,' 'result of the act of,' 'means,' 'instrument.'

PRESENT INFINITIVE	BASE	LATIN COMPOUND NOUN	ENGLISH LOAN WORD
docēre 'to teach'	**doc-**	**documentum**	*document*

2. Present-infinitive base plus **-men** (genitive **-minis**) >
-*men* 'act of,' 'result of the act of,' 'means.'

PRESENT INFINITIVE	BASE	LATIN COMPOUND NOUN	ENGLISH LOAN WORD
regere 'to rule'	**reg–**	**regimen**	*regimen*

3. Present-infinitive base plus **-bulum, -bula,** or **-culum** >
-*ble,* -*cle* 'place,' 'result of the act of,' 'means,' or 'instrument.'

PRESENT INFINITIVE	BASE	LATIN COMPOUND NOUN	ENGLISH LOAN WORD
stāre 'to stand'	**st–**	**stabulum**	*stable*
vehere 'to carry'	**veh–**	**vehiculum**	*vehicle*

4. Present-infinitive base plus **-or** > -*or,* forming abstract
nouns in which it denotes 'state of' or 'result of the act of.'

PRESENT INFINITIVE	BASE	LATIN COMPOUND NOUN	ENGLISH LOAN WORD
languēre 'to be faint'	**langu–**	**languor**	*languor*

This suffix is used principally with verbs of the Second Conjugation. It must be distinguished from the suffix **-or** that denotes agent (see Lesson 29).

5. Present-infinitive base plus **-ium.** This suffix forms nouns in which it has the meaning 'act of,' 'result of the act of,' 'place,' 'means.' Nouns so formed are neuters of the Second Declension; for their appearance in English, see Lesson 2.

PRESENT INFINITIVE	BASE	LATIN COMPOUND NOUN	ENGLISH LOAN WORD
studēre 'to be eager'	**stud–**	**studium**	*study*
fugere 'to flee'	**fug–**	**refugium**	*refuge*

In a few cases (for example, *initial, initiate, interstices*), the perfect-participial base has been used instead of the present-infinitive base.

6. Present-infinitive base plus **-īna.** This suffix forms abstract nouns in which it has the meaning 'act of,' 'or result of

the act of.' Nouns so formed belong to the First Declension; for their appearance in English, see Lesson 1.

PRESENT INFINITIVE	BASE	LATIN COMPOUND NOUN	ENGLISH LOAN WORD
ruere 'to tumble down'	**ru-**	**ruīna**	*ruin*

ETYMOLOGICAL NOTES

Homicide may be used as an abstract noun ("he committed *homicide*") or as an agent noun ("the police arrested the *homicide*.") The abstract noun comes from **homicīdium** 'the act of (**-ium**) killing (**-cīd-**, from **caedere** 'to cut,' 'to kill') a man (**homō**).' The agent noun, however, comes from **homicīda** 'one who kills a man.' This double derivation is true of *patricide*, *suicide*, and so on, as well.

Stāmen, etymologically an abstract noun (**stāre** 'to stand' + **-men**), appears in Latin as concrete (cf. Lesson 14), meaning 'a standing thread' in an upright loom. This sense was later generalized to 'thread'; so, today, a *stamen* is a 'threadlike' part of a flower. The standing threads in the old upright looms had to be very strong—hence the current meaning of *stamina*, originally merely the plural of **stāmen.**

Auspice comes from **auspicium,** a multiple-base compound which means etymologically 'bird-watching.' The second element derives from **-spicere** 'to watch' plus **-ium,** the first from **avis** 'bird.' The Romans believed that the cries and flights of birds were omens from the gods; accordingly special priests would, before any undertaking, make observations of them and decide whether they boded well or ill. If the 'bird-watching' indicated success for your project, you were starting under favorable *auspices*. The priest whose job it was to watch birds was called an **augur.** One of the common occasions on which he carried out his duties was the installation of an official—hence the meaning of *inaugurate*.

Frontispiece has nothing to do with *piece* etymologically. Its form in Latin is **frontispicium;** the **-spicium** here has the same source as in the case of *auspices*, and the **front-** comes from **frōns, frontis** 'brow,' 'face.' A *frontispiece* is etymologically, therefore, a 'face-looking' or 'that which (first) faces the eye.' In English it originally referred to the title page of a book, since this was the first page to meet the eye, then was shifted to refer to an illustration placed alongside the title page. It can also mean 'façade,' since this is the first part of a building to be seen.

Binnacle, the box that houses a ship's compass, is derived, with considerable specialization of meaning, from **habitāculum** 'dwelling place' (**habitāre** 'to dwell'). Its earlier form was *bittacle,* which came to English through Spanish. It was in Spanish that the first syllable of the original Latin (**ha-**) was dropped. *Nasturtium* means 'nose-twisting' etymologically. It's a multiple-base compound consisting of **nas-** from **nāsus** 'nostril,' **-turt-** from **tortus** the perfect participle of **torquēre** 'to twist,' and **-ium.** The ancients believed that the pungent odor of the plant caused the nose to twitch. *Pigment* and *pimento* are doublets. The first means etymologically 'means for painting,' from **pig-**, the root of **pingere** 'to paint,' and **-mentum.** In mediaeval Latin, **pigmentum** was first the name of a spiced drink and then came to mean simply 'spice,'— hence *pimento.*

EXERCISES

1. Give the etymological meaning of the following words, paying careful attention to the force of the suffix in each:
    (a) *armament, instrument, ligament, liniment, sediment*
    (b) *acumen, specimen*
    (c) *curriculum, miracle, receptacle, tentacle*
    (d) *fetor, furor, stupor, terror, torpor, valorous*
    (e) *armistice, remedy, sacrifice*

2. Analyze the words *colloquial, delirious, documentation, fabulous, fluorescent, incendiary, initiate, officiate, pronunciamento, soliloquy, vocabulary.*

3. Analyze each italicized word and determine the meaning

of the expression in which it appears: *antediluvian* military tactics, a clever *artifice*, a handy *compendium* of American history, the unmeasurable *firmament*, *internecine* strife, *interstices* in the weave, accused of *matricide*, bring *obloquy* on oneself, his *obsequious* manner, the *orifice* of a tube, *primordial* instincts, *stertorous* breathing, a clever *subterfuge*.

4. Analyze each italicized word and determine its meaning in the context.

A His *candor* makes his contest an *invigorating spectacle*.—NEW YORK TIMES

B He hath perverted a young gentlewoman here in Florence . . . he hath given her his *monumental* ring.
—SHAKESPEARE

C [The German sky] is clearer than the English sky and is not loaded with its dreary fogs, but has its own *nocuments*, which are madness and defeat.
—REBECCA WEST

D Come, come, be every one *officious*
To make this banquet.—SHAKESPEARE

E *Opprobrium* sometimes falls upon the innocent, when circumstances seem to convict them of guilt.—CRABBE

F A robber city, founded by outlaws and living by *rapine* . . .

G (a) A *regimen* which included careful diet, fresh air and sunshine; (b) The many lucrative government positions available under the old *regime*.

5. (a) What is the force of the prefix in each of the following: *complement, obstacle, subsidy, supplement*? Does a fulcrum *complement* or *supplement* a lever?

(b) What is the meaning of the suffix in *spectacle* in the expression "a pair of *spectacles*"? in the expression "an awesome *spectacle*"?

(c) Judging by the etymology of *testament* what, to the Romans, was the most important step in drawing up a will?

6. The following list contains seven pairs of words that are linguistically related. Select the pairs and show in each case what the relationship is: *ablutions, affection, antediluvian, arti-*

fice, auspices, continent, destruction, dilate, hospice, incipient, incorrect, inspection, instrument, intense, irruption, receptacle, regimen, tenor.

LESSON 29

Compound Nouns (*Concl'd*)

(c) *Perfect-Participial Base Plus Noun-Forming Suffix.*

1. Perfect-participial base plus **-or** > *-or*, forming agent nouns in which it denotes 'that which' or 'the person who' performs the action indicated in the base.

PRESENT INFINITIVE	PERFECT PARTICIPLE	BASE	LATIN COMPOUND NOUN	ENGLISH LOAN WORD
movēre 'to move'	mōtus	mōt-	mōtor	*motor*

This suffix must be distinguished from the *-or* that is attached to the bases of present infinitives to form abstract nouns (see Lesson 28).

2. Perfect-participial base plus **-rīx** > *-rix*, forming feminine agent nouns in which it denotes 'she who' performs the action indicated in the base.

PRESENT INFINITIVE	PERFECT PARTICIPLE	BASE	LATIN COMPOUND NOUN	ENGLISH LOAN WORD
testārī 'to be a witness,' 'to make a will'	testātus	testāt-	testātrīx	*testatrix*

3. Perfect-participial base plus **-ūra** > *-ure*, forming abstract nouns in which it denotes 'act of' or 'result of the act of.'

LATIN

PRESENT INFINITIVE	PERFECT PARTICIPLE	BASE	COMPOUND NOUN	ENGLISH LOAN WORD
frangere 'to break'	frāctus	frāct-	frāctūra	*fracture*

ETYMOLOGICAL NOTES

Savior, curiously enough, is connected etymologically with *salvo*, a simultaneous discharge of cannon. The ancestor of *savior* is **salvātor**, an agent noun from **salvātus**, perfect participle of **salvāre** 'to save.' Now, **salvāre** is a denominative verb from **salvus** 'safe,' 'well.' Another denominative verb from the same adjective is **salvēre** 'to be well.' **Salvē,** the imperative of the verb, was used as a greeting (hail!) and from it *salvo* is probably derived. A *salvo*, then, was originally a volley fired as a salutation.

Escalator, echelon, and *scale* 'graded system' are closely related. **Scāla** is the Latin word for the ladders used in clambering up the walls of an enemy city. *Scale* comes directly from it. *Echelon*, etymologically 'large scaling-ladder,' has been borrowed through modern French from **scāla** plus an augmentative suffix. An *escalator* (from **scālātus**, the perfect participle of the denominative verb **scālāre**, + **-or**) is a device which enables you to 'scale' the stories in a building.

Here are a few agent nouns altered from their original form as the result of having passed through French. A *governor* is etymologically a 'helmsman'; the word comes from **gubernātor** (**gubernāre** 'to steer'). A *commodore* is 'one who commands,' from **commandātor** (**commandāre** 'to command'). A *connoisseur* is 'a knower' (**cōgnōscītor**, ultimately from **cōgnōscere** 'to know'). **Dōnātor** 'one who gives (**dōnāre**)' has become *donor*; **antecessor** 'one who goes before (**antecēdere, antecessus**)' has become *ancestor*; **jūrātor** 'one who has taken the oath (**jūrāre**)' has, with specialization of meaning, given *juror*; **trāditor** 'one who betrays (**trādere, trāditus**)' has given *traitor*.

EXERCISES

1. Analyze the words *aviatrix, commentator, competitor, curvature, dictatorial, doctor, equatorial, incinerator, investiture, literature, natural, orator, picture, predecessor, structure, transgressor.*

2. Analyze each italicized word and determine the meaning of the expression in which it appears: a recompense *commensurate* with one's effort, a *conjectural* reconstruction of the crime, dangerous *fissures* in the surface, the *posture* of affairs, a wise *preceptor,* the whole line of his *progenitors.*

3. Note how Shakespeare uses the italicized words in the following passages. In each instance the etymological meaning provides the clue to the poet's usage:

A Fain would mine eyes be witness with mine ears,
To give their *censure* of these rare reports.
(Henry VI, Part 1)

B To you all three,
The senators alone of this great world,
Chief *factors* for the gods . . .
(Antony and Cleopatra)

C The firm *fixture* of thy foot would give an excellent motion to thy gait in a semi-circled farthingale.
(Merry Wives of Windsor)

D (*The speaker has been rescued from a shipwreck*)
And spite of all the *rapture* of the sea,
This jewel holds his biding on my arm.
(Pericles)

4. Analyze each italicized word and determine its meaning in the context.

A He said Thomson was a great poet, rather than a good one; his style was as *meretricious* as his thoughts were natural.—HAZLITT

B Groups of bad statues, tables, chairs, and pictures,
On which I cannot pause to make my *strictures* . . .
—BYRON

C   Nature, like a cautious *testator*, ties up her estate so
as not to bestow it all on one generation.—THOREAU

D   Being men of birth, educated according to the custom of the age without *tincture* of letters, the Knights
Templar scorned the ignoble occupations of a monastic
life.—STEVENSON

E   The old sea dog started *triturating* some shavings of
hard tobacco between his huge palms.—STEVENSON

5. Analyze the word *floriculture*.   What is the chief product of *apiculture*? of *viticulture*?

6. Determine the etymological meaning of *actor, executor,
incisor, pasture, Scripture, tractor*.   What semantic change is
illustrated by the current meaning of each?

7. Form two abstract nouns from each of the following
Latin verbs (for example, **creāre**—*creature, creation*): **capere,
frangere, jungere, nāscī, stāre, torquēre.**

8. Judging by the etymology of the word, (a) how was
manufacturing done in ancient times?   (b) how were *lectures*
original y delivered?   (c) what color is traditionally connected with *miniatures*?

LESSON 30

Compound Adjectives

(a) *Present-Infinitive or Perfect-Participial Base Plus Adjective-Forming Suffix.*

1. Present-infinitive or perfect-participial base plus **-bilis**
> -*ble*.   This suffix most often expresses a passive capacity:
'capable of being,' 'able to be'; occasionally an active capacity: 'able to,' 'causing,' 'suitable for,' 'given to.'

When **-bilis** is attached to the base of a First-Conjugation
verb, the connecting vowel **-a-** is used, otherwise **-i-.**   In

many words borrowed through French, however, and in formations made in English, -a- is used indiscriminately.

PRESENT INFINITIVE	PERFECT PARTICIPLE	BASE	LATIN COMPOUND ADJECTIVE	ENGLISH LOAN WORD
penetrāre 'to pierce'		penetr-	penetrābilis	*penetrable*
horrēre 'to shudder'		horr-	horribilis	*horrible*
crēdere 'to believe'		crēd-	crēdibilis	*credible*
flectere 'to bend'	flexus	flex-	flexibilis	*flexible*
But:				
tenēre 'to hold'		ten-	*tenibilis	*tenable*

2. Present-infinitive or perfect-participial base plus -ilis > -ile, with the same meanings as -ble.

PRESENT INFINITIVE	PERFECT PARTICIPLE	BASE	LATIN COMPOUND ADJECTIVE	ENGLISH LOAN WORD
docēre 'to teach'		doc-	docilis	*docile*
mittere 'to send'	missus	miss-	missilis	*missile*

(b) *Present-Infinitive Base Plus Adjective-Forming Suffix.*

1. Present-infinitive base plus -āx (genitive -ācis). Adjectives so formed almost always appear in English in combination with the suffix -ous (< -ōsus) or -ity (< -itās). The compound suffixes -acious and -acity so formed produce, the one, adjectives in which it means 'inclined to,' 'abounding in,' the other, abstract nouns in which it means 'the quality of being inclined to,' 'the quality of abounding in.'

PRESENT INFINITIVE	BASE	LATIN COMPOUND ADJECTIVE	ENGLISH LOAN WORD
audēre 'to dare'	aud-	audāx (genitive audācis)	*audacious, audacity*

2. **Present-infinitive base plus -uus.** Adjectives so formed almost always appear in English in combination with the suffix *-ous* (< **-ōsus**). The compound suffix *-uous* so formed produces adjectives in which it means 'inclined to.'

PRESENT INFINITIVE	BASE	LATIN COMPOUND ADJECTIVE	ENGLISH LOAN WORD
nocēre 'to harm'	noc-	nocuus	*nocuous*

3. **Present-infinitive base plus -ulus.** Adjectives so formed appear in English with the suffix *-ous* (<**-ōsus**) attached. The compound suffix *-ulous* thus formed means 'tending to,' 'addicted to,' or 'inclined to.'

PRESENT INFINITIVE	BASE	LATIN COMPOUND ADJECTIVE	ENGLISH LOAN WORD
tremere 'to tremble'	trem-	tremulus	*tremulous*

4. **Present-infinitive base plus -idus** > *-id* 'inclined to.'

PRESENT INFINITIVE	BASE	LATIN COMPOUND ADJECTIVE	ENGLISH LOAN WORD
vīvere 'to live'	vīv-	vīvidus	*vivid*

Adjectives formed with *-id* often parallel abstract nouns formed with *-or* 'state of' (see Lesson 28). Thus alongside *pallid* we have *pallor* 'the state of being pale (**pallēre** 'to be pale')'; alongside *rigid, rigor* 'the state of being stiff (**rigēre** 'to be stiff').'

ETYMOLOGICAL NOTES

Shingles, the skin disease that often manifests itself as an inflamed band around the waist, and *shingles,* the slips of wood used on roofs and exterior walls, are not at all related. The name of the disease goes back to **cingulum** 'girdle,' a

combination of **cingere** 'to gird' and **-ulum,** neuter of **-ulus.**
The salient characteristic of the ailment etymologically is the
encircling band that it forms.   The *shingle* that goes on a
roof has a completely different etymology, one which, incidentally, illustrates a bit of ancient folk-etymology.   The
word comes from **scindula** which is clearly formed from **scindere** 'to split' and **-ula,** feminine of **-ulus.** *Shingles* were in
ancient times—and are often still today—made by splitting
logs.   But records show that the earlier Latin form of **scindula**
was **scandula,** from **scandere** 'to mount,' 'to rise' + **-ula.**   In
other words, *shingles* originally got their name from the fact
that, always overlapping when laid, they seemed to rise or
mount toward the peak of a roof.   Later speakers of Latin,
not realizing this, thought they were named from the way
they were manufactured and changed the old correct **scandula**
to **scindula.**

EXERCISES

1. For each of the following words determine whether the
suffix (a) is used with passive or active force, (b) has been
attached to the base of the present infinitive or of the perfect
participle: *accessible, durable, eligible, fusible, immutable, in-
tangible, irresistible, reptile, terrible.*
2. Give the etymological meaning of each of the following:
   (a) *affable, flexible, interminable, reprehensible, visible*
   (b) *agile, ductile, missile*
   (c) *capacity, pugnacity, tenacious*
   (d) *conspicuous, innocuous, promiscuous*
   (e) *bibulous, garrulous, tremulous*
   (f) *humid, squalid, stupid.*   Form an abstract noun end-
       ing in *-or* to parallel each of these three adjectives.
3. Analyze the words *audibility, continuation, incapacitate,
ineradicable, invalidate, rapidity, rehabilitate, residual, tractable,
versatile.*
4. Analyze each italicized word and determine the meaning
of the expression in which it appears: *arable* land, *commensu-*

rable factors, *florid* language, the *habiliments* necessary for such an occasion, *irrevocable* moments, his *inexorable* decision, an *ineluctable* conclusion, *palpable* movement, *pendulous* jowls, *querulous* voice, the *rapacity* of the greedy, a *tenable* supposition.

5. Analyze each italicized word and determine its meaning in the context.

A   The *contumacious* resist only occasionally; the rebel resists systematically.—CRABBE

B   The stream of time, which is continually washing the *dissoluble* fabrics of other poets, passes without injury by the adamant of Shakespeare.—JOHNSON

C   (a) Compared with this, all other purposes in literature . . . are bastard in nature, *facile* of execution, and feeble in result.—STEVENSON   (b) He was endowed with a pleasing personality, a ready wit, and a *facile* tongue.

D   The face of the presiding magistrate, clean shaved and *impassible*, looked at him.—CONRAD

E   I was *indocile* at an age
    When better boys were taught,
  But thou at length hast made me sage,
    If I am sage in aught.—LANDOR

F   The mystic sees the *ineffable*, and the psychopathologist the unspeakable.—MAUGHAM

G   Not much would now remain unexplained and uncorrected except the *inexplicable* and the *incorrigible*.
      —HOUSMAN

H   The Tomb is now my *inexpugnable* Fortress.
      —CARLYLE

I   His village mildness masked, like any woodland creature's, a sharp *retractile* claw.—VAN WYCK BROOKS

J   She was left an opulent widow of forty, with strong *sensibility*, *volatile* fancy, and slender judgement.
      —MACAULAY

6. (a) What is the meaning of the suffix in the word *sensible* in each of the following uses: (1) She was an honest, *sensible* person; (2)

Art thou not, fatal vision, *sensible*
To feeling as to sight?

(b) What is the meaning of the suffix in each of the italicized words: (1) After the horse is stolen, the *stable* is locked. (2) In times of unrest, nothing is *stable*.

(c) What is the meaning of the prefix in *perfervid* and *pertinacious*?

7. The following contain pairs of words that are sometimes confused. Determine the distinction in meaning between the members of each pair.

(a) an *incredible* story; an *incredulous* person

(b) weather reports are *fallible*; newspaper reports are often *fallacious*

(c) a well-trained, *perspicacious* writer; a fluent *perspicuous* exposition of a difficult problem

8. (a) Judging by the etymology of *deciduous*, what is the outstanding characteristic of *deciduous* trees?

(b) How, so far as etymology is concerned, are *fossils* found?

(c) What metaphor is involved in the shift of *assiduous* from its original to its present meaning?

LESSON 31

Compound Adjectives (*Concl'd*)

(c) *Perfect-Participial Base Plus Adjective-Forming Suffix.*

1. Perfect-participial base plus **-ōrius** > *-ory*, forming adjectives from verbs.

PRESENT INFINITIVE	PERFECT PARTICIPLE	BASE	LATIN COMPOUND ADJECTIVE	ENGLISH LOAN WORD
amāre 'to love'	**amātus**	**amāt-**	**amātōrius**	*amatory*

The suffix -ōrium, neuter singular of -ōrius, was used to form nouns in which it has the meaning 'place for or of,' 'that which pertains to or serves for.' (Cf. Lesson 9 for a similar use of -ārium.) It appears in English sometimes without change, more commonly in the form -ory.

PRESENT INFINITIVE	PERFECT PARTICIPLE	BASE	LATIN COMPOUND NOUN	ENGLISH LOAN WORD
audīre 'to hear'	audītus	audīt-	audītōrium	*auditorium*
dormīre 'to sleep'	dormītus	dormīt-	dormītōrium	*dormitory*

2. Perfect-participial base plus -īvus > -ive 'given to,' 'tending to.'

PRESENT INFINITIVE	PERFECT PARTICIPLE	BASE	LATIN COMPOUND ADJECTIVE	ENGLISH LOAN WORD
agere 'to do'	actus	act-	actīvus	*active*

Adjectives formed with -īvus frequently appear in English as nouns—for example, *motive*, *detective*.

3. Perfect-participial base plus -īcius. Adjectives so formed always appear in English in combination with the suffix -ōsus. -īcius combined with -ōsus appears as -itious (*c* and *t* were frequently confused in later Latin) in English, meaning 'of the nature of,' 'characterized by.'

PRESENT INFINITIVE	PERFECT PARTICIPLE	BASE	LATIN COMPOUND ADJECTIVE	ENGLISH LOAN WORD
fingere 'to fashion,' 'to feign'	fictus	fict-	fictīcius	*fictitious*

Etymological Notes

When the suffix -īvus passes through Old French, it frequently appears in English in the form -iff. Thus from *planctīvus 'lamenting' (**plangere, planctus** 'to lament'), we have derived, through Old French, the noun *plaintiff* 'one who laments injustice done him and consequently brings action against a defendant.' *Plaintive* 'expressive of sorrow,' the doublet of *plaintiff*, is much closer in meaning to the original Latin. Similarly, from **captīvus** (**capere** 'to seize'), we have borrowed *captive* directly and its doublet *caitiff* through Old French. When borrowed through Modern French, -īvus may appear in English in the form -*if*—for example, *motif*, doublet of *motive*.

EXERCISES

1. What is the meaning of the suffix in each of the following words: *conservatory, exclamatory, laboratory, laudatory, lavatory, preparatory, purgatory, reformatory, respiratory.*

2. (a) Give the Latin verb, with its meaning, that has supplied the base for each of the following: *cohesive, comprehensive, conjunctive, consumptive, digestive, disruptive, effusive, exclusive, expressive, inquisitive, interrogative, native, objective, restrictive, superlative.*

    (b) Give the Latin noun or adjective, with its meaning, that is connected with each of the following derivatives of denominative verbs: *circulatory, confirmatory, declarative, defamatory, inoperative.*

3. Analyze the words *captivate, compensatory, compulsory, motivation, meritorious, radioactivity, surreptitious, tentative, valedictory.*

4. Analyze each italicized word and determine the meaning of the expression in which it appears: an *abortive* attempt at revolution, a *cursory* examination, *desultory* reading, *dilatory* tactics, *discursive* treatment of a topic, *gustatory* pleasure, *predatory* raids, *provocative* statements, a *refractory* child, *repository* of knowledge, *sensory* perceptions, basing his claim on *supposititious* treaties, the *trajectory* of a projectile, *votive* offerings.

5. Analyze each italicized word and determine its meaning in the context.

A   The art of composition is merely *accessory* to the poetical talent.—NEWMAN

B   But Shakespeare always makes nature predominate over accident, and if he preserves the essential character, is not very careful of distinctions superinduced and *adventitious*.   His story requires Romans or kings, but he thinks only on men.—JOHNSON

C   QUEEN.   Come hither, my good Hamlet, sit by me.
　　 HAMLET.   No, good mother, here's metal more *attractive*.—SHAKESPEARE

D   Our sight [is] . . . a more delicate and *diffusive* kind of touch, that spreads itself over an infinite number of bodies.—ADDISON

E   This is in others a *factitious* state,
　　 An opium dream of too much youth and reading.
　　　　　　　　　　　　　　　　　　　　　　　　—BYRON

F   The diligence of the editor has not been wasted on trivial researches or *nugatory* commentaries.
　　　　　　　　　　　　　　　　　　　　　—ISAAC D'ISRAELI

G   The Highlander gives to every question an answer so prompt and *peremptory*, that scepticism is dared into silence.—JOHNSON

H   Bungay sit down, for by *prospective* skill
　　 I find this day shall fall out ominous.
　　　　　　　　　　　　　　　　　　　　　—ROBERT GREENE

I   O it was a pleasure to see the sable younkers [chimney-sweepers] lick in the *unctuous* meat, with his [their host's] more *unctuous* sayings.—LAMB

6. (a) What is the difference between a *deprecatory* remark and a *derogatory* remark?

(b) What is the difference between an *illusive* dream and an *elusive* dream?

7. (a) Give an example of a *transitive* verb and of an *intransitive* verb.

(b) Give an example of a word used in a *pejorative* sense.

(c) What is the opposite of an *augmentative* suffix?

(d) Show how the analysis of *sanatorium* differs from that of *sanitarium*.

(e) The *infinitive* is the form of a verb that is 'not limited.' 'Not limited' by what?

Lesson 32

Review

1. Analyze the following words:
    (a) *affectionate, detestation, explanation, extortionate, modulation, regeneration, renunciation, suspicion, variation*
    (b) *acumen, candor, curricle, documentary, insecticide, rapine, regiment, subsidiary, vocabulary*
    (c) *administratrix, adventure, competitor, incisor, rotator, structure*
    (d) *agile, durable, execrable, extensible, incalculable, probable, textile, variable*
    (e) *assiduous, efficacious, invalidate, loquacity, lucid, pendulous, sagacity, salacious*
    (f) *aggressive, consecutive, descriptive, impassive, instinctive, missive, obtrusive, repository, secretive, statutory, supererogatory, surreptitious*

2. Analyze the words *activate, argumentative, conversation, initiative, mortification, nationality, orientation, revolutionary, tergiversation, transubstantiation.*

3. The following list contains ten pairs of words that are linguistically related. Select the pairs and show in each case what the relationship is: *artifact, belligerent, compromise, compulsory, conference, efficacious, evident, impassivity, impel, implicit, improvise, inarticulate, inception, intermittent, multiply,*

participant, parturition, patent, patient, pertinacity, suggestion, supply, tenor, translation.

4. Determine the etymological meaning of *operation* and *prohibition.* What semantic change is revealed by the use of the first in the expression 'an *operation* requiring a local anaesthetic'? by the second in the expression 'the repeal of *prohibition*'?

5. Give the etymological meaning of *auspices, governor, nasturtium, plaintiff, salvo, season, shingle, treason.*

General Vocabulary

[All words involved in the exercises are included. Words marked with the dagger (†) have been assigned to be memorized in the exercises. The double dagger (‡) indicates words that have produced no more than two or three common derivatives.]

NOUNS, ADJECTIVES, ADVERBS

acerbus 'harsh,' 'bitter'
acētum 'vinegar'
acus (acu-) 'needle'
‡adeps, adipis 'fat'
aedēs, aedis 'building,' 'house'
†aequus 'equal'
aestus (aestu-) 'heat,' 'tide'
aevum 'age'
ager, agrī 'field'
albus 'white'
‡aliās (adv.) 'at another time'; aliās dictus = 'otherwise called'
‡alibī (adv.) 'elsewhere,' 'at another place'
‡almus 'food-giving,' 'nurturing'
altus 'high'
‡alumna 'foster-daughter,' 'pupil'
‡alvus 'belly'
‡amoenus 'pleasant,' 'charming'
amplus 'spacious'
‡amulētum 'charm worn against evils'

‡ancilla 'maid-servant'
angulus 'angle,' 'corner'
anima 'air,' 'breath,' 'life,' 'soul'
†animus 'mind,' 'feeling'
†annus 'year'
annuus 'yearly'
‡antenna 'ship's sailyard'
antīquus 'ancient'
‡anus (an-) 'old woman'
‡apex, apicis 'point,' 'top'
apis 'bee'
aptus 'fit,' 'suitable'
†aqua 'water' (adj. aqueus 'watery')
‡aquila 'eagle'
arbiter, arbitrī 'judge'
arbor, arboris 'tree'
arca 'chest,' 'box'
arcus (arcu-) 'bow'
‡ārea 'vacant plot of land in town'
‡arēna 'sand,' 'sandy place'
†arma (nom. plu.) 'arms'
†ars, artis 'skill,' 'art'
artus (artu- or art-) 'joint'
‡asinus 'ass'

157

‡atavus, 'ancestor'
‡ater, atrī 'black'
‡augustus 'reverend,' 'majestic'
aureus 'golden'
auris 'the ear'
‡aurum 'gold'
‡avārus 'grasping,' 'greedy'
avis 'bird'
axis 'axle'
‡bacca 'berry'
barba 'beard'
bellum 'war'
bellus 'pretty'
bene 'well'
bīlis 'bile,' 'anger'
†bonus 'good'
‡bōs, bovis 'ox,' 'bull,' 'cow'
brūtus 'dull,' 'irrational'
‡bucca 'cheek'
bulla 'water-bubble,' 'amulet'
caecus 'blind'
‡caelum 'sky'
‡caerimōnia 'religious usage,' 'sacred rite'
‡calumnia 'false accusation'
calx, calcis 'limestone,' 'pebble'
†camera 'vault,' 'chamber'
campus 'plain,' 'open country'
cancer, cancrī 'crab'
canis 'dog'
caper, caprī 'he-goat'
‡capillus 'hair'
†caput, capitis (n) 'head'

carbō, carbōnis 'coal'
‡cardō, cardinis 'hinge'
†carō, carnis 'flesh'
‡carpentum 'carriage'
cārus 'dear,' 'precious'
‡castrum 'fort'
castus 'pure'
cauda (or cōda) 'tail'
†causa 'motive'
‡cavilla 'mockery'
cavus 'hollow'
cella 'cell,' 'store-room'
cerebrum 'the brain'
‡Cerēs Ceres (*goddess of agriculture*)
certus 'sure'
‡cervīx, cervīcis 'neck'
‡cilium 'eyelid' (supercilium 'eyebrow')
cinis, cineris 'ashes'
‡circā (*adv.*) 'about,' 'around'
†circus 'ring'
‡citrus 'citrus-tree,' 'citron-tree'
cīvis 'citizen'
†clārus 'clear'
‡claustrum 'bolt,' 'shut place'
clāvis 'key'
‡cliēns, clientis 'dependant,' 'follower'
clīvus 'slope,' 'hill'
cōdex, cōdicis 'ancient form of book'
‡comes, comitis 'companion'
‡cōmis 'courteous'
commūnis 'common'
‡congeriēs 'heap,' 'mass'

‡cōnus 'cone'
†cor, cordis (n) 'heart'
‡corium 'skin,' 'hide'
corōna 'garland,' 'crown'
cornū 'horn'
†corpus, corporis (n) 'body'
‡coruscus 'waving,' 'flashing,'
   'glittering'
costa 'rib,' 'side'
‡coxa 'hip'
crassus 'thick,' 'gross'
‡crispus 'curled'
‡crūdus 'raw'
‡crūs, crūris (n) 'leg'
†crux, crucis 'cross'
‡cubitum 'elbow'
‡culīna 'kitchen'
culpa 'fault,' 'blame'
cuneus 'wedge'
cūpa 'cask,' 'barrel'
†cūra 'care,' 'trouble,' 'attention'
‡curtus 'shortened'
†curvus 'bent,' 'curved'
cutis 'skin'
damnum 'loss,' 'harm'
decor, decōris 'comeliness'
‡decōrus 'becoming,' 'seemly'
dēns, dentis 'tooth'
†deus (or dīvus) 'god'
dexter, dexterī (or dextrī)
   'right'
diēs 'day'
digitus 'finger,' 'toe'
dignus 'worthy'
‡dīrus 'ill-omened,' 'fearful,'
   'dread'

dominus 'lord'
dorsum 'back'
†dūrus 'hard'
dux, ducis 'leader'
ego 'I'
equus 'horse'
‡exemplum 'sample,' 'copy,'
   'pattern'
†exterus 'outside'
‡facētiae (nom. plu.) 'witty
   sayings'
faciēs 'appearance,' 'surface.'
   'shape,' 'face'
‡falx, falcis 'sickle,' 'pruning-
   hook'
fāma 'report,' 'rumor'
fānum 'shrine,' 'temple'
‡farrāgō, farrāginis 'mixture'
fascis 'bundle,' 'bundle of
   faggots'
fatuus 'silly'
febris 'fever'
fēlīx, fēlīcis 'fortunate'
fēmina 'woman'
ferrum 'iron'
‡ferus 'wild,' 'untamed'
fēstus 'joyful'
fētus (fētu-) 'offspring'
fidēs 'trust,' 'faith'
fīlum 'thread'
†fīnis 'limit,' 'boundary,'
   'end'
†fīrmus 'steadfast,' 'fixed'
fiscus 'basket,' 'money-
   basket,' 'purse'
†flōs, flōris 'flower'
focus 'hearth'

folium 'leaf'

†fōrma 'shape'

fortior comparative of fortis

†fortis 'strong'

fortissimus superlative of fortis

fortūna 'fate,' 'fortune'

francus 'of the Franks'

‡frīgus, frīgoris (n) 'coldness'

frōns, frontis 'forehead'

‡frūgēs (nom. plu.) 'fruit'

‡fulcrum 'bedpost,' 'prop'

‡fulmen, fulminis (n) 'lightning,' 'thunderbolt'

fūmus 'smoke,' 'steam'

‡fūnis 'rope'

‡fūnus, fūneris (n) 'funeral,' 'death'

‡fuscus 'dark'

‡gelidus 'icy cold'

genius 'guardian deity'

gēns, gentis 'tribe,' 'race'

‡genū (genu-) 'knee'

†genus, generis (n) 'race,' 'kind,' 'sort'

germen, germinis (n) 'seed'

‡glaciēs 'ice'

‡gladius 'sword'

‡glans, glandis 'acorn'

globus 'ball,' 'sphere'

glōria 'renown'

†gradus (gradu-) 'step,' 'degree'

†grandis 'great,' 'lofty'

†grānum 'grain,' 'seed'

†grātus 'pleasing,' 'agreeable,' 'grateful'

†gravis 'heavy'

†grex, gregis 'flock,' 'herd'

herba 'blade of grass,' 'herb'

‡hircus 'he-goat'

‡histriō, histriōnis 'actor'

‡hoc 'this'

homō, hominis 'man'

hospes, hospitis 'host,' 'guest'

‡hostia 'sacrifice'

hostis 'enemy'

hūmor 'liquid,' 'fluid'

īgnis 'fire'

imperium 'sovereign power'

inānis 'empty'

‡index, indicis 'forefinger'

†īnferus 'under'

īnsula 'island'

integer, integrī 'untouched,' 'whole'

‡interim (adv.) 'meanwhile,' 'in the meantime'

†interior 'inner'

‡ipse 'self,' 'own'

‡iter, itineris (n) 'journey'

‡iterum (adv.) 'again'

‡jējūnus 'hungry,' 'scanty,' 'barren,' 'insignificant'

jocus 'jest'

jūdex, jūdicis 'judge'

Juppiter, gen. Jovis Jupiter, Jove (chief of the gods)

jūs, jūris (n) 'law,' 'right'

jūstus 'upright,' 'righteous'

juvenis (adj.) 'young'; (noun) 'young man'

labium 'lip'

†labor, labōris 'work'

lāc, lactis (n) 'milk'

‡lacrima 'tear'

‡lacūna 'hole,' 'gap'

laevus 'left'

lapis, lapidis 'stone'

‡Larēs Lares (*household gods*)

‡lassus 'languid,' 'weary'

‡lātus 'wide'

latus, lateris (n) 'side'

laus, laudis 'praise'

‡leō, leōnis 'lion'

†levis 'light (in weight),' 'light-minded'

lēx, lēgis 'law'

liber, līberī 'free,' 'unrestrained'

liber, librī 'book'

līgnum 'wood'

limbus 'border,' 'edge'

līmen, līminis (n) 'threshold,' 'entrance'

†līnea 'line'

†lingua 'tongue,' 'language'

‡līra 'furrow'

†lītera 'letter'

‡līvidus 'blue,' 'black and blue'

†locus 'place'

longus 'extended'

‡lucrum 'gain,' 'profit'

lūdus 'game'

‡lumbus 'loin'

†lūmen, lūminis (n) 'light'

lūna 'moon'

‡lūridus 'pale yellow,' 'wan,' 'ghastly'

lūx, lūcis 'light'

magister, magistrī 'master,' 'teacher'

†magnus 'great'

†malus 'bad'

†manus (manu-) 'hand'

mare, maris (n) 'sea'

margō, marginis 'border,' 'edge'

Mārs, Mārtis Mars (*god of war*)

māter, mātris 'mother'

māteria 'matter,' 'wood'

‡mātrōna 'married woman'

mātūrus 'ripe'

‡Mātūta Matuta (*goddess of dawn*)

†medius 'middle'

medicus 'physician'

‡medulla 'marrow'

‡mel, mellis (n) 'honey'

memor, memoris 'mindful'

mēns, mentis 'mind'

‡mentum 'chin'

Mercurius Mercury (*messenger of the gods, god of dexterity, of eloquence, of traders*)

‡merx, mercis 'wares,' 'merchandise'

‡metus (met- *or* metu-) 'fear'

mīles, mīlitis 'soldier'

minera 'mine,' 'ore'

minister, ministrī 'servant'

‡minium 'red-lead'

‡minūtiae (*nom. plu.*) 'details,' 'trifles'

miser, miserī 'wretched'

‡mītis 'mild,' 'soft'
†modus 'measure,' 'method,'
    'fashion'
 mollis 'soft'
 mōns, montis 'mountain'
†mōnstrum 'wonder,' 'mira-
    cle'
‡morbus 'disease'
†mors, mortis 'death'
 mūcus 'mucus'
†mōs, mōris 'habit,' 'custom'
†multus 'much,' 'many'
‡mundus 'the world,' 'the
    earth'
‡mūnus, mūneris (n) 'duty,'
    'gift,' 'reward'
 mūrus 'wall'
 mūs, mūris 'mouse'
 nāsus 'nose'
‡ne (adv. and conj.) 'not'
 nebula 'mist,' 'vapor,' 'fog'
‡nefās (nef-) 'sin,' 'impious
    deed'
‡nepōs, nepōtis 'grandson,'
    'nephew'
 nervus 'sinew'
‡nex, necis 'slaughter'
‡niger, nigrī 'black'
 nihil 'nothing'
‡nimbus 'thick shower,'
    'cloud'
 nōdus 'knot,' 'node'
†nōmen nōminis (n) 'name'
 norma 'measure,' 'standard,'
    'pattern'
‡noster, nostrī 'our'

†nota 'mark'
 novus 'new'
 nox, noctis 'night'
 noxa 'harm'
‡nūgae (nom. plu.) 'jests,'
    'trifles'
‡nullus 'not any,' 'none'
†numerus 'number'
‡nunc 'now'
†nuncius 'messenger'
 nux, nucis 'nut'
†oculus 'eye'
‡odium 'hatred,' 'ill-will'
 officium 'service,' 'duty'
 oleum 'oil'
 ōmen, ōminis (n) 'forebod-
    ing,' 'sign'
 omnis 'all'
 onus, oneris (n) 'burden'
†opera 'work'
 ops, opis 'influence,'
    'wealth'
†opus, operis (n) 'work,' 'la-
    bor'
†ōrdō, ōrdinis 'order,' 'regular
    succession'
 orīgō, orīginis 'beginning,'
    'source'
†ōs, ōris (n) 'mouth'
 os, ossis (n) 'bone'
‡ōscillum 'swing'
‡ōstium 'door'
 ōtium 'leisure,' 'idleness'
‡ovis 'sheep'
 ōvum egg
 paene 'nearly,' 'almost'

‡**Palātium** the Palatine hill (*site of Augustus' residence*)

pālus 'stake'

pānis 'bread'

pār, paris 'equal'

†**pars, partis** 'portion'

†**parvus** 'small'

passus (**passu-**) 'pace'

pater, patris 'father'

‡**paucus** 'few'

‡**paulus** 'little'

pāx, pācis 'peace'

pectus, pectoris (n) 'breast'

‡**pecūnia** 'money'

Penātēs Penates (*household gods*)

penna 'feather'

‡**pēnūria** 'want,' 'destitution'

†**persōna** 'mask,' 'role,' 'character,' 'person'

†**pēs, pedis** 'foot'

pestis 'disease,' 'plague'

pīla 'ball'

pilus 'a hair'

piscis 'fish'

pius 'dutiful,' 'loyal,' 'pious'

†**plānus** 'level,' 'flat'

‡**plēbs, plēbis** (**pleb-** *or* **plebē-**) 'common people'

plēnus 'full'

plumbum 'lead'

plūs, plūris 'more'

poena 'penalty,' 'punishment'

populus 'people'

‡**porcus** 'hog,' 'pig'

portus (**portu-**) 'port,' 'harbor'

†**posterus** 'coming after,' 'following'

praeda 'plunder,' 'prey'

†**pretium** 'value' 'worth'

prex, precis 'prayer'

prīmus 'first'

†**prior** 'former,' 'previous,' 'earlier'

‡**prīstinus** 'early,' 'original'

prīvus 'one's own,' 'private'

‡**probrum** 'reproach,' 'infamy'

†**probus** 'good'

prōlēs, prōlis 'offspring'

‡**prōlixus** 'extended' (*see* **liquēre**)

‡**prōnus** 'bent over,' 'leaning'

proprius 'one's own,' 'special,' 'characteristic'

puer 'boy'

pūgna 'fight'

‡**pūlmō, pūlmōnis** 'lung'

‡**pulpitum** 'scaffold'

pūpa 'girl'

pūpus 'boy'

pūrus 'pure,' 'unstained'

pūs, pūris (n) 'pus'

‡**pusillus** 'very little,' 'petty'

‡**quadrāgintā** 'forty'

quantus 'of what size?' 'how much?' 'how great?'

‡**quid** 'what?'

‡**quondam** (*adv.*) 'formerly'

quot 'how many?'

‡rabiēs 'madness'
racēmus 'bunch,' 'cluster'
†radius 'staff,' 'rod,' 'spoke of
   a wheel'
rādīx, rādīcis 'root'
rāmus 'branch'
‡rārus 'rare'
†rēctus 'upright,' 'straight'
   (see regere)
‡rēgīna 'queen'
rēgnum 'government,' 'rule,'
   'sovereignty'
rēnēs (nom. plu.) 'kidneys'
rēs (re-) 'thing,' 'matter'
rēte, rētis (n) 'net'
rēx, rēgis 'king'
‡rīpa 'bank of a river'
‡rītus (rītu-) 'form of religious
   observance,' 'ceremony'
‡rōbur, roboris (n) 'oak,'
   'strength'
rōbustus 'of oak-wood,' 'firm'
†rota 'wheel'
rotundus 'rolling,' 'circular'
‡ruber, rubrī 'red'
rūga 'wrinkle'
†sacer, sacrī 'sacred'
‡saeculum 'generation,' 'lifetime,' 'the world'
sagāx, sagācis 'keen-scented'
sal, salis 'salt'
salūs, salūtis 'health,'
   'safety'
salvus 'safe'
sanguis, sanguinis 'blood'
†sānus 'sound,' 'healthy,'
   'rational'

satis 'enough'
‡Saturnus Saturn (god of
   time)
‡scamnum 'bench,' 'stool'
scintilla 'spark'
‡scrūpus 'sharp stone'
scūtum 'shield'
sēmen, sēminis (n) 'seed'
senex, senis (adj.) 'old';
   (noun) 'old man'
‡septuāgintā 'seventy'
‡seriātim 'in order'
seriēs 'row,' 'succession,'
   'series'
‡sermō, sermōnis 'talk,' 'conversation'
servus 'slave'
sexus (sexu-) 'sex'
†sīgnum 'mark,' 'token'
†similis 'like' (neuter simile)
sinister 'on the left hand'
sinus (sinu-) 'curve'
‡sōbrius 'sober,' 'moderate'
†socius 'associate,' 'ally'
sōl, sōlis 'sun'
solidus 'firm,' 'compact'
†sōlus 'alone,' 'single'
somnus 'sleep'
†sonus 'sound'
‡sopor, sopōris 'deep sleep'
sors, sortis 'lot,' 'fate'
spatium 'space'
†speciēs 'appearance'
‡specula 'watch-tower'
spīna 'thorn,' 'spine'
stella 'star'
stimulus 'prick,' 'goad'

‡stirps, stirpis 'stem,' 'root'
‡stultus 'foolish'
subter (*prep. and adv.*)
  'beneath'
‡sūcus 'juice,' 'sap,' 'taste'
†summus 'highest'
†superus 'upper'
‡supīnus 'lying on the back'
‡suus 'its own'
‡taberna 'rude dwelling,'
  'hut'
tabula 'plank,' 'tablet'
‡taedium 'weariness,'
  'disgust'
‡taurus 'bull'
†tempus, temporis (n) 'time'
‡tenebrae (*nom. plu.*) 'dark-
  ness'
tenuis 'slender'
‡tergum 'back'
†terminus 'boundary stone,'
  'boundary'
†terra 'earth'
‡tessera 'a cube,' 'a square
  piece,' 'a die'
†testis 'witness'
tōtus 'all,' 'the whole'
trux, trucis 'savage,' 'wild'
tūber, tūberis (n) 'bump,'
  'swelling;' 'truffle'
‡turba 'turmoil,' 'commotion'
‡tūtēla 'a watching,' 'safe-
  guard,' 'protection'
ultrā (*adv.*) 'beyond,' 'far-
  ther,' 'in addition'
umbra 'shadow'
unda 'wave'

urbs, urbis 'city'
‡ursus 'a bear'
‡ūsūra 'a using,' 'loan,' 'payment for use of money'
‡vacca 'cow'
†vacuus 'empty'
vānus 'empty,' 'vain'
‡vapidus 'flat,' 'stale'
†varius 'varied'
vās, vāsis (n) 'vessel,' 'dish'
vēlōx, vēlōcis 'swift'
vēna 'blood-vessel,' 'vein'
‡venia 'pardon'
venter, ventris 'belly'
‡vēnum 'sale'
‡verbātim 'word for word'
‡verber, verberis (n) 'lash,'
  'whip'
†verbum 'word'
‡vērē (*adv.*) 'truly,' 'rightly'
vermis 'worm'
‡vertebra 'joint'
‡vertex, verticis 'peak,' 'tip'
†vērus 'true'
vēsīca 'bladder,' 'blister'
†vestis 'garment'
vetus, veteris 'old'
†via 'way,' 'road'
vicis (*gen. sing.*) 'change,'
  'alternation'
vīnum 'wine'
‡vīpera 'serpent'
vir, virī 'man'
‡virāgō, virāginis 'man-like
  woman'
‡viridis 'green'
‡vīrus 'venom,' 'potent juice'

‡vīs (vi-) 'force'
‡vīscera (*neuter plu*.) 'inter-
    nal organs'
vīta 'life'
‡vītis 'vine'
vitium 'defect,' 'flaw'
vīvus 'alive,' 'living'

‡voluntās (volunt-) 'free-will,'
    'choice'
‡vortex, vorticis 'center of a
    whirlpool'
†vōx, vōcis 'voice'
†vulgus 'the masses,' 'the
    crowd'
‡vulpēs, vulpis 'fox'

VERBS

‡acuere, acūtus 'to sharpen'
‡adolēscere, adultus 'to grow
    up' (*see* olēre)
‡affīdāre 'to take oath,' 'to
    pledge' (*see* fidēs)
†agere, actus (-igere, -actus)
    'to do,' 'to act', 'to drive'
amāre 'to love'
ambulāre 'to walk'
‡arāre 'to plow'
‡audēre, ausus 'to dare'
audīre, audītus 'to hear'
augēre, auctus 'to increase'
beāre 'to make happy,' 'to
    bless'
bibere, —— 'to drink'
‡bullīre, bullītus 'bubble,'
    'boil'
†cadere, cāsus (-cidere,
    -cāsus) 'to fall'
†caedere, caesus (-cīdere,
    -cīsus) 'to cut'
candēre, —— 'to be a
    glowing white'
canere, *cantus 'to sing'
†capere (-iō), captus (-cipere,

-ceptus) 'to take,' 'to
    grasp,' 'to hold'
‡carēre, —— 'to lack'
carpere, carptus (-cerpere,
    -cerptus) 'to pick,' 'to
    pluck'
cavēre, cautus 'to take care,'
    'to beware,' 'to guard
    against'
†cēdere, cessus 'to go,' 'to
    yield'
-cendere, -census 'to burn'
    (*see* incendere)
cēnsēre, cēnsus 'to rate,' 'to
    assess'
†cernere, crētus 'to sift,' 'to
    distinguish'
citāre 'to rouse,' 'to mention'
†clāmāre 'to cry out'
‡clangere, —— 'to ring,'
    'to clang'
†claudere, clausus (-clūdere,
    -clūsus) 'to shut'
clīnāre 'to lean'
colere, cultus 'to till,' 'to
    cultivate'

‡comminīscī, commentus 'to invent,' 'to reflect upon'

‡condere, conditus 'to store'

‡cōnfūtāre 'to check'

‡cōnsīderāre 'to examine,' 'to reflect'

cōnsulere, cōnsultus 'to take counsel'

coquere, coctus 'to cook'

‡coruscāre 'to glitter' (*see* coruscus)

creāre 'to bring into being'

crēdere, crēditus 'to believe,' 'to trust'

†crēscere, crētus 'to grow'

‡crūdēscere 'to become hard or raw,' 'to worsen' (*see* crūdus)

‡-culere, -cultus 'to hide' (*see* occulere)

-cumbere, -cubitus 'to lie' (*see* incumbere)

cupere (-iō), cupītus 'to long for,' 'to desire'

†currere, cursus 'to run'

dare, datus (-dere -ditus) 'to give'

‡dēficere (-iō), dēfectus 'to make absent or lacking,' 'to fail,' 'to be wanting' (*see* facere)

‡dēsīderāre 'to desire,' 'to long for'

†dīcere, dictus 'to say,' 'to tell'

dīvidere, dīvīsus 'to divide'

docēre, doctus 'to teach'

dormīre, dormītus 'to sleep'

†dūcere, ductus 'to lead'

emere, ēmptus (-imere, -ēmptus) 'to buy,' 'to take'

errāre 'to wander'

‡exīre, exitus 'to go out'

†facere (-iō), factus (-ficere, -fectus) 'to make,' 'to do'

fallere, falsus 'to deceive'

†fārī, fātus 'to speak'

‡ferīre, —— 'to strike'

†ferre (*base* fer-), lātus 'to bring,' 'to bear' (*irregular verb of the Third Conjugation*)

fervēre, —— 'to seethe'

‡fētēre, —— 'to stink'

fīdere, fīsus 'to trust,' 'to rely on'

‡fīerī, factus 'to be made,' 'to be done' (*irregular passive of* facere)

†fīgere, fīxus 'to fix,' 'to fasten'

findere, fissus 'to split'

fingere, fictus 'to fashion,' 'to feign'

flāre 'to blow'

†flectere, flexus 'to bend'

flōrēre, —— 'to bloom,' 'to flourish' (*see* flōs)

†fluere, fluxus 'to flow'

‡fodere (-iō), fossus 'to dig'

†frangere, frāctus (-fringere, -frāctus) 'to break'

fugere (-iō), *fugitus 'to flee'

fulgēre, —— 'to flash'

†fundere, fūsus 'to pour'

fungī, fūnctus 'to do,' 'to perform'

‡furere, —— 'to rage'

-fūtāre (see confūtāre, refūtāre)

‡garrīre, —— 'to chatter'

†gerere, gestus 'to bear,' 'to carry on'

gignere, genitus 'to beget,' 'to bring forth'

†gradī (-ior), gressus (-gredī, -gressus) 'to step'

‡gubernāre 'to steer'

†habēre, habitus (-hibēre, -hibitus) 'to have,' 'to hold'

habitāre 'to have possession of,' 'to dwell,' 'to reside' (see habēre)

†haerēre, haesus 'to stick'

‡haurīre, haustus 'to draw out'

‡hiāre 'to stand open,' 'to gape'

†horrēre, —— 'to shrink,' 'to shudder'

hūmēre, —— 'to be moist'

‡īgnōrāre 'to be ignorant,' 'to have no knowledge of'

incendere, incēnsus 'to set fire to,' 'to burn'

‡incumbere, incubitus 'to lie on,' 'to pay attention to'

‡interesse, —— 'to be of importance'

†īre, itum (pres. part. base ient-) 'to go'

†jacere (-iō), jactus (-jicere, -jectus) 'to throw'

†jungere, jūnctus 'to join'

†jūrāre 'to swear'

lābī, lapsus 'to fall,' 'to slip'

laedere, laesus (-līdere, -līsus) 'to strike'

‡lambere, —— 'to lick'

languēre, —— 'to be faint'

‡latēre, —— 'to lie hid'

laudāre 'to praise' (see laus)

lavāre, lavātus or lōtus 'to wash'

†legere, lēctus (-ligere, -lēctus) 'to gather,' 'to read,' 'to choose'

licēre, licitum 'to be allowable,' 'to be permitted'

ligāre 'to bind'

‡linere, litus 'to smear,' 'to anoint'

linquere, —— (-lictus) 'to leave'

liquēre, *lixus 'to be liquid'

†loquī, locūtus 'to speak'

lūcēre, —— 'to be light,' 'to shine'

luctārī 'to struggle'

†lūdere, lūsus 'to play'

luere (pres. inf. base lu- and luv-), —— (-lūtum) 'to wash,' 'to loosen,' 'to atone for'

manēre, mānsus 'to remain'

medērī, —— 'to heal'

merēre, meritus 'to earn'

mergere, mersus 'to dip,' 'to plunge'

mētīrī, mēnsus 'to measure'

mīlitāre 'to be a soldier,' 'to fight' (see mīles)

-minēre, —— 'to project,' 'to threaten'

-minīscī, -mentus (see comminīscī)

mīrārī 'to wonder,' 'to admire'

miscēre, mīxtus 'to mingle'

†mittere, missus 'to let go,' 'to send'

monēre, monitus 'to warn'

mordēre, morsus 'to bite'

†movēre, mōtus 'to move'

‡mulctāre 'to fine,' 'to penalize'

†mūtāre 'to change,' 'to alter'

†nāscī, nātus 'to be born'

‡necāre 'to kill' (see nex)

nectere, nexus 'to bind'

nocēre, —— 'to harm'

nōscere, nōtus 'to know'

‡obsolēscere, obsolētus 'to wear out,' 'to fall into disuse' (see olēre ['increase'] and -olēscere)

‡occulere, occultus 'to cover up,' 'to hide'

‡olēre, —— 'to smell'

olēre, —— 'to increase'

-olēscere (see adolēscere, obsolēscere and olēre 'increase')

‡opīnārī 'to suppose,' 'to think'

ōrdināre 'to arrange' (see ōrdō, ōrdinis)

‡ōrdīrī, ōrsus 'to begin'

orīrī, ortus 'to arise'

ōrnāre 'to equip,' 'to adorn'

‡ōscillāre 'to swing' (see ōscillum)

‡pacīscī, pactus 'to make an agreement'

paenitēre, —— 'to repent'

pallēre, —— 'to be pale'

‡palpāre 'to stroke,' 'to feel'

pangere, pāctus (-pingere, -pāctus) 'to strike,' 'to fasten'

parāre 'to prepare'

parere (-iō), partus 'to give birth'

partīrī, partītus 'to share' (see pars)

pāscere, pāstus 'to feed,' 'to graze'

‡patēre, —— 'to stand open'

†pati (-iōr), passus 'to suffer,' 'to bear'

†pausāre 'to cease' (see Etymological Notes, Lesson 20)

†pellere, pulsus 'to drive'

†pendēre, —— (-pēnsus) 'to hang'

†pendere, pēnsus 'to weigh,' 'to pay'

‡penetrāre 'to pierce'

†petere, petītus 'to seek'

pingere, pictus 'to paint'

placēre, placitus 'to please'

plangere, planctus 'to strike,' 'to lament'

plaudere, plausus (*or* plōdere, plōsus) 'to clap'

†-plēre, -plētus 'to fill'

†plicāre, plicātus *or* plicitus 'to fold'

‡polīre, polītus 'to smooth,' 'to polish'

†pōnere, positus 'to place,' 'to put' (*see* Etymological Notes, Lesson 20)

†portāre 'to carry'

posse, —— (*pres. part.* base pot-) 'to be powerful,' 'to be able'

postulāre, postulātus 'to ask,' 'to demand'

precārī 'to beg,' 'to pray' (*see* prex)

†prehendere, prehensus 'to grasp'

†premere, pressus (-primere, -pressus) 'to press'

prīvāre 'to deprive' (*see* prīvus)

‡prōpāgāre 'to multiply,' 'to spread'

‡prūrīre, —— 'to itch'

pūgnāre 'to fight' (*see* pūgna)

†pungere, punctus 'to prick'

pūrgāre 'to make clean or pure,' 'to cleanse'

†putāre, putātus 'to reckon,' 'to think'

†quaerere, quaesītus (-quīrere, -quīsītus) 'to seek'

quatere (-iō), quassus (-cutere, -cussus) 'to shake'

‡querī, questus 'to complain'

quiēscere, quiētus 'to be quiet'

rādere, rāsus 'to scrape'

rapere (-iō), raptus (-ripere, -reptus) 'to seize and carry off,' 'to rob'

‡recipere (-iō), receptus 'to take back,' 'get back,' 'take' (*see* capere)

‡refūtāre 'to check,' 'to disprove'

†regere, rēctus (-rigere, -rēctus) 'to straighten,' 'to rule'

‡rēpere, rēptus 'to creep,' 'to crawl'

rērī, ratus 'to think,' 'to reckon'

‡rigēre, —— 'to be stiff'

†rogāre 'to ask,' 'to propose a law'

‡ruere, rutus 'to tumble down'

‡rūgāre 'to wrinkle' (*see* rūga)

†rumpere, ruptus 'to break'

‡saepīre, saeptus 'to enclose'

‡sāgīre, —— 'to discern acutely'

†salīre, saltus (-silīre, -sultus) 'to leap'

salvēre, —— 'to be well'

‡sānāre 'to make sound,' 'to heal' (*see* sānus)

sancīre, sānctus 'to make holy'

scandere, scānsum (-scendere, -scēnsum) 'to rise,' 'to climb'

scindere, scissus 'to cut,' 'to split'

scīre, scītus 'to know'

†scrībere, scrīptus 'to write'

†secāre, sectus 'to cut'

‡sēdāre 'to calm'

†sedēre, sessus (-sidēre, -sessus) 'to sit'

†sentīre, sēnsus 'to feel'

†sequī, secūtus 'to follow'

‡serere, satus 'to sow'

serere, sertus 'to bind,' 'to join,' 'to connect'

†servāre 'to save'

servīre, servītus 'to serve' (see servus)

-sīderāre (see cōnsīderāre, dēsīderāre)

†sistere, status (-sistere, -stitus) 'to cause to stand,' 'to stand'

sōlārī 'to comfort'

†solvere, solūtus 'to loose,' 'to free'

sonāre 'to sound' (see sonus)

‡sortīrī, sortītus 'to cast lots' (see sors)

spargere, sparsus (-spergere, -spersus) 'to scatter'

†specere (-iō), spectus (-spicere, -spectus) 'to look'

‡speculārī 'to spy out,' 'to observe' (see specula)

†spīrāre 'to breathe'

spondēre, spōnsus 'to promise'

‡squālēre, —— 'to be foul'

†stāre 'to stand'

†statuere, statūtus (-stituere, -stitūtus) 'to set up'

sternere, strātus 'to spread'

‡stertere, —— 'to snore'

-stinguere, -stinctus 'to prick,' 'to quench'

†stringere, strictus 'to draw tight'

†struere, strūctus 'to build'

‡studēre, —— 'to be eager'

stupēre, —— 'to be struck senseless'

-sulere, -sultus (see cōnsulere)

†sūmere, sūmptus 'to take'

‡tacēre, tacitus (-ticēre) 'to be silent'

†tangere, tāctus (-tingere, -tāctus) 'to touch'

tegere, tēctus 'to cover'

†tendere, tentus or tēnsus 'to stretch,' 'to hold a course'

†tenēre, tentus (-tinēre, -tentus) 'to hold'

†terere, trītus 'to rub,' 'to wear'

terrēre, territus 'to frighten'

texere, textus 'to weave'

‡tinguere, tinctus 'to dip,' 'to dye'

torpēre, —— 'to be stiff,' 'to be numb'

†torquēre, tortus 'to twist'

††trahere, tractus 'to draw,' 'to drag'

tremere, —— 'to tremble'

tribuere, tribūtus 'to assign,' 'to allot'

†trūdere, trūsus 'to push'

tumēre, —— 'to swell'

‡unguere, ūnctus 'to smear,' 'to anoint'

‡urgēre, —— 'to press'

ūtī, ūsus 'to employ,' 'to use'

‡vacillāre 'to waver,' 'to totter'

vādere, —— 'to go,' 'to walk'

vagārī 'to wander'

†valēre, —— 'to be strong,' 'to be worth'

vehere, vectus 'to carry'

velle (*pres. inf. base* **vol-**) 'to wish'

vellere, —— (-vulsus) 'to pluck'

†venīre, ventum 'to come'

‡verērī, veritus 'to fear,' 'to feel awe for'

vergere, —— 'to bend,' 'to turn,' 'to incline'

†vertere, versus 'to turn'

‡vetāre, vetitus 'to oppose,' 'to forbid,' 'to prohibit'

†vidēre, vīsus 'to see'

vigēre, —— 'to thrive'

†vincere, victus 'to conquer'

vīvere, vīctum 'to live'

volāre 'to fly'

†volvere, volūtus 'to roll'

vorāre 'to devour'

vovēre, vōtus 'to vow'

vulgāre 'to make general,' 'to spread abroad' (*see* **vulgus**)

Part Two
GREEK

CHAPTER ONE

Introduction

IN THE Introduction to Part One we pointed out (pp. 4–6) that Greek was a sister tongue of Latin, English, and the other Indo-European languages. Greek, therefore, will not be something completely strange to you. Many of its words are cognate with native English and with Latin words, and some of these cognates show extremely close resemblance. Consider, for example, the following pairs:

LATIN	GREEK
ferō 'I bear'	phérō
duo 'two'	dúo
trēs 'three'	treis
sex 'six'	hex
septem 'seven'	heptá
octō 'eight'	októ

Greek, then, is a sister tongue of Latin, but an older sister. By the fifth century B.C., when the incomparable literary works of Sophocles, Euripides, Herodotus, and others were produced, Greek was a fully developed language. Latin did not reach its prime until the second and first centuries B.C. During the period when Latin was developing, it started to borrow from Greek and kept this up even after it became a fully developed language. The Roman trader who had business connections in the Greek-speaking Near East brought in the names of Greek merchandise; the Roman soldier, returned from years of service in Greece or Egypt or Syria, came back with a miscellany of Greek terms; the wealthy young Roman who was tutored as a child by a Greek slave and took his degree at the University of Athens brought in Greek mathematical and philosophical terms; the Roman gentleman who, like all the members of his set, spoke Greek as fluently as Latin, sprinkled his Latin conversation with a variety of Greek expressions.

The rise of Christianity brought into Latin a whole new group of Greek words. Christianity arose in the East and its early adherents spoke and wrote Greek. When the Church spread to the western part of the Roman empire it was forced to use Latin, a language lacking equivalents for the religious technical terms that were so necessary a part of the vocabulary of Christianity. These were, accordingly, borrowed wholesale from Greek.

In the Introduction to Part One we gave the history of the contact between Latin and English. Until the Revival of Learning in the fifteenth century (see page 10), English was in contact solely with Latin, and the only Greek words to enter our language were those that Latin had previously borrowed from Greek. These words entered English, naturally, in their Latinized form. With the Revival of Learning the first large-scale borrowing from Greek itself began and has never stopped, for the sciences today still turn largely to Greek to supplement their technical vocabularies. The fact that until the fifteenth century all Greek words passed through Latin before entering English has influenced all subsequent borrowing: even today words taken from Greek or made up from Greek elements are almost always Latinized in form before being adopted by English.

The history of the Greek alphabet is totally different from that of the Greek language. This circumstance is true, incidentally, of all alphabets, since an alphabet is not something linguistic but merely a series of stereotyped pictures, as it were. Greek adopted an alphabet which was originally Semitic. It did this with as little difficulty as English experienced in adopting Arabic numbers. An alphabet used by the Phoenicians—an ancient Semitic race which carried on trade all over the Mediterranean—was borrowed by the Greeks at some time before the eighth century B.C. and split into two branches. One developed into the Greek alphabet of ancient and modern times. The other, carried by Greek colonists to Italy and borrowed there by the Romans, gave rise to the Roman alphabet, from which our English alphabet is derived.

The Greek Alphabet.

FORMS		NAMES	GREEK FORMS IN ENGLISH LETTERS	GREEK SOUNDS
A	α	alpha	a	*a* as in *father*
B	β	bēta	b	*b* as in *bed*
Γ	γ	gamma	g	*g* as in *go*
Δ	δ	delta	d	*d* as in *do*
E	ε	epsīlon	e	*e* as in *met*
Z	ζ	zēta	z	*dz* as in *adze*
H	η	ēta	ē	*e* as in *prey*
Θ	θ	thēta	th	*th* as in *thin*
I	ι	iōta	i	*i* as in *machine*
K	κ	kappa	k	*k* as in *kill*
Λ	λ	lambda	l	*l* as in *land*
M	μ	mū	m	*m* as in *man*
N	ν	nū	n	*n* as in *now*
Ξ	ξ	xī	x	*x* as in *tax*
O	o	omīcron	o	*o* as in *obey*
Π	π	pī	p	*p* as in *pet*
P	ρ	rhō	r	*r* as in *road*
Σ	σ,s	sigma	s	*s* as in *see*
T	τ	tau	t	*t* as in *tip*
Y	υ	upsīlon	y	like German *ü* or French *u*
Φ	φ	phī	ph	*ph* as in *philter*
X	χ	chī	ch	*ch* as in *loch*
Ψ	ψ	psī	ps	*ps* as in *lips*
Ω	ω	ōmega	ō	*o* as in *lone*

αβγδεζηθικλμνξοπραστυφχψω

Transliteration. For those who do not know the Greek alphabet, most English dictionaries give Greek words, not in Greek characters, but in transliterated English characters. The column headed GREEK FORMS IN ENGLISH LETTERS gives the English transliterated equivalent of each Greek letter according to the system used by Webster's *New Collegiate Dictionary.*

In writing and transliterating Greek the following peculiarities must be noted:

1. In order to distinguish ε (epsilon), which is a short vowel, from η (eta), which is long, the former is written e and the latter ē. In order to distinguish o (omicron), which is short, from ω (omega), which is long, the former is written o and the latter ō. Thus, σκηνή 'tent' is transliterated skēnḗ and ἰδέα 'idea' is transliterated idéa; γλῶσσα becomes glṓssa and ὄργανον becomes órganon.

2. The small sigma has two forms. The second (s) is used at the end of a word, the other (σ) everywhere else.

3. Gamma (γ) before another gamma or before kappa (κ), xi (ξ), or chi (χ) has the sound of *n* in *singer* instead of its usual sound and is consequently transliterated in these positions as *n*.

GREEK	ENGLISH TRANSLITERATION
ἄγγελος 'messenger'	ángelos
ἐγκώμιον 'eulogy'	enkṓmion
λάρυγξ 'larynx'	lárynx
βρόγχος 'windpipe'	brónchos

4. In most English derivatives, *ch* (from χ) is pronounced like *k* (cf. *chaos*); *ps* (from ψ) is pronounced like *ps* in *psychology* if it begins a word, but otherwise like *ps* in *ellipsis.*

5. There is no independent letter *h* in the Greek alphabet. Within words the sound of *h* is taken care of by the double letters theta (θ), phi (φ), and chi (χ). At the beginning of words it is taken care of by the 'rough breathing.' The rough breathing is a symbol resembling an apostrophe turned the wrong way ('). It is found over the initial vowel of a word

or, if the word begins with a diphthong, over the second member thereof. The rough breathing is pronounced and transliterated as *h*:

GREEK	ENGLISH TRANSLITERATION
ὑπό 'under'	**hypó**
αἵρεσις 'choice'	**haíresis**

In writing Greek a symbol called the 'smooth breathing' is also used. This symbol resembles an apostrophe turned as it is in English (') and is placed over the initial vowel or initial diphthong of those words where no *h* sound is wanted. Thus every Greek word beginning with a vowel or diphthong will have either a rough or smooth breathing; the former indicates that the word begins with an *h* sound, the latter is disregarded in pronunciation and transliteration.

GREEK	ENGLISH TRANSLITERATION
ὑπέρ 'over'	**hypér**
αἵρεσις 'choice'	**haíresis**
ὄργανον 'tool'	**órganon**
αὐτός 'self'	**autós**

Aside from initial vowels and the second member of initial diphthongs, the rough breathing is used in only two other positions: (1) initial rho is always given a rough breathing; (2) where two successive rhos occur, the first is given a smooth breathing, the second a rough. Rho combined with the rough breathing in this way is transliterated *rh*.

GREEK	ENGLISH TRANSLITERATION
ῥυθμός 'measure,' 'proportion'	**rhythmós**
μύρρα 'myrrh'	**mýrrha**

When words begin with a capital letter, the breathings are placed to the left of the letter instead of above it.

GREEK	ENGLISH TRANSLITERATION
Ἀριστοφάνης	**Aristophánēs**

6. Greek words, with certain exceptions, are given a written accent. These accents are of three types: acute ('), grave (`), and circumflex (^). The distinction among them does not concern us: simply accent words on the syllable that bears any one of the above accents.

Diphthongs. There are seven diphthongs in Greek:

FORMS	GREEK FORMS IN ENGLISH LETTERS	GREEK SOUNDS
αι	ai	*ai* as in *aisle*
ει	ei	*ei* as in *rein*
οι	oi	*oi* as in *soil*
υι	ui	*we*
αυ	au	*ow* as in *cow*
ευ	eu	*éh-oo*
ου	ou	*ou* as in *you*

Note that upsilon, when part of a diphthong, is transliterated **u** and not **y** as elsewhere.

Latinization. For the reasons mentioned above (pp. 175–76) Greek words, with very few exceptions, were Latinized in form before entering English. In Latinizing Greek words the Romans used the same equivalents we use in English transliteration except for the following:

	GREEK	LATIN
kappa (κ)		
becomes *c:*	ἀκακία **akakía**	*acacia*
alpha iota (αι)		
becomes *ae:*	σφαῖρα **sphaíra**	*sphaera*
omicron upsilon (ου)		
becomes *ū:*	Μοῦσα **Moúsa**	*Mūsa*
epsilon iota (ει)		
becomes *ī:*	εἰρωνεία **eirōneía**	*īrōnīa*
or *ē:*	Μουσεῖον **Mouseíon**	*Mūsēum*
omicron iota (οι)		
becomes *oe:*	ἀμοιβή **amoibḗ**	*amoeba*

It must always be remembered that practically every Greek word to enter English underwent first the changes listed above. In the case of nouns still further changes connected with declensional endings take place. These are discussed below in Lessons 1–4.

CHAPTER TWO

Greek Nouns

GREEK NOUNS, like Latin nouns, are declined. Unlike Latin, however, Greek has but three declensions.

Lesson 1

The First Declension

The First Declension. This includes both feminine and masculine nouns. The former end in **-a** or **-ē** in the nominative case, the latter in **-ēs.** The base may be found by dropping these endings.

GREEK NOUN	BASE
γλῶσσα **glṓssa** 'tongue'	**glōss-**
ἀκμή **akmḗ** 'point,' 'prime'	**akm-**
χάρτης **chártēs** 'sheet of papyrus'	**chart-**

Nouns ending in **-ē,** when Latinized, generally, but not always, change this ending to **-a,** since **-a** is the regular ending for Latin First-Declension nouns.

GREEK NOUN	LATIN NOUN
ἀμοιβή **amoibḗ** 'change'	*amoeba*

For the same reason nouns ending in **-ēs,** when Latinized, generally change this ending to **-a.** This is not true, however, of proper names.

182

	GREEK NOUN		LATIN NOUN
	χάρτης **chártēs** 'sheet of papyrus'		*charta*
but:			
	Θουκυδίδης **Thoukydídēs** (name of Greek historian)		*Thūcydidēs*

First-Declension Nouns in English. As mentioned before, Greek nouns were, with few exceptions, Latinized before being borrowed by English. Whenever, therefore, we refer to a word as having been borrowed 'unchanged' or 'without change,' it is to be understood that its Latinized form, unless specific mention to the contrary is made, has been so borrowed.

First-Declension Greek nouns have been borrowed either without change or Anglicized; that is, their ending either drops off or is replaced by silent *-e.*

	GREEK NOUN	LATIN NOUN	ENGLISH LOAN WORD
ENDING UNCHANGED:	χίμαιρα **chímaira** 'she-goat,' 'chimera'	*chimaera*	*chimera*
	λήθη **léthē** 'forgetfulness'	*Lēthē*	*Lethe*
	ἀμοιβή **amoibé** 'change'	*amoeba*	*amoeba*
	Θουκυδίδης **Thoukydídēs** (name of Greek historian)	*Thūcydidēs*	*Thucydides*
ENDING DROPPED:	γλῶσσα **glóssa** 'tongue'	*glōssa*	*gloss*
	νύμφη **nýmphē** 'nymph,' 'bride,' 'young woman'	*nympha*	*nymph*
	χάρτης **chártēs** 'sheet of papyrus'	*charta*	*chart*

| | LATIN | ENGLISH |
| GREEK NOUN | NOUN | LOAN WORD |

ENDING RE-
PLACED BY
SILENT -*e*:   γάγγραινα **gángraina** *gangraena*   *gangrene*
'cancerous ulcer'

ᾠδή **ōidế** 'poem sung *ōda*   *ode*
to music'

ἐρημίτης **erēmítēs**   *erēmīta*   *eremite*
'hermit'

Many nouns that end in -ia have this ending replaced in English by -*y*, as in **harmonía** which becomes *harmony*.

Hybrids are frequently formed in English by combining Greek elements with Latin elements. Thus *orchestral* represents a combination of the base of the Greek noun **orchế̄stra** with the Latin-derived suffix -*al* (< -*ālis*).

EXERCISES

1. Give the English form of the following proper names: Ἀφροδίτη, Ἀρκαδία, Εὐριπίδης, Ἥρα, Λιβύη.

2. (a) Using the General Vocabulary, find the Greek noun and its meaning from which each of the following is derived: *artery, choler, chord, conch, lyre, mitre, myrrh, stele.*

    (b) Latinize each of the Greek words referred to in (a).

    (c) Determine the current meaning of the words listed in (a).

3. Analyze each of the following (use the General Vocabulary to find the Greek word involved): *bursar, disburse, reimburse, scenario, scholar.*

4. Determine the meaning of each italicized word in the context. Using the General Vocabulary, find the Greek noun and its meaning from which each is derived.

    A   There was not a sound of life save that *acme* and sublimation of all dismal sounds, the bark of a fox.

                                                     —HARDY

    B   The wits even of Rome are united into a rural group

of nymphs and swains under the appellation of modern *Arcadians.*—GOLDSMITH

C Plato—and the Hayes Office—would have to prohibit or alter Shakespeare, provided . . . that the *aura* of sanctity which protects and neutralizes his work did not exist.—THE NEW YORK TIMES

D A man who could propose, even playfully, to quench old McNab's thirst must have been a Utopist, a pursuer of *chimaeras.*—CONRAD

E In fact, he was the victim of too many gifts, no mere Janus with a double head but a sort of accomplished *Hydra.*—VAN WYCK BROOKS

F Come, let's all take hands,
Till that the conquering wine hath steep'd our sense in soft and delicate *Lethe.*—SHAKESPEARE

G There are few people who have not groaned under the *plethora* of goods that fell to the lot of the Swiss Family Robinson.—STEVENSON

5. (a) What is the etymological meaning of *diet*? What semantic change is illustrated by *diet* in the expression 'lost eight pounds by a new *diet*'?

(b) Consider the expressions 'a benevolent *despot*,' and 'the oppression of a *despot* like Ivan the Terrible.' In which is *despot* closer to its etymological meaning? What semantic change is illustrated by the other?

6. What is the meaning of the Christian names *Cora, Daphne, Irene, Rhoda, Zoe*?

LESSON 2

Suffixes.   Multiple-Base Compounds

Suffixes. For the sake of convenience we are introducing at this point several important Greek noun- and adjective-forming suffixes which may be attached to the base of Greek nouns and adjectives.

1. Noun base plus **-ikos** > *-ic*, forming adjectives from nouns.

GREEK NOUN	BASE	GREEK COMPOUND ADJECTIVE	ENGLISH LOAN WORD
λύρα **lýra** 'lyre'	**lyr-**	λυρικός **lyrikós**	*lyric*

When a base ends in **-i-**, **-akos** > *-ac* is used instead of **-ikos**.

GREEK NOUN	BASE	GREEK COMPOUND ADJECTIVE	ENGLISH LOAN WORD
καρδία **kardía** 'heart'	**kardi-**	καρδιακός **kardiakós**	*cardiac*

In English, *-al* (< *-ālis*) is frequently added to such adjectives. Thus alongside *lyric* we have *lyrical*, alongside *cardiac*, *cardiacal*.

2. Noun or adjective base plus **-ia** (sometimes **-eia**) > *-ia*, *-y*, forming abstract nouns.

GREEK NOUN	BASE	GREEK ABSTRACT NOUN	ENGLISH LOAN WORD
διφθέρα **diphthéra** 'piece of leather'	**diphther-**	*διφθερια ***diphtheria**	*diphtheria*
βοτάνη **botánē** 'plant'	**botan-**	βοτανία **botanía**	*botany*

3. The suffixes *-ism* and *-ist* have already been discussed in connection with Latin (see page 79). They were frequently attached to Greek bases in English, as in *mechanism* from **mēchanē** 'machine,' *botanist* from **botánē** 'plant.' Since they are ultimately derived from verb elements, they will be studied in full detail below (Lesson 18).

Multiple-Base Compounds. Multiple-base compounds may be formed by combining Greek words or bases. Thus *telephone* consists of the Greek adverb **tēle** 'afar' and **phōnē** 'voice.' Hybrid multiple-base compounds may be formed by combining Greek with Latin or English elements. Thus *petroleum* consists of the base of the Greek noun **pétra** 'rock' and the Latin noun *oleum* 'oil.' The connecting vowel most commonly used is *-o-*, as in *sociology*.

Certain elements called *combining forms* are used consistently to form multiple-base compounds. Four of these follow; others will be introduced in the succeeding lessons.

COMBINING FORM	ENGLISH MULTIPLE-BASE COMPOUND
-λογια **-logia**[1] > *-logy* 'collection of'	*terminology*
'study of,' 'science of'	*psychology*
-μαντεια **-manteia** > *-mancy* 'divination by'	*geomancy*
-τομια **-tomia**[1] > *-tomy* 'cutting,' 'cutting of'	*glossotomy*
-εκτομια **-ektomia**[1] > *-ectomy* 'cutting out of'	*glossectomy*

ETYMOLOGICAL NOTES

Diphtheria, etymologically 'leatheriness,' gets its name from the fact that the most striking characteristic of the disease is a leathery false membrane which coats the air passages. *Stoicism*, etymologically 'the philosophy of the porch (stoá)' is so called because the founder of the philosophy, Zeno, used to address his disciples under a famous colonnade or porch in Athens.

The Greek noun **chártēs** 'sheet of papyrus (the ancient writing paper)' has had an interesting career. In Latin it became **charta**, a form preserved in the name of England's great charter of liberty, the Magna *Charta*. **Charta** passed through French to give us *chart*, and through Italian and French to produce the doublet *card*. A Latin diminutive **chartula** underwent a similar double development: through Old French it became *charter*, and through Italian and French, *cartel*. Combined with an augmentative suffix, **charta** produced *carton*

---

[1] The composition of this combining form is shown below, in Lesson 16.

and its doublet *cartoon*. *Cartridge*, too, is derived from it. From **charta** the Italians formed **cartoccio**, which the French transformed to **cartouche,** subsequently borrowed without change by English as an architectural and archaeological term. *Cartridge* is simply a corruption of *cartouche*. The semantic connection with the original **chártēs** becomes clear when you realize that *cartridges* were at first rolled in paper.

The noun **kánna** 'reed,' 'tube' has flourished in English almost as much as **chártēs**. *Canna,* the name of the large brilliantly colored flower, and *cane* are from it, the first through Latin, the second through Latin and Old French. Combined with the same suffix that appears in *carton,* it produced through French *cannon,* etymologically 'a great tube.' Closely related to *cannon* is *canyon,* a sort of 'great tube' formed through rock by a stream. *Canyon* was borrowed through Spanish.

EXERCISES

1. Memorize the following Greek nouns with their meanings. Determine the current meaning of the English derivative listed alongside each.

γῆ **gē** (base **ge-**) 'earth'	*geology*
γλῶσσα **glóssa** (or γλῶττα **glótta**) 'tongue'	*glossary*
	glottal
καρδία **kardía** 'heart'	*cardiac*
κεφαλή **kephalḗ** 'head'	*cephalic*
μορφή **morphḗ** 'form'	*morphology*
φωνή **phōnḗ** 'voice,' 'sound'	*phonology*
ψυχή **psychḗ** 'breath,' 'life,' 'soul,' 'mind'	*psychology*
σφαῖρα **sphaíra** 'ball,' 'globe'	*spherical*
τέχνη **téchnē** 'art,' 'skill'	*technical*

2. Using the General Vocabulary, find the Greek noun and its meaning from which each of the following is derived: *phial, pyre, spiral*. Determine the current meaning of these words.

3. Analyze each of the following (where necessary, use the General Vocabulary to find the Greek noun involved): *dieti-*

cian, idealistic, ideology, mechanical, sociology, stoical, strato-sphere, technicolor.

4. Determine the etymology and meaning in the context of each italicized word:

A He appraised debentures and went through the whole rigmarole with the ease of a Jewish rabbi's disciple going through the countless compilations of the Law and the Commentaries and excreting rabbinical *glosses*, or of a scholastic mastering a thousand theses and antitheses on a single aspect of the essence of the Trinity.—BLAKE

B "Making generalizations and pursuing knowledge are amusements. Among the most entertaining, to my mind." Philip went on to develop his *hedonistic* justification of the mental life.—ALDOUS HUXLEY

C Here, too, the bride's aunt, and next relation; a widowed female of a *Medusa* sort, in a stony cap, glaring *petrifaction* at her fellow-creatures.—DICKENS

5. (a) Consider the expressions '*a petrified forest*' and '*petrified with fear.*' In which is *petrify* closer to its etymological meaning? What semantic change is illustrated by the other expression?

(b) What is the etymological meaning of *music*? What semantic change does its current meaning illustrate?

LESSON 3

Second-Declension Masculine Nouns

The Second Declension includes masculine and neuter nouns. The study of neuters is reserved for the subsequent lesson.

Masculine nouns of this declension end in **-os** in the nominative case. The base may be found by dropping this ending.

GREEK NOUN	BASE
ὕμνος hýmnos 'song of praise'	hymn-

When Latinized, the ending -os is almost always changed to -us, since -us is the regular ending for Latin Second-Declension masculines.

GREEK NOUN	LATIN NOUN
ἰσθμός isthmós 'neck of land'	*isthmus*

Second-Declension masculines have been borrowed (1) unchanged in their Greek form or only partially Latinized, (2) unchanged in their Latinized form, (3) Anglicized, that is, with their ending either dropped or replaced by silent -e.

	GREEK NOUN	ENGLISH LOAN WORD
(1)	δῆμος démos 'people'	*demos*
	κόσμος kósmos 'order,' 'universe'	*cosmos*
(2)	ἰσθμός isthmós 'neck of land'	*isthmus*
(3)	ὕμνος hýmnos 'song of praise'	*hymn*
	θρόνος thrónos 'chair of state'	*throne*

ETYMOLOGICAL NOTES

Comedy and *tragedy* mean 'revel-song' and 'goat-song, respectively. The first is a combination of kõmos 'revel' and -ōidia (= ōidé 'song' + -ia), the second of trágos 'goat' and -ōidia. The development of the meaning of the first offers no difficulty: *comedy* apparently grew out of the rude jesting and fun-making that went on during certain primitive holiday revels. No satisfactory explanation of the semantics of *tragedy* has been found.

A group of varied derivatives has come from the Greek noun kólaphos meaning 'a blow,' 'a cuff.' In Latin kólaphos was shortened to *colpus.* French reduced this to *coup,* a form which we have taken over without change. From *coup,* the French made *couper* 'to cut.' This word is the source of *coupé,* a car that is 'cut down' in size, and *coupon,* a ticket that is 'cut off.' *Coppice* and its doublet *copse* are related to this group of words   They refer to a small thicket or grove that is, strictly speaking, grown for periodical cutting.

The Greek noun **dáktylos** means fundamentally 'finger.' It is also applied to a metrical foot of one long and two short syllables (–⌣⌣), because of a fancied resemblance between this foot and the one long and two short bones of a finger. It is this sense which is preserved in the English loan word *dactyl*. *Date* (the fruit of the date palm) is a doublet of *dactyl*, and comes into English through Old French. The palm tree derived its name from the resemblance of its leaves to the palm of the hand (Latin *palma*). It is natural that the fruit of this tree should be termed its 'fingers (**dáktyloi**).'

The Greek **dískos** was a flat circular piece of stone or metal, differing only in this last respect from the modern *discus*, which is made of wood, weighted with metal. The discus throw was a standard Greek field event as far back as heroic times. The development of the word in English has been almost as rich as that of **chártēs**. The noun was borrowed by Latin in the form *discus,* and passed from Latin into English to yield the doublets *discus* and *disc*. The Latin word had the meaning 'plate,' a sense which a third derivative, *dish*, preserves. From the meaning 'table,' which *discus* had in Mediaeval Latin, the meaning of *desk* may easily be understood. From 'table' to 'raised platform' is a simple step; hence the sense of *dais*, the fifth derivative.

EXERCISES

1. Memorize the following Greek nouns with their meanings. Determine the current meaning of the English derivative listed alongside each.

ἄνθρωπος **ánthrōpos** 'man'	*anthropology*
βίος **bíos** 'life'	*biology*
χρόνος **chrónos** 'time'	*chronology*
χρυσός **chrysós** 'gold'	*chrysolite*
δάκτυλος **dáktylos** 'finger'	*dactyl*
δῆμος **démos** 'people'	*demos*

γάμος **gámos** 'marriage'	*bigamy*
ἵππος **híppos** 'horse'	*hippopotamus*
κόσμος **kósmos** 'order,' 'harmony,' 'universe'	*cosmic*
κύκλος **kýklos** 'wheel,' 'circle'	*cycle*
λίθος **líthos** 'stone'	*lithotomy*
νεκρός **nekrós** 'corpse'	*necrology*
οἶκος **oîkos** 'house'	*ecology*
ὀφθαλμός **ophthalmós** 'eye'	*ophthalmology*
θεός **theós** 'god'	*theism*
τόπος **tópos** 'place'	*topic*
ξένος **xénos** 'stranger'	*xenolith*

2. Give the Greek form of the following names: *Aeschylus, Bacchus, Daedalus, Pyrrhus.*

3. Using the General Vocabulary, find the Greek noun and its meaning from which each of the following is derived. Show, where it is not obvious, the connection between the Greek and the current meaning: *chorus, cone, crocus, style, thesaurus.*

4. Analyze each of the following (where necessary, use the General Vocabulary to find the Greek noun involved): *atmosphere, ceramics, colossal, cylindrical, elegy, gyration, hippodrome, hymnody, mythology, porous, strategy, tyrannicide.*

5. Determine the etymology of each italicized word and the meaning of the expression in which it appears: *anthropomorphic* representation of a god, the *bacchic* orgies of the prohibition era, *bucolic* poetry, *chronic* good spirits, a *lay* opinion, the *lotus* of escapism, *pander* to popular taste, a bitter *polemic*, Whitman's *threnody* on the death of Lincoln.

6. Determine the etymology and meaning in the context of each italicized word.

A   The wind played on the tent-cords in *Aeolian* improvisations.—HARDY

B   (a) Certain skilled writers—modestly dubbing themselves 'reporters'—are admitted, and by them *cosmos* is conjured out of chaos.—BEERBOHM   (b) One of the greatest contrasts between mediaeval thinking and the more critical thought of today lies in the general conception of man's relation to the *cosmos*.

C Persons . . . travel around the country telling seductively dark and horrible stories of innocent virgins dragged into polygamy by the hair of their heads . . . Now, of course, this is a fascinating picture, a dainty dish to set before King *Demos,* just the sort of dish he likes.—LOUIS SHERMAN

D (a) A delightful *labyrinth* of hazel copse;—HARDY

  (b)   They so embellish, that 'tis quite a bore
    Their *labyrinth* of fables to thread through.

—BYRON

E They say he is a brave *necromancer,* that he can make women of devils, and he can juggle cats into costermongers.—ROBERT GREENE

F Shade after shade goes grimly over your soul, till you have the fixed, starless, *Tartarean* black.—CARLYLE

7. What is the meaning of the Christian names *George, Peter, Stephen?*

8. Determine the etymological meaning of *angel.* What semantic change does its current meaning reveal?

LESSON 4

Second-Declension Neuter Nouns.   Multiple-Base Compounds

Second-Declension Neuters. These nouns end in **-on** in the nominative case. The base may be found by dropping this ending.

GREEK NOUN	BASE
κρανίον **kraníon** 'skull'	**krani-**

When Latinized, the ending **-on** is almost always changed to **-um,** since **-um** is the regular ending for Latin Second-Declension neuters.

GREEK NOUN	LATIN NOUN
κρανίον **kraníon** 'skull'	*crānium*

Second-Declension neuters have been borrowed (1) unchanged in their Greek form or only partially Latinized, (2) unchanged in their Latinized form, (3) Anglicized—that is, with their ending either dropped or replaced by silent *-e.*

	GREEK NOUN	ENGLISH LOAN WORD
(1)	γάγγλιον **gánglion** 'tumor'	*ganglion*
	κῶλον **kõlon** 'limb,' 'clause'	*colon*
(2)	κρανίον **kraníon** 'skull'	*cranium*
(3)	πέταλον **pétalon** 'leaf'	*petal*
	προῦνον **proúnon** 'plum'	*prune*

Multiple-Base Compounds. The following combining forms appear in numerous English words.

COMBINING FORM	ENGLISH MULTIPLE-BASE COMPOUND
-λατρεια **-latreia** > *-latry* 'worship of'	*bibliolatry*
-λατρης **-latrēs** > *-later* 'worshipper of'	*bibliolater*
-μετρον **-metron** > *-meter* 'measure,' 'instrument for measuring'	*chronometer*
-μετρια **-metria** (= **métron** + **-ia**) > *-metry* 'art, process, or science of measuring'	*geometry*
-νομια **-nomia**[1] > *-nomy* 'law,' 'arrangement of,' 'science of'	*economy*
-μανια **-mania**[1] > *-mania* 'madness for or about,' 'admiration for,' 'eager pursuit of'	*bibliomania*
-παθεια **-patheia**[1] > *-pathy* 'feeling,'	*telepathy*
'disease of,'	*psychopathy*
'treatment of or by'	*osteopathy*

---

[1] The composition of this combining form is discussed below, in Lesson 16.

	ENGLISH
	MULTIPLE-BASE
COMBINING FORM	COMPOUND

-παθος -pathos > *-path*
'one subject to disease of,'   *psychopath*
'one who treats of or by'   *osteopath*
φιλ- phil- > *phil-* 'loving'   *philharmonic*
-φιλος -philos > *-phile* 'lover of' *Russophile*
-φοβια -phobia (= **phóbos** 'fear' + **-ia**) >
  -phobia 'fear of'   *agoraphobia*
-φοβος -phobos > *-phobe* 'one who fears' *Russophobe*
-σκοπος -skopos > *-scope* 'instrument for *telescope*
  examining'
-σκοπια -skopia[1] > *-scopy* 'viewing,'   *telescopy*
  'observation of'

Etymological Notes

Margarine derives from the Greek noun **márgaron** 'pearl.' The word was coined in the nineteenth century by the French chemist Chevreul. Chevreul came across a certain fatty acid which he believed was new to chemistry. Because of the pearly lustre of its crystals, he called it *margarique* (*margaric* in English) and named a fatty substance derived from it *margarine.* It turned out, however, that Chevreul's acid was not something new, but merely a combination of two fatty acids already known. As a consequence, *margaric* and *margarine* in their original meanings, those which they were created to convey, have become obsolete. The former has subsequently taken on another chemical meaning and the latter has become the official name for artificial butter.

Electric goes back to **élektron**, a Greek noun meaning 'amber.' The semantic connection lies in the fact that the property of developing electricity when excited by friction was first observed in amber. The newer word *electron* is not

---

[1] The composition of this combining form is discussed below, in Lesson 16.

the Greek form borrowed without change but rather a combination of *electr-*, from *electric*, and *-on*, an ending which appears in certain scientific terms used in the study of *electronics*.

EXERCISES

1. Memorize the following Greek nouns with their meanings.   Determine the current meaning of the English derivative listed alongside each.

κέντρον **kéntron** 'sharp point,' 'center'	*center*
νεῦρον **neúron** 'nerve,' 'sinew'	*neurology*
ὄργανον **órganon** 'tool,' 'instrument'	*organ*
ὀστέον **ostéon** 'bone'	*osteotomy*
πτερόν **pterón** 'feather,' 'wing'	*pterodactyl*
ξύλον **xýlon** 'wood'	*xylophone*
ζῷον **zôon** 'animal'	*zoology*

2. Give the Greek form of the following place names:
Cyprus, Ilium, Pĕrgamum.

3. Using the General Vocabulary, find the Greek noun and
its meaning from which each of the following is derived.
Show, where it is not obvious, the connection between the
Greek and the current meaning: *idol, metal, opium, talent* (the
clue to the explanation of the current meaning of *talent* can
be found in the New Testament parable recorded in St. Mat-
thew xxv:14–30).

4. Analyze each of the following (where necessary, use the
General Vocabulary to find the Greek noun involved): *cen-
trifugal, centripetal, chrysanthemum, concentrate, dipsomaniac,
electricity, fluoroscope, gyroscope, horoscope, oleomargarine, phi-
lanthropy, rhododendron.*

5. Give the current meaning of each of the following: *an-
thropometry, anthroponomy, astronomy, cardiopathy, centimeter,
egomania, electropathy, Francophile, hippophile, millimeter, ne-
crolatry, necrophobia, neuropathic, ophthalmoscope, thanatoma-
nia, thanatophobia.*

6. Determine the etymology and meaning in the context of each italicized word.

A   The village folk in general, mainly of the purest English stock, carried on their ancient village ways, not in a spirit of *Anglophobia*, but rather as if England had never existed.—VAN WYCK BROOKS

B   Dante seems to be a *cosmic* poet and to have escaped the *anthropocentric* conceit of romanticism.—PATER

C   The scene depicting Mr. Crawley's collision with the Bishop's wife in Vanity Fair is the chief *ganglion* of the tale.—STEVENSON

D   I had had brothers myself, and it was no revelation to me that little girls could be slavish *idolaters* of little boys.—HENRY JAMES

E   In France, patriotism is considered respectable, and its worst characteristic, *xenophobia*, is general.

7.   (a) What is the meaning of the proper nouns *Philip* and *Philadelphia*?

(b) Determine the etymological meaning of *Bible* and *organ*.   What semantic change do their current meanings reveal?

Lesson 5

The Third Declension

Third-Declension nouns offer a variety of endings in the nominative singular.   Most of these endings may be divided into three classes, according to the way the base is found:

(1) **-an, -ar, -ēn, -ēr, -ōn, -ōr, -yr**
(2) **-as, -is, -ps, -ōs, -ys, -x**
(3) **-ma, -sis, -os**

In the case of most nouns having the endings listed in (1), the base is virtually identical with the nominative.

GREEK NOUN	ENGLISH DERIVATIVE CONTAINING BASE
Τιτάν **Titán** 'Titan'	*titanic*
νέκταρ **néktar** 'drink of the gods'	*nectarine*
Ἕλλην **Héllēn** 'a Greek'	*Hellenic*
κλιμακτήρ **klimaktér** 'rung of a ladder'	*climacteric*
πνεύμων **pneúmōn** 'lung'	*pneumonia*
ῥήτωρ **rhétōr** 'teacher of rhetoric'	*rhetoric*
μάρτυρ **mártyr** 'witness'	*martyrolatry*

In the case of most nouns having the endings listed in (2), the base is found by dropping the ending of the genitive which, in the Third Declension, is **-os**. The genitive of these nouns will, therefore, always be given alongside the nominative.

GREEK NOUN	ENGLISH DERIVATIVE CONTAINING BASE
Ἄτλας, Ἄτλαντος **Átlas, Átlantos** 'Atlas'	*Atlantic*
πυραμίς, πυραμίδος **pyramís, pyramídos** 'pyramid'	*pyramidal*
φλέψ, φλεβός **phleps, phlebós** 'vein'	*phlebotomy*
ἥρως, ἥρωος **hérōs, hérōos** 'hero'	*heroic*
ἰχθύς, ἰχθύος **ichthýs, ichthýos** 'fish'	*ichthyology*
λάρυγξ, λάρυγγος **lárynx, láryngos** 'larynx'	*laryngeal*

The three endings grouped under (3) must be considered separately. The genitive of nouns ending in **-ma** is **-matos**. The base of these nouns is most often found by dropping the **-os** of the genitive, but frequently by dropping the **-a** of the nominative.

GREEK NOUN	ENGLISH DERIVATIVE CONTAINING BASE
χρῶμα, χρώματος **chrŏma, chrŏmatos** 'color'	*chromatic* *chromosome*

The base of nouns ending in **-sis** is generally found by dropping **-is,** of nouns ending in **-os** by dropping **-os.**

GREEK NOUN	ENGLISH DERIVATIVE CONTAINING BASE
βάσις **básis** 'step,' 'stand'	*basic*
ἄνθος **ánthos** 'flower'	*anthology*

When Latinized, the nominative ending of Third-Declension nouns remains unchanged with the exception of **-ōn** which occasionally becomes **-ō**—for example, **Plátōn** becomes *Platō*. The **-os** of the genitive is changed in Latin to **-is,** the genitive ending of the Latin Third Declension.

Most Greek Third-Declension nouns that have produced simple derivatives in English have been borrowed in their nominative form without change. A number have been Anglicized in easily recognizable ways.

GREEK NOUN	ENGLISH LOAN WORD
νέκταρ **néktar** 'drink of the gods'	*nectar*
λάρυγξ, λάρυγγος **lárynx, láryngos** 'larynx'	*larynx*
ἄρωμα, ἀρώματος **árōma, arōmatos** 'fragrance'	*aroma*
πυραμίς, πυραμίδος **pyramís, pyramídos** 'pyramid'	*pyramid*
ἀψίς, ἀψῖδος **apsís, apsídos** 'arch'	*apse*

ETYMOLOGICAL NOTES

A number of the words in this lesson involve Greek mythology. The following notes will help to clarify the semantic development of some of them.

The *Titans* were a race of giants who ruled the world until they were overthrown by the Olympian deities. *Atlas*, the son of one of the Titans, was forced by Zeus to carry the heavens on his shoulders. He took up his stand far west of Greece, near the ocean, which was accordingly named after him. The covers of books of maps traditionally bore a picture of Atlas supporting the globe; hence the origin of *an atlas*. *Nestor* and *Laocoön* were figures in the story of the Trojan

War. The former was an aged wise leader who played the part of senior counselor to the Greek forces. The latter was a Trojan priest, and the only person among the Trojans to distrust completely the wooden horse. Shortly after he had uttered the immortal line, "I fear the Greeks even when they bring gifts," unfriendly gods sent out two sea serpents which strangled him and his two sons in their coils.

Ichor was the substance that flowed in the veins of the gods in place of blood. The *aegis* was the shield of Athena and Zeus, which, naturally, offered unique protection to the carrier. The *Styx* was the dread river beyond which Hades lay and over which all dead souls were ferried by the famous ferryman, Charon.

EXERCISES

1. Memorize the following Greek nouns with their meanings. Determine the current meaning of the English derivative listed alongside each.

ἀήρ **aér** 'air'	*aeroplane*
ἄλγος **álgos** 'pain'	*neuralgia*
ἄνθος **ánthos** 'flower'	*anthology*
βάρος **báros** 'weight'	*barometer*
χείρ, χειρός **cheir, cheirós** 'hand'	*chiropodist*
χρῶμα, χρώματος **chróma, chrómatos** 'color'	*chromatic*
δέρμα, δέρματος **dérma, dérmatos** 'skin,' 'hide'	*dermatology*
γαστήρ, γαστρός **gastér, gastrós** 'stomach'	*gastric*
γυνή, γυναικός **gyné, gynaikós** (base **gyn-** or **gynaik-**) 'woman'	*gynecology*
ἠώς, ἠόος **ēós, ēóos** 'dawn'	*eolithic*
ὕδωρ **hýdōr** (**hydr-**) 'water'	*hydrophobia*
ἶρις, ἴριδος **íris, íridos** 'rainbow,' 'Iris (goddess of the rainbow)'	*iris*
κάλλος **kállos** 'beauty'	*callisthenic*
κέρας or κέρως, κέρατος **kéras or kérōs, kératos** 'horn'	*rhinoceros*
κύστις **kýstis** 'sac'	*cyst*
μῦς, μυός **mys, myós** 'mouse,' 'muscle'	*myotomy*

ὀδούς, ὀδόντος **odoús, odóntos** 'tooth'   *odontology*

ὤψ, ὠπός **ōps, ōpós** 'eye,' 'face'   *Cyclops*

φῶς, φωτός **phōs, phōtós** 'light'   *photometer*

πόλις **pólis** 'city'   *necropolis*

πούς, ποδός **pous, podós** 'foot'   *chiropodist*

πῦρ **pyr** 'fire'   *pyromaniac*

ῥίς, ῥινός **rhis, rhinós** 'nose'   *rhinoceros*

σῶμα, σώματος **sōma, sōmatos** 'body'   *chromosome*

2. Determine the etymology of each italicized word and the meaning of the expression in which it appears: under the *aegis* of a wealthy patron, the *canons* of art, *canon* law, statues of *chryselephantine*, to lie *comatose*, to pass through countless *eons*, *halcyon* days, the *hegemony* of central Europe, *myriads* of people, the *Nestor* of American politics, the sound of a mighty *paean*, *psychosomatic* medicine, huge *pylons*, *stygian* caverns.

3. Analyze the words *agony, dehydrate, erotic, helicopter, hydrant, hydraulic, iridescent, irony, nostalgia, mastodon, pyrotechnics.*

4. Determine the etymology and meaning in the context of each italicized word.

A   Vulgarization of words that should not be in common use robs them of their *aroma.*—FOWLER

B   "Soothe yourself ever so little with alcohol, and you don't get QUITE the full sensation of gambling.   You do lose a little something of the proper tremors before a coup, the proper throes during a coup, the proper thrill of joy or anguish after a coup . . . You're bound to, you know," he added, purposely making this *bathos* when he saw me smiling at the heights to which he had risen.

—BEERBOHM

C   The Editor of these Sheets was led to regard Teufelsdröckh as a man not only who would never wed, but who would never even flirt; whom the grand-*climacteric* itself . . . would crown with no new myrtle garland.

—CARLYLE

D   One thought of him as the man in Plutarch's story

who conversed with men one day only in the year and spent the rest of his days with the nymphs and *demons*.

—VAN WYCK BROOKS

E   The sweat poured from her skin as if the wounds of her whole life were shedding their salt *ichor*.

—KATHERINE ANNE PORTER

F   The long-tied espaliers . . . had grown so stout, and cramped, and gnarled that they had pulled their stakes out of the ground and stood distorted and writhing in vegetable agony, like leafy *Laocoöns*.—HARDY

G   (a) Little knowest thou of the burning of a World-*Phoenix*, who fanciest that she must first burn-out, and lie as a dead cinereous heap; and therefrom the young one start-up by miracle, and fly heavenward.—CARLYLE

(b) For every man alone thinkes he hath got
To be a *Phoenix*, and that then can bee
None of that kinde, of which he is, but hee.

—DONNE

5. (a) What shape would an *apsidal* addition to a building have?

(b) Judging by the current meaning of *laconic*, what was one of the chief characteristics of ancient Spartans?

(c) What was the habitat of the mythological nymphs known as *dryads*? as *naïads*? as *oreads*?

6. What is the difference between

(a) *climactic* signs and *climatic* signs?

(b) classifying people *ethically* and classifying people *ethnically*?

(c) the *history* of the Homeric Age and the *historicity* of the Homeric Age?

7. The *Academy*, the *Stoics*, and the *Cynics* refer to three schools of ancient Greek philosophy.   How did each of these names arise?

LESSON 6

Suffixes.   Multiple-Base Compounds

In addition to the suffixes mentioned in Lesson 2, the following may be attached to noun bases to form compound
nouns.

1. Noun or adjective base plus **-iskos** > *-isk*, forming diminutive nouns.

		GREEK	ENGLISH
GREEK NOUN	BASE	COMPOUND NOUN	LOAN WORD
ἀστήρ **astḗr** 'star'	**aster-**	ἀστερίσκος **asterískos**	*asterisk*

2. Noun or adjective base plus **-ion** > *-ium* 'thing connected
with.'   (This suffix is actually the neuter of an adjective-
forming suffix **-ios.**)

		GREEK	ENGLISH
GREEK NOUN	BASE	COMPOUND NOUN	LOAN WORD
Παλλάς **Pallás** 'Pallas' (an epi-thet of Athena)	**Pallad-**	Παλλάδιον **Pallá-dion** 'thing con-nected with Athena,' 'statue of Athena'	*palladium*

The suffix **-ion** is also used to form diminutives.

		GREEK	ENGLISH
GREEK NOUN	BASE	COMPOUND NOUN	LOAN WORD
πούς **pous** 'foot'	**pod-**	πόδιον **pódion** 'little foot'	*podium*

3. Noun or adjective base plus **-eion, -aion** > *-eum, -aeum*,
'place for.'

GREEK NOUN	BASE	GREEK COMPOUND NOUN	ENGLISH LOAN WORD
Μοῦσα Moúsa 'Muse'	Mous-	Μουσεῖον Mouseíon	museum
Ἀθήνη Athḗnē 'goddess of wisdom'	Athēn-	Ἀθήναιον Athḗnaion	athenaeum

4. Noun or adjective base plus -itēs > -ite 'one having to do with,' 'inhabitant of,' 'descendant of'; also used to form names of chemicals, minerals, and so forth.

GREEK NOUN OR ADJECTIVE	BASE	GREEK COMPOUND NOUN	ENGLISH LOAN WORD
ἐρῆμος erḗmos 'solitary'	erēm-	ἐρημίτης erēmítēs	eremite
δύναμις dýnamis 'force'	dynam-	*δυναμιτης *dynamitēs	dynamite

5. Noun or adjective base plus -itis > -itis 'inflammation of.'

GREEK NOUN	BASE	GREEK COMPOUND NOUN	ENGLISH LOAN WORD
ἄρθρον árthron 'joint'	arthr-	ἀρθρῖτις arthrítis	arthritis

6. Many English medical terms contain the suffixes -osis 'process of,' 'disease connected with,' 'diseased condition of' (for example, psychosis) and -oma 'morbid affection of' (for example, sarcoma). These are ultimately derived from verbs and will be studied in greater detail below (Lesson 18).

Multiple-Base Compounds. The following combining forms appear in numerous English words.

COMBINING FORM	ENGLISH MULTIPLE-BASE COMPOUND
ἀρχ- arch- (base of archós 'chief') > arch- 'chief,' 'leading'	archdeacon
-αρχια -archia[1] > -archy 'rule by'	gynarchy
-κρατια -kratia (= krátos 'power' + -ia) > -cracy 'rule by'	democracy

---
[1] The composition of this combining form is shown below (Lessons 16, 17).

COMBINING FORM	ENGLISH MULTIPLE- BASE COMPOUND
-κρατης **-kratēs** > -*crat* 'supporter of the rule by'	*democrat*
-γραφος **-graphos** > -*graph* 'writing,' 'writer,' 'instrument for writing or recording'	*telegraph*
-γραφια **-graphia**[1] > -*graphy* 'writing,' 'art or science of writing or describing'	*geography*
-γραμμα **-gramma**[1] > -*gram* 'thing written or drawn'	*telegram*
-ουργια **-ourgia** (= **érgon** 'work' + **-ia**) > -*urgy* 'art of working'	*metallurgy*

EXERCISES

1. Analyze the words *aerate, geopolitics, hydrangea, matriarch, obelisk, patriarch, police, polity.*

2. Give the current meaning of each of the following: *archangel, archduke, calligraphy, demonolatry, dermatitis, iconolatry, lithograph, multigraph, neuritis, neurosis, phonograph, photography, plutocrat, psittacosis, pyromancy, rhinitis, stethoscope, technarchy, technocracy, theocracy, topography.*

3. Determine the etymology and meaning in the context of each italicized word.

    A Make me not sighted like the *basilisk:*
        I have look'd on thousands, who have sped the better
        By my regard, but kill'd none so.—SHAKESPEARE

    B "As one that was ever an ornament to human life," says Mr. Wegg, again holding out Mr. Venus's palm as if he were going to tell his fortune by *chiromancy.*

                        —DICKENS

    C The wild goose is more of a *cosmopolite* than we; he breaks his fast in Canada, takes luncheon in Ohio, and plumes himself for the night in a southern bayou.

    D The form of government under which he lives is an

---

[1] The composition of this combining form is shown below (Lessons **16, 17**).

absolute *gastrocracy*—the belly tyrannizing over the members whom it used to serve.—BEERBOHM

E　The liberty of the press is the *palladium* of all the civil, political, and religious rights of an Englishman.

—LETTERS OF JUNIUS

F　Here and there one found a *Sybarite*. Harrison Gray Otis, at the age of eighty, after forty years of gout, breakfasted every morning on pâté de foie gras.

—VAN WYCK BROOKS

G　Darwin gave the death-blow to *teleology* by showing that apparently purposive structures could arise by means of a non-purposive mechanism.—JULIAN HUXLEY

H　Who has learned, or begun learning, the grand *thaumaturgic* act of Thought!—CARLYLE

I　Whatever skill . . . of medicine he possessed, he eked it out with *theurgic* pretenses.—FREDERICK FARRAR

4. (a) The noun *surgery* has been considerably altered in form as a result of having passed through French. What combining form is involved in its etymology?

(b) Judging by the etymology of the word, what is a characteristic shape of *bacteria*?

(c) *Lyceum* and *Odeum* are frequently seen as the names of theatres. Etymologically speaking, which is more suitable? Explain your answer.

5. Determine the etymological meaning of *mausoleum* and *architect*. What semantic change does the current meaning of each reveal?

LESSON 7

Review

1. Give the English form of the following Greek names: Ἀλκαῖος, Ἀπόλλων, Ἀριστείδης, Ἡρακλῆς, Ἡρόδοτος, Κροῖσος, Ὅμηρος.

2. Give the Greek form of the following names: *Aphrŏdĭtē, Hĕphaestus, Oedipūs, Pŏseidōn*.

3. The Latin-derived word *local* (= **locus** 'place' + **-ālis**) is etymologically equivalent, element for element, to the Greek-derived word *topic* (= **tŏpos** 'place' + **-ikos**). Give a Greek-derived word that is etymologically equivalent in this fashion to each of the following Latin-derived words: *animal, cordial, morals, ocular, temporal*.

4. Write the Greek words meaning:
   (a) body, sinew, skin, bone, head, eye, nose, tooth, tongue
   (b) fire, air, earth, water

5. Give the current meaning of the following words and the Greek combining form, with its meaning, involved in each: *anthomania, archipelago, biography, cardiograph, gerontocracy, hydropathy, metrology, necromancy, philhellenic, pyrolatry*.

6. Give the current meaning of the following words and the Greek suffix, with its meaning, that appears in each: *asterisk, bronchitis, clinic, gastritis, geranium, hypnosis, lycanthropy*.

7. Give the etymological meaning of each italicized word: He made a checking list of his favorite neurasthenic fears: *agoraphobia, claustrophobia, pyrophobia, anthropophobia*, and the rest, ending with what he asserted to be "the most fool pretentious witch doctor term of the whole bloomin' lot," namely *siderodromophobia*, the fear of a railway journey.

—SINCLAIR LEWIS

8. Give the meaning of the Christian names *Chloë, Dorothea, Theodore, Theophilus*.

CHAPTER THREE

Greek Adjectives, Numerals, Prefixes

LESSON 8

Adjectives

THERE are two types of Greek adjectives, those of the First and Second Declension, and those of the Third Declension. This lesson is devoted to the former.

The nominative singular masculine (the form under which adjectives are given in both Greek and English dictionaries) of regular First- and Second-Declension adjectives ends in **-os.** The base may be found by dropping this ending. The nominative singular neuter ends in **-on.**

NOMINATIVE SINGULAR MASCULINE	BASE	NOMINATIVE SINGULAR NEUTER
χλωρός chlōrós 'light green'	chlōr-	chlōrón

A few Greek adjectives have been borrowed as nouns in their Greek neuter form without change. Thus *moron* comes from **mōrón,** the neuter of **mōrós** 'dull,' 'stupid.' In a few cases, such as *asylum* from **ásylon,** neuter of **ásylos** 'inviolable,' this form has been Latinized. The great majority of Greek adjectives, however, have been borrowed as the first base in multiple-base compounds. For example, *chlorophyll,* the name given to the green coloring matter in plants, consists of *chlor-* the base of **chlōrós** 'light green,' the connecting vowel *-o-,* and *-phyll* from **phýllon** 'leaf.'

208

EXERCISES

1. Memorize the following Greek adjectives with their meanings. Determine the current meaning of the English derivative listed alongside each.

ἄκρος **ákros** 'topmost,' 'outermost'	*acropolis*
ἄλλος **állos** 'another,' 'different'	*allopathy*
ἀρχαῖος **archaíos** 'old,' 'ancient'	*archaeology*
αὐτός **autós** 'self'	*autonomy*
χλωρός **chlōrós** 'light green'	*chlorine*
ἕτερος **héteros** 'other'	*heterodox*
ἱερός **hierós** 'holy'	*hierarchy*
ὅλος **hólos** 'whole,' 'entire'	*holograph*
ὅμοιος **hómoios** 'similar'	*homeopathy*
ὁμός **homós** 'same'	*homogeneous*
ἴσος **ísos** 'equal'	*isosceles*
κακός **kakós** 'bad'	*cacophony*
μέσος **mésos** 'middle'	*Mesopotamia*
νέος **néos** 'new'	*neon*
ὀρθός **orthós** 'straight,' 'right,' 'true'	*orthodox*
παλαιός **palaiós** 'old'	*paleography*
σοφός **sophós** 'wise'	*philosophy*

2. Analyze the words *autobiography*, *automobile*, *chloroform*, *neo-classical*, *paleobotany*.

3. Analyze each italicized word and determine the meaning of the expression in which it appears: an *acrostic* that spelled out his name, an *archaic* use of a word, *autochthonous* inhabitants of a region, the military *hierarchy*.

4. Analyze each italicized word and determine its meaning in the context.

A   Hie thee to hell for shame, and leave this world, Thou *cacodemon*!—SHAKESPEARE

B   The puns [of Thackeray] and the *cacographies*, the little *gastronomical* diversions, and the flittings to Brighton and Paris, are its [his melancholy's] palliatives and its *allopathic* drugs.—SAINTSBURY

C Prussia is a mild despotism to be sure. 'Tis the *homeopathic* tyranny—small doses, constantly administered, and strict diet and regimen.—MOTLEY

D When a national hero is to be commemorated by a street we should ask him to design the street himself. Assuredly, the mere plastering-up of his name is no *mnemonic*.—BEERBOHM

E And he who draws the lowest
    Shall (so 'twas said)
    Be thenceforth dead—
  In fact, a legal "ghoest"
(When exigence of rhyme compels,
Orthography forgoes her spells,
  And "ghost" is written "ghoest").—W. S. GILBERT

5. (a) What is the etymological meaning of *brontosaurus, dinosaur, tyrannosaurus*?

(b) The *Mesozoic, Paleozoic*, and *Cenozoic* eras are divisions of geologic time. Arrange them in chronological order.

(c) The prehistoric period of human culture has been divided into the *neolithic, eolithic*, and *paleolithic* ages. Arrange these in chronological order.

6. (a) From what Greek adjective is the first base in *cenobite* derived? in *cenotaph*? in *Cenozoic*? Give an example of a group of *cenobites*. How does a *cenotaph* differ from an ordinary tomb?

(b) Give an example of a country with a *heterogeneous* population and one with a *homogeneous* population.

(c) What sort of work does a specialist in *orthodontia* do? a specialist in *orthopedics*?

(d) What is the antonym of *homosexual*?

7. (a) Compare the etymological meanings of *autonomy* and *autocracy*. What type of semantic change does the current meaning of the latter reveal?

(b) Determine the etymological meaning of *aristocracy*. What type of semantic change does its current meaning reveal?

8. What is the meaning of the Christian names *Agatha, Barbara, Phoebe, Sophia?*

LESSON 9

Adjectives (*Concl'd*). Adverbs

Adjectives (*Concl'd*). Irregular adjectives of the First-Second Declension and adjectives of the Third Declension have such a variety of endings that it is difficult to set up rules for determining the base. Accordingly, in our vocabularies, the base of such adjectives will be given in parentheses alongside the nominative singular masculine.

In Lesson 2, the adjective-forming suffix **-ikos** was taken up. A second important adjective-forming suffix is **-oeidēs.** This suffix appears in English in the form *-oid*, meaning 'like,' 'resembling.'

GREEK NOUN	BASE	GREEK COMPOUND ADJECTIVE	ENGLISH LOAN WORD
σφαῖρα **sphaíra** 'ball'	**sphair-**	σφαιροειδής **sphairoeidēs**	*spheroid*

Adverbs. The adverbs **tēle** 'afar' and **pálin** 'back,' 'again' appear in a number of commonly used English words. The adverbs **entós** or **éndon** 'within' and **ektós** or **éxō** 'outside' are found in numerous learned terms—for example, *endogamy* 'marriage within the tribe, caste, social group; inbreeding' and its opposite *exogamy; entozoon* 'internal parasite' and *ectozoon* 'external parasite.'

Exotic and *esoteric* derive from adjectives which were formed from adverbs. The first comes from **exōtikós** 'foreign,' 'alien,' a formation from **éxō**, the second comes from **esōtérō** 'inner,' the comparative of the Greek adverb **ésō** 'within,' combined with **-ikos.**

ETYMOLOGICAL NOTES

Greek adjectives appear in a number of well-known place names. *Mesopotamia*, for example, is etymologically '(the land in) the middle of the rivers (**mésos** 'middle' and **potamós** 'river'),' so called because it lies between the Tigris and the Euphrates. *Naples* goes back to the Greek **Neápolis** 'new city' from **néa,** feminine of **néos** 'new,' and **pólis** 'city.' The word **pólis,** incidentally, appears in the names of a number of cities. *Tripoli* is the ancient **Trípolis** 'triple city'; it received the name in the third century A.D. when it was created by the union of three pre-existing towns. *Constantinople* is 'Constantine's city'; the great Roman emperor of that name founded it. *Gallipoli* is the 'beautiful city' (**kállos** 'beauty' + **pólis**). The Solomons, the Bismarck Archipelago, and other islands northeast of Australia, where the natives are predominantly black, form the area known as *Melanesia*, a combination of **mélas** 'black,' **nêsos** 'island,' and the suffix **-ia.** The tiny islands of the Marianas, the Carolines, the Marshalls, and others make up *Micronesia*, and the numberless islands in the central Pacific, *Polynesia*.

Plateía hodós is the Greek for 'broad street.' **Plateía** is the feminine of **platýs** 'broad,' and **hodós** is a feminine noun meaning 'way,' 'road.' In time **hodós** was dropped and **plateía** by itself came to mean 'broad street,' just as we often say 'the deep' for 'the deep sea' or 'the blue' for 'the blue sky.' We have borrowed **plateía** with this meaning three times, each time through a different language. Through French it gave us *place*, through Italian *piazza*, and through Spanish *plaza.*

EXERCISES

1. Memorize the following Greek adjectives with their meanings. Determine the current meaning of the English derivative listed alongside each.

λευκός **leukós** 'white'   *leukemia*
μακρός **makrós** 'long'   *macron*
μέγας **mégas** (**mega-** or **megal-**) 'great'   *megaphone*

μέλας **mélas** (**mela-** or **melan-**) 'black'   *melancholy*
μικρός **mikrós** 'small'   *microphone*
ὀλίγος **olígos** 'few'   *oligarchy*
ὀξύς **oxýs** (**ox-** or **oxy-**) 'sharp,' 'acid'   *oxygen*
παχύς **pachýs** (**pachy-**) 'thick'   *pachyderm*
πᾶς **pas** (**pan-** or **pant-**) 'all,' 'every'   *Pan-American*
πλατύς **platýs** (**plat-** or **platy-**) 'broad'   *platypus*
πολύς **polýs** (**poly-**) 'much,' 'many'   *polyglot*
ψευδής **pseudḗs** (**pseud-**) 'lying,' 'false'   *pseudo-intellectual*
στενός **stenós** 'narrow'   *stenography*
στερεός **stereós** 'solid'   *stereoscope*
θερμός **thermós** 'hot'   *thermos*

2. Analyze the words *anthropoid, asteroid, chameleon, mega-cycle, megalith, microbe, pantomime, polyandry, polygamous, televise.*

3. Determine the etymological and current meanings of *micrometer, microscope, pantograph, thermometer.*

4. Analyze each italicized word and determine the meaning of the expression in which it appears: *exotic* flowers, the *mega-lomania* of would-be conquerors of the world, *panegyrical* orations, *polychrome* painting on Greek vases, the *polyphony* of certain native chants.

5. Analyze each italicized word and determine its meaning in the context.

    A   If the [literary] club had not existed, Dr. Holmes would have invented it . . . —a club strung like a harp, with a dozen ringing intelligences, each answering to some chord of the *macrocosm.*—VAN WYCK BROOKS

    B   The ocean-going ship of today is a sort of *microcosm.*

    C   For Boston was controlled by an *oligarchy,* an unofficial caste of leading men for whom a "republic" and a "democracy" had next to nothing in common.

                               —VAN WYCK BROOKS

    D   Balmawhapple [had given satisfaction] by such a *palinode* as rendered the use of the sword unnecessary.

                                      —SCOTT

E Old wine is a true *panacea*
　　For ev'ry conceivable ill,
　　When you cherish the soothing idea
　　　That somebody else pays the bill!—w. s. GILBERT
F Alas, the *panoply* of Sarcasm was but as a buckram
case, wherein I had striven to envelop myself.—CARLYLE
G (a) The *Pantheon* at Rome, built hundreds of years
ago and still standing; (b) Gods in the Norse *pantheon*
with counterparts in the Greek.

6. Give an example of a *polytheistic* religion; of an *esoteric*
field of study.

7. (a) Judging by the etymology of the word, what is the
chief characteristic of *panchromatic* film? of a *polytechnic*
school?

(b) What is a *polyglot* Bible?

Lesson 10

Numerals

The following Greek numerals appear frequently as the first
element in English multiple-base compounds:

GREEK NUMERAL	FORM IN MULTIPLE-BASE COMPOUNDS	EXAMPLE
ἥμισυς **hēmisys** 'half'	*hemi-*	*hemisphere*
ἕν **hen** 'one'	*hen-*	*henotheism*
μόνος **mónos** 'one,' 'single,' 'alone'	*mon-*	*monocle*
πρῶτος **prōtos** 'first'	*prot-*	*protozoa*
δύο **dýo** 'two'	*dy-*	*dyarchy*
δίς **dis** 'twice'	*di-*	*dimeter*

GREEK NUMERAL	FORM IN MULTIPLE-BASE COMPOUNDS	EXAMPLE
δεύτερος **deúteros** 'second,' 'secondary'	deuter-	deuterogamy
τρίς **tris** 'thrice'	tri-	trimeter
τέτταρα **téttara** 'four times'	tetra-, tetr-	tetrameter
πέντε **pénte** 'five'	penta-, pent-	pentameter
ἕξ **hex** 'six'	hexa-	hexameter
ἑπτά **heptá** 'seven'	hepta-	heptameter
ὀκτώ **oktṓ** 'eight'	octo-, octa-	octameter
ἐννέα **ennéa** 'nine'	ennea-, enne-	enneaphyllous
δέκα **déka** 'ten'	deca-	decaliter
ἑκατόν **hekatón** 'one hundred'	hecat-, hecto-	hectoliter
χίλιοι **chílioi** 'one thousand'	kilo-	kilogram

The following combining forms are frequently found in combination with Greek numerals:

COMBINING FORM	ENGLISH MULTIPLE-BASE COMPOUND
-γωνος **-gōnos** (from **gōnía** 'angle') > -gon '-angled figure'	octagon
-έδρον **-hedron** (from **hédra** 'seat,' 'base') > -hedron '-faced figure'	octahedron
-μερος **-meros** (from **méros** 'part') > -merous denoting, in botany, 'of — parts'	octamerous
-μετρος **-metros** (from **métron** 'measure') > -meter denoting, in prosody, 'verse of — metrical feet'	octameter

EXERCISES

1. Explain the fact that many of the Greek numerals listed above are very similar to the corresponding Latin numerals.

2. (a) How many faces does a *tetrahedron* have? a *hepta-hedron*? a *polyhedron*?

(b) How many angles does a *pentagon* have? an *octagon*? a *decagon*? a *polygon*?

(c) What is *trochaic tetrameter*? *iambic pentameter*? *dactylic hexameter*?

(d) Webster defines *dimeter* as "a verse consisting of two metrical feet or of two *dipodies*." Explain this distinction.

3. Analyze the words *dimity, heptarchy, kilocycle, monody, monogamy, monopoly, monotheism, octopus, tetrarch, trigonometry*. What is the antonym of *monogamy*? of *monotheism*?

4. (a) What is the current meaning of *decagram, hectogram, kilometer, monophobia*?

(b) What is the etymological meaning of *heptamerous, trimerous, proton*?

5. Analyze each italicized word and determine the meaning of the expression in which it appears: to make a *hecatomb* of mankind with atomic warfare, the *monochromatic* sky, a *monolithic* dictatorship, the time-consuming demands of diplomatic *protocol*, *proto-Hellenic* civilization, a *triptych* by an early Flemish artist.

6. (a) Explain the title of Boccaccio's collection of tales, *The Decameron*.

(b) The *pentathlon* and *decathlon* are events in the modern Olympic games. Why are they so called?

(c) Why is a *tripod* so called?

(d) What is the *Pentateuch*?

7. Distinguish between (a) a *monogram* and a *monograph*, (b) *bigamy* and *deuterogamy*, (c) *monomania* and *megalomania*.

Lesson 11

Prefixes

Greek prefixes may be placed before nouns and adjectives to form compound nouns or adjectives. Thus *anodyne* 'serving to assuage pain' comes from the prefix **an-** 'without' and

odýnē 'pain'; *emporium* 'market,' 'commercial center' consists of *en-* from the prefix **en-** 'on,' *-por-* base of **póros** 'way,' 'journey' and *-ium* from **-ion** 'thing connected with.'

The following Greek prefixes appear in numerous English words:

BASIC FORM	BEFORE VOWELS	MEANING	ENGLISH EXAMPLE
ἀμφι- **amphi-**	**amph-**	'both,' 'of both kinds,' 'on both sides,' 'around'	*amphibrach*
ἀ- **a-**	**an-**	'not,' 'without'	*anarchy*
ἀνα- **ana-**	**an-**	'up,' 'upward,' 'back-ward,' 'again,' 'anew'; also used intensively	*anabasis*
ἀντι- **anti-**	**ant-**	'opposite,' 'against,' 'ri-valing,' 'in exchange'	*antipodes*
ἀπο- **apo-**	**ap-**	'from,' 'away from,' 'off,' 'quite'	*aphelion*
δια- **dia-**	**di-**	'through,' 'between,' 'apart,' 'across'	*diameter*
δυσ- **dys-**		'ill,' 'bad,' 'hard,' 'diffi-cult'	*dysentery*
ἐν- **en-, em-, el-**		'in,' 'into'	*endemic*
ἐκ- **ek-**	**ex-**	'out,' 'out of'	*eccentric*
ἐπι· **epi-**	**ep-**	'upon,' 'at,' 'for (of time)', 'to,' 'on the ground of,' 'in addi-tion to'	*epidermis*

The prefixes **anti-, apo-,** and **epi-** before the rough breathing become **anth-, aph-,** and **eph-** respectively.

Note that **a-** and **ana-** before words beginning with a vowel both appear in English as *an-*.

ETYMOLOGICAL NOTES

Toxophilite, intoxicate, toxicological, and *antitoxin* are all related. In each we find the base of the Greek word **tóxa** 'bow and arrows.' Only *toxophilite* 'lover of archery' has preserved the meaning of **tóxa**; the others all show the effects of alternate specialization and generalization. The adjective **toxikós** means 'pertaining to bows and arrows.' The neuter **toxikón** was first specialized to mean 'poison in which arrows are dipped' and then generalized to include any kind of poison. Hence *toxicology* is the 'study of poisons.' In *toxin* 'poison secreted by a microbe' and *antitoxin* 'serum neutralizing a toxin,' the clipped base *tox-* has been used instead of *toxic-*. *Intoxicate* has lost a good deal of the grimness of its original meaning. It comes from **intoxicāre,** a late Latin derivative of **toxikón,** which means 'to poison,' 'to drug.'

Diapason, used commonly today in the sense 'swelling sound,' 'rich, full, deep outburst of sound,' consists of **diá** 'through' and **pasôn,** the genitive plural of **pas** 'all.' In Greek the expression ἡ διὰ πασῶν χορδῶν συμφωνία **hē diá pasôn chordôn symphōnía** means 'the (**hē**) concord (**symphōnía**) through (**diá**) all (**pasôn**) the strings (**chordôn**) or notes of the scale.' This, shortened to **diá pasôn** and run together, has given us *diapason*.

EXERCISES

1. What Latin prefix or prefixes are in general synonymous with each of the prefixes listed above?

2. Analyze the words *atheism, diagonal, diathermy, eccentricity, encephalitis, energy, epicycle, epitaph.*

3. Analyze each italicized word and determine the meaning of the expression in which it appears: an *acephalous* political movement, an *amorphous* group of buildings, an *antinomy* between federal and state restrictions, a social *antinomian*, the *apogee* of human achievement, the *diapasons* of a full symphony orchestra, study a problem *empirically*, *ephemeral* fads.

4. Analyze each italicized word and determine its meaning in the context.

    A   Experts tell us that a one-room school is an *anachronism* in a population of 143,000,000.

B   If you are depressed by modern life, you are unlikely to find an *anodyne* in the self-appointed task of cutting certain capers which your ancestors used to cut because they, in their day, were happy.—BEERBOHM

C   A capital without a country is an apparent *anomaly*.
—DISRAELI

D   *Amphibians* are terrestrial when they reach their full development, but aquatic until then.
—LECOMTE DU NOÜY

E   "He's a no-'count varmint," said the woman . . . "She keeps a-throwin' skillet lids," came Ransie's *antiphony*.—O. HENRY

F   (a) And men, to sound depths, so much line untie,
    As one might justly thinke, that there would rise
    At end thereof, one of th' *Antipodies*.—DONNE

(b) I have met with my moral *antipodes*, and can [hence] believe the story of two persons meeting (who never saw one another before in their lives) and instantly fighting.—LAMB

G   Learning was *endemic* in the Boston mind, as befitted a town whose first inhabitant, the Cambridge scholar Blaxton . . . had brought his library with him.
—VAN WYCK BROOKS

H   Passions are themselves physical impulses, maturing in their season, and often *epidemic*, like contagious diseases.—SANTAYANA

I   What had at first appeared as an *epicene* shape, the decreasing space resolved into a cloaked figure.—HARDY

J   Then set the merry joybells ringing! Let festive *epithalamia* resound through these ancient halls!
—W. S. GILBERT

5. (a) What astronomical feature is involved in the etymology of *antarctic*?

(b) Judging by the etymology of the word, where did *encomiums* first take place?

(c) What is the general difference between an *epidemic* and an *epizootic*?

LESSON 12

Prefixes (*Concl'd*)

The following Greek prefixes appear in numerous English words:

BASIC FORM	BEFORE VOWELS	MEANING	ENGLISH EXAMPLE
εὐ- **eu-**		'well,' 'good,' 'advantageous'	*euthanasia*
ὑπερ- **hyper-**		'over,' 'above,' 'beyond,' 'exceedingly,' 'excessive'	*hypersensitive*
ὑπο- **hypo-**	**hyp-**	'under,' 'below,' 'slightly'	*hypodermic*
κατα- **kata-**	**kat-**	'down,' 'away,' 'concerning,' 'mis-'; also used intensively	*catholic*
μετα- **meta-**	**met-**	'with,' 'after,' 'beyond,' 'over,' 'change'	*metamorphic*
παρα- **para-**	**par-**	'beside,' 'beyond,' 'contrary to,' 'irregular,' 'amiss'	*paradox*
περι- **peri-**		'around,' 'about,' 'near'	*perimeter*
προ- **pro-**		'before,' 'in front of'	*proscenium*
προσ- **pros-**		'to,' 'towards,' 'in addition'	*prosody*
συν- **syn-, sym-, syl-, sys-**		'with,' 'along with,' 'together,' 'like'	*symmetry*

The prefixes **hypo-**, **kata-**, and **meta-** before the rough breathing become **hyph-**, **kath-**, and **meth-**, respectively.

Before a vowel **eu-** is changed in English to *ev-*.

ETYMOLOGICAL NOTES

Cathedral derives from **kathédra** 'seat,' 'throne' (**kata-** + **hédra**). The name arose from the fact that, unlike other churches, a *cathedral* contains the throne of a bishop. The original meaning of **kathédra** is seen in the expression *ex cathedra*, literally 'from the chair,' but specialized to mean 'from the teacher's chair' and hence 'authoritative' (or, as an adverb, 'authoritatively'). The *cathedra* of this expression and *chair* and *chaise* are triplets. The Greek **kathédra** became *chaëre* in Old French, which was altered to *chair* in English. A local Parisian pronunciation of the French word was *chaise*, which we took over without change. The form *shay* (as in 'one-horse *shay*') is the result of an error. *Chaise* was wrongly thought to be a plural, the *s* was lopped off, and *shay* was the result. This sort of mistake occurs frequently. *Pea*, for example, was *pise* in Old English (plural *pisan*), from the Latin **pīsum**. *Cherry* was formed in the same erroneous way from the Norman French **cherise,** a derivative of the Greek **kerasós**. The *s* has been properly retained in the doublet *cerise*, which was borrowed later, through French.

In the Etymological Notes of Part One, Lesson 10, we described how ancient medical beliefs have affected the meaning of *bilious, sanguine*, and certain other words. Another example is *hypochondria* which means etymologically 'the under-cartilage.' *Hypochondria*, the ancients believed, was caused by the spleen. And the spleen is located under (**hypó**) the breastbone cartilage (**chóndros**).

EXERCISES

1. Memorize the following Greek nouns with their meanings.

αἷμα, αἵματος **haíma, haímatos** (**haim-** or   *anemia*
   haimat-) 'blood'

ὁδός **hodós** 'way,' 'road'   *method*

ὄνυμα, ὀνύματος **ónyma, onýmatos** (**onym-**   *synonym*
   or **onomat-**) 'name,' 'noun'

2. What Latin prefix or prefixes are in general synonymous with each of the prefixes listed above?

3. Analyze the words *hemophilia, hyphen, hypodermic, parallel, paranoia, parody, period, prognathous, symphony, symposium, syndicate.*

4. Analyze each italicized word and determine the meaning of the expression in which it appears: penetrate deep into *hyperborean* regions, the Russian use of a Christian name and a *patronymic, peristyle* temples, *synchronous* events, a *synod* of the highest dignitaries.

5. Analyze each italicized word and determine its meaning in the context:

A   There is no such thing as a singly *euphonious* or a singly *cacophonous* name.   There is no word which, by itself, sounds ill or well.—BEERBOHM

B   He was a great lover of form, more especially when he could dictate it *ex cathedra.*—SCOTT

C   The mysteries of John Bidlake's personal religion were quite as obscure and *paradoxical* as any of those in the *"theolatrous" orthodoxies* which he liked to deride.

—ALDOUS HUXLEY

D   A man is not better adapted to his environment than the flea which lives upon him as a *parasite.*

—JULIAN HUXLEY

E   Boldwood had felt the *symmetry* of his existence to be slowly getting distorted in the direction of an ideal passion.—HARDY

6. (a) Give the meaning of the prefix in *anonymous, antonym, eponymous, metonymy, synonym.*

(b) Give three examples of sets of *homonyms.*

(c) Give three examples of *metonymy.*

(d) Name an *eponymous* founder of a city.

7. (a) Analyze the words *catholic* and *parochial.*

(b) What is the difference between *catholic* and *parochial* tastes in literature?

(c) Give a word whose base comes from the same word that has supplied the base for *parochial.*

8. Determine the etymological meaning of *paraphernalia*. What semantic change does its current meaning reveal?

9. What is the antonym of *perigee*?

10. What is the meaning of the Christian name *Eunice*?

LESSON 13

Review

1. The words in the following groups contain bases of Greek nouns with which you are familiar. Determine the etymology, pronunciation, and current meaning of each of these words. Wherever possible, show how the basic meaning of the one Greek noun from which each group is derived is reflected in the current meaning of each word.

(a) *Anachronism, chronic, chronicle, synchronous*

(b) *Apogee, geography, geology, geomancy, geometry, geophysics, perigee*

(c) *Epiglottis, gloss, glossary, glottal, monoglot, polyglot*

(d) *Cacophonous, cacophony, euphonious, euphony, homophone, megaphone, microphone, symphonic, symphony, telephone, xylophone*

(e) *Bicycle, cycle, cyclic, cyclist, cyclone, cyclonic, Cyclopean, cyclopedia, cyclopedist, Cyclops, encyclopedia, kilocycle, megacycle, tricycle*

(f) *Anonymous, antonym, homonym, metonymy, pseudonym, synonym*

(g) *Comedy, monody, parody, threnody, tragedy*

2. Give a Greek-derived word that is etymologically equivalent, element for element (cf. Lesson 7, Question 3), to the following Latin-derived words: *canine, contemporary, informal, multiped, quadrangle, sanguinary, subcutaneous.*

3. Analyze each italicized word and determine the meaning of the expression in which it appears: *anodyne* translations

from Homer in sleepy prose, the *encomiums* of uncritical followers, *ex cathedra* statements, fear was *pandemic*.

4. Analyze each italicized word and determine its meaning in the context.

> A   The trees . . . chanted to each other in the regular *antiphonies* of a *cathedral* choir.—HARDY
>
> B   There is a *chorus* of voices, almost distressing in their *harmony*, raised in favor of the doctrine that education is the great *panacea* for human troubles.—T. H. HUXLEY
>
> C   There came a new malady of the spiritual sort on Europe: I mean the *epidemic*, now *endemical*, of View-hunting.—CARLYLE

5. The italicized words below are all technical. On the basis of the etymology, answer the question in which each appears.

(a) With what process in dentistry is *exodontia* concerned?

(b) What shape does an *ovoid* object have?

(c) With what is the science of *paleozoology* concerned?

(d) Is clover generally *trimerous* or *tetramerous*?

(e) What sort of morbid condition is *toxemia*?

6. *Metropolis* means etymologically 'mother city,' that is, a Greek city which sent out a colony and acted, as it were, as parent to it. What semantic change does the current meaning reveal?

CHAPTER FOUR

Greek Verbs

IN THE etymological notes of most American dictionaries, Greek verbs are given in the present infinitive active. In most cases this form ends in **-ein**. In addition to **-ein, -an** and **-oun** and **-nai** are occasionally found. Every now and then verbs ending in **-esthai** or the like will appear. These are deponent verbs (cf. pp. 90–91). Greek dictionaries and some British dictionaries give Greek verbs in the first person singular active indicative. This form for most verbs ends in **-ō**, for a few in **-mi**, for deponents in **-omai**.

Greek verbs, with but a few exceptions, have not been borrowed by English as verbs. What have been borrowed are numerous adjectives and nouns which were formed, usually in Greek itself, by combining verb bases with certain suffixes. For our purposes, therefore, the most important part of a Greek verb is its base.

The rules for determining the base of Greek verbs are rather complicated. We have, therefore, in this book adopted the procedure of giving the present infinitive and, in parentheses alongside, the base. A typical listing, for example, would run:

λέγειν **légein** (**log-** or **lek-**) 'speak,' 'say,' 'gather'

That is to say, the present infinitive of the Greek verb meaning 'speak,' 'say,' or 'gather' is **légein**. This verb has two bases to which suffixes may be attached: **log-** (as in, for example, *monologue*) and **lek-** (as in, for example, *dialect*).

All the prefixes studied in the previous chapter may be used with verbs. Thus among the English derivatives of **légein** we find *analogy, apology, eulogy, epilogue, prologue,* and so on.

LESSON 14

Adjectives from Verbs

1. Verb base plus **-tos** (neuter **-ton**), forming adjectives that are equivalent in meaning to Latin perfect participles (see p. 95). Since adjectives so formed were often used as nouns in Greek, their English derivatives are very often nouns. The suffix appears in English as *-t, -te,* and, rarely, *-ton.*

GREEK VERB	BASE	GREEK COMPOUND ADJECTIVE	ENGLISH LOAN WORD
σκέλλειν **skéllein** 'dry up'	**skele-**	σκελετός **skeletós** 'dried up'	*skeleton*
διδόναι **didónai** 'give'	**do-**	δοτός **dotós** 'given'	*antidote*

2. Verb base plus **-tikos** > *-tic,* forming adjectives from verbs.

GREEK VERB	BASE	GREEK COMPOUND ADJECTIVE	ENGLISH LOAN WORD
ἀκούειν **akoúein** 'hear'	**akous-**	ἀκουστικός **akoustikós**	*acoustic*

This suffix is closely related to **-ikos,** the suffix that forms adjectives from nouns (see Lesson 2).

ETYMOLOGICAL NOTES

The feminine form of **kryptós** 'hidden,' from **krýptein** 'hide,' is **kryptế.** It means in Greek 'vault,' 'hidden chamber.' So, today, the underground burial chambers beneath old churches are called *crypts.* In Italian, **kryptế** became *grotta,* from which we derived *grotto*, a picturesque chamber buried in rock. Many ancient grottoes excavated in Italy have curious paintings on their walls. This type of painting the Italians called **grottesca**—whence our *grotesque*.

Ink is related to the word *caustic*. The latter comes from **kaustikós**, an adjective from **kaíein (kaus-)** 'burn.' *Ink* comes from **encaustum**, the name of the purple-red ink employed by the Roman emperors for signing edicts. *Encaustum* is the Latinized form of the Greek **énkauston** 'burnt in,' 'painted in *encaustic'*—that is, with colors mixed with wax and fused by means of hot irons.

EXERCISES

1. Memorize the following Greek verbs. Analyze the English derivative listed alongside each.

διδόναι **didónai (do-)** 'give'	*anecdote*
κρύπτειν **krýptein (kryp-** or **kryph-)** 'hide'	*cryptogram*
λέγειν **légein (log-** or **lek-)** 'speak,' 'say,' 'gather'	*dialect*
πάσχειν **páschein (path-** or **pathē-)** 'suffer,' 'feel'	*pathetic*
φύειν **phýein (phy-)** 'grow'	*neophyte*
σκέπτεσθαι **sképtesthai (skop-** or **skep-)** 'watch,' 'examine'	*skeptic*

2. Analyze the words *acrobat, asbestos, cryptography, drastic, elastic, emetic, practical, static.*

3. Analyze each italicized word and determine the meaning of the expression in which it appears: the *Analects* of Confucius, an *apocryphal* story, a *cryptic* message, *didactic* poetry, an *eclectic* philosophy, a terrifying *holocaust.*

4. Analyze each italicized word and determine its meaning in the context.

A Man, even to himself, is a *palimpsest*, having an ostensible writing, and another beneath the lines.—HARDY
B False teachers commonly make use of . . . little tricks and devices to make disciples and gain *proselytes.*
—JOHN TILLOTSON

C The invisible hosts of *saprophytics* had already begun
their unresisted invasion. They would live among the
dead cells, they would grow and prodigiously multiply,
and in their growing and procreation all the chemical
building of the body would be undone.—ALDOUS HUXLEY

5. What is the difference between an *ascetic* existence and
an *aesthetic* existence?

6. (a) Determine the meaning of *caustic* in the expressions
'*caustic* soda' and '*caustic* remarks.'   In which is *caustic* closer
to its etymological meaning?   What semantic change is illustrated by the other?

(b) What is the precise meaning of the prefix in *epithet*?

7. What is the etymological meaning of *anapaest*?   Why is
an *anapaest* so called?

8. (a) Judging by the etymology of *septic*, what action
takes place in a *septic* tank?

(b) Judging by the etymology of *styptic*, how does a
styptic medicine cause bleeding to stop?

LESSON 15

Nouns from Verbs

1. Verb base plus **-a** or **-ē**.   Nouns so formed belong to the
First Declension and appear in English in the ways previously
described for that declension (see Lesson 1).

GREEK VERB	BASE	GREEK COMPOUND NOUN	ENGLISH LOAN WORD
φέρειν **phérein** 'carry'	**phor-**	μεταφορά **metaphorá** 'a carrying across,' 'transfer'	*metaphor*
πέμπειν **pémpein** 'send'	**pomp-**	πομπή **pompḗ** 'a sending,' 'procession'	*pomp*

2. Verb base plus **-os** (rarely **-on**). Nouns so formed belong to the Second Declension and appear in English in the ways previously described for that declension (see Lessons 3 and 4).

GREEK VERB	BASE	GREEK COMPOUND NOUN	ENGLISH LOAN WORD
τρέπειν **trépein** 'turn'	**trop-**	τρόπος **trópos** 'a turning'	*trope*

The noun **páthos** 'suffering,' which has been borrowed by English without change, is derived from **path-**, base of **páschein** 'suffer,' 'feel.' The omicron sigma that ends this word, however, is not the Second-Declension suffix listed above, but a Third-Declension ending (cf. p. 197).

The first step in analyzing English words that contain the suffixes involved in this lesson is to determine from the dictionary the form of the Greek compound noun from which the word in question is derived, for this will reveal all the etymological elements. In its etymological note on *symbol*, for example, Webster's *New Collegiate Dictionary* states: "F. *symbole*, fr. L. *symbolus*, *symbolum*, fr. Gr. *symbolon* a sign by which one knows or infers a thing, fr. *symballein* to throw together, to compare, fr. *syn* with + *ballein* to throw." This note reveals that the Greek compound noun from which *symbol* is derived is **sýmbolon,** which can be broken down into:

> **syn-** 'with,' 'together'
> **-bol-,** base of **bállein** 'throw'
> **-on,** suffix forming nouns from verbs.

Etymological Notes

Parabolḗ 'comparison,' the noun formed from **parabállein** 'place side by side,' is the ultimate source of a large group of English words. Derived from it, with only a slight change in form and meaning, are the doublets *parabola* and *parable*. Its other derivatives, however, reveal the influence of Latin, Old French, and even Hebrew.

There existed in Hebrew a noun *māshāl* 'comparison,' which

was translated in Greek by **parabolḗ**. However, since *māshāl* also meant 'word,' this was added to **parabolḗ** as a second meaning. **Parabolḗ** was subsequently borrowed by Latin in this second sense in the form *parabola,* and a verb *parabolāre* 'to talk' was coined to accompany it. These two words soon drove out the Classical Latin words *verbum* 'word' and *loquī* 'to talk,' and yielded the common words for 'talk' in all the Romance languages. *Parabola* is, consequently, the ultimate source of the Portuguese *palabra* 'word,' from which our *palaver* is derived, and of the French *parole* 'word.' English *parole* is a clipped form of *parole d'honneur.* Alongside *parabolāre* there existed in Latin the modified form *parlāre,* from the perfect participle of which, in Mediaeval Latin, the noun *parlātōrium* 'place for speaking' was formed. This word became our *parlor.*

EXERCISES

1. Memorize the following Greek verbs. Analyze the English derivative listed alongside each.

ἄγειν **ágein** (**agog-**) 'lead'	*synagogue*
βάλλειν **bállein** (**ball-, bol-,** or **blē-**) 'throw'	*hyperbola*
γλύφειν **glýphein** (**glyph-** or **glyp-**) 'carve'	*hieroglyph*
φέρειν **phérein** (**pher-** or **phor-**) 'bear,' 'carry'	*phosphorus*
στέλλειν **stéllein** (**stol-**) 'send'	*epistle*
στρέφειν **stréphein** (**stroph-** or **strep-**) 'turn,' 'twist'	*strophe*
τείνειν **teínein** (**ton-**) 'stretch'	*tone*
τέμνειν **témnein** (**tom-**) 'cut'	*tome*
τρέπειν **trépein** (**trop-**) 'turn'	*tropical*
τύπτειν **týptein** (**typ-**) 'strike'	*type*

2. Analyze the words *barytone, catarrh, catastrophe, diphthong, metronome, monologue, pedagogue, phosphorescent, prologue, scope, semaphore, stereotype.*

3. Analyze each italicized word and determine the meaning

of the expression in which it appears: discover an *analogue* in a related field, an *apostrophe* to the heavens, a lengthy *diatribe*, write an *eclogue*, the *prototype* of the modern automobile.

4. Analyze each italicized word and determine its meaning in the context.

A Schools are little societies, where a boy of any observation may see in *epitome* what he will afterwards find in the world at large.—FIELDING

B Other dramatists can only gain attention by *hyperbolical* or aggravated characters, by fabulous and unexampled excellence or depravity.—JOHNSON

C Teufelsdröckh rose into the highest regions of the Empyrean, by a natural *parabolic* track, and returned thence in a quick perpendicular one.—CARLYLE

5. (a) Give an example of a *hyperbole;* of a *palindrome;* of a *trope.* What phenomenon of the sun is involved in the etymology of *tropics?*

(b) What is the *Decalogue?*

6. Give the meaning of the prefix in each of the following: *epilogue, episcopal, dialogue.*

7. (a) The Greek word **apóstolos** means 'messenger' (etymologically 'one who is sent off'). What semantic change does its English derivative *apostle* reveal?

(b) Determine the etymological meaning of *demagogue.* What semantic change does its current meaning reveal?

8. Determine the etymological meaning of *atom.* Show how the expression '*atomic* fission' is, etymologically speaking, self-contradictory.

9. What is the etymological meaning of *streptococcus?*

Lesson 16

Nouns from Verbs (*Cont'd*)

In addition to those listed in the previous lesson, the following suffixes may be attached to Greek verb bases to form compound nouns.

3. Verb base plus **-ia** > *-ia, -y*, forming abstract nouns.

GREEK VERB	BASE	GREEK COMPOUND NOUN	ENGLISH LOAN WORD
μαίνεσθαι **maínesthai** 'to be mad'	**man-**	μανία **manía** 'madness'	*mania*
λέγειν **légein** 'speak'	**log-**	ἀπολογία **apología** 'a speaking off,' 'defense'	*apology*

This suffix appears in many of the combining forms described in previous lessons. Thus, **-logia,** from which *-logy* is derived (see Lesson 2), is a combination of **log-**, base of **légein** 'speak' and **-ia**; **-skopia,** from which *-scopy* is derived (see Lesson 4), is a combination of **skop-,** base of **sképtesthai** 'examine' and **-ia**; and so forth.

We have already noted the use of **-ia** with noun and adjective bases (see Lesson 2).

4. Verb base plus **-tēs** > *-t, -te* (rarely *-tes*), forming agent nouns in which it denotes 'one who' or 'that which' performs the action indicated in the base.

GREEK VERB	BASE	GREEK COMPOUND NOUN	ENGLISH LOAN WORD
πλανᾶσθαι **planásthai** 'wander'	**planē-**	πλανήτης **planétēs** 'wanderer'	*planet*

5. Verb base plus **-tēr** > *-ter*, forming agent nouns.

GREEK VERB	BASE	GREEK COMPOUND NOUN	ENGLISH LOAN WORD
κεραννύναι **kerannýnai** 'mix'	**kra-**	κρατήρ **kratḗr** 'mixing bowl'	*crater*

6. Verb base plus **-tron** > *-ter* 'place for,' 'means for,' 'instrument for.'

GREEK VERB	BASE	GREEK COMPOUND NOUN	ENGLISH LOAN WORD
σκήπτειν **skḗptein** 'support'	**skēp-**	σκῆπτρον **skḗptron**	*scepter*

7. Verb base plus **-tērion** > *-tery* (rarely *-terion*) 'place for,' 'means for,' 'instrument for.'

GREEK VERB	BASE	GREEK COMPOUND NOUN	ENGLISH LOAN WORD
κοιμᾶν **koimán** 'put to sleep'	**koimē-**	κοιμητήριον **koimētḗrion**	*cemetery*

ETYMOLOGICAL NOTES

In Greek, **krínein** 'to judge' also means 'to question,' since judging people who have been brought to trial most often involves questioning them. The deponent compound **hypo-krínesthai** meant originally 'to reply to questions.' Since question and answer is the core of dramatic dialogue, **hypo-krínesthai** came to mean 'to speak dialogue,' 'to play a part on the stage,' and a **hypokrítēs** was 'one who plays a part on the stage,' 'actor.' From 'actor' to *hypocrite* is an easy step.

Although its current meaning hardly shows it, *character* was in origin an agent noun. The Greek verb **charássein** (base **charak-**) means 'to scratch,' 'to engrave,' and a **charaktḗr** was originally either the instrument with which engraving was done or the man who wielded it. The meaning later shifted from agent to result, from the instrument with which engraving was done to that which was engraved.

EXERCISES

1. Memorize the following Greek verbs.　Analyze the English derivative listed alongside each.

αἰσθάνεσθαι **aisthánesthai** (**aisthē-**) 'feel,' 'perceive'	*aesthete*
γίγνεσθαι **gígnesthai** (**gon-, gen-,** or **genē-**) 'be born,' 'become'	*cosmogony*
ἱστάναι **histánai** (**sta-**) 'set,' 'stand'	*apostate*
κλᾶν **klan** (**klas-**) 'break'	*iconoclast*
κρίνειν **krínein** (**kri-**) 'judge'	*criterion*
νέμειν **némein** (**nom-** or **neme-**) 'deal out,' 'arrange'	*astronomy*
φαγεῖν **phageín** (**phag-**) 'eat'	*anthropophagy*
φάναι **phánai** (**pha-** or **phē-**) 'speak,' 'say'	*prophet*
τρέφειν **tréphein** (**troph-**) 'nourish'	*atrophy*

2. Determine the composition of the combining forms -*tomy*, -*ectomy*, -*nomy*, -*pathy*, -*graphy*.

3. Analyze the words *anatomy, apathy, cataract, cautery, dynast, genetics, hypercritical, kleptomania, photostat, thermostat, troglodyte.*

4. Analyze each italicized word and determine the meaning of the expression in which it appears: an *analogy* between two phenomena, monks and *anchorites*, the *antipathy* between them, a *deleterious* effect, a fulsome *eulogy*, the *periphery* of the social aristocracy.

5. Analyze each italicized word and determine its meaning in the context.

　　A　We have in this world men whom Rabelais would call *agelasts* . . . It is but one step from being *agelastic* to *misogelastic* . . . We have another class of men, who are pleased to consider themselves antagonists of the foregoing, and whom we may term *hypergelasts*.

—MEREDITH

　　B　The cultural *euphoria* that overtook Italy after Mussolini's fall seems to be already a thing of the past.

C The Puritans . . . seem mere savage *Iconoclasts,* fierce destroyers of Forms; but it were more just to call them haters of untrue Forms.—CARLYLE

D You are pleased by the sound of such words as GONDOLA, VESTMENTS, CHANCEL . . . They seem to be fraught with a subtle *onomatopoeia,* severally suggesting by their sounds the grace or sanctity . . . of the things which they connote.—BEERBOHM

E The Model T was distinguished from all other makes of cars by the fact that its transmission was of a type known as *planetary* . . . Engineers accepted the word "planetary" in its epicyclic sense, but I was always conscious that it also meant "wandering," "erratic."

—LEE STROUT WHITE

F "He has a motive, and of course his motive is a dark motive. Now, whatever his motive is, it's necessary to his motive"—Mr. Fledgeby's constructive powers were not equal to the avoidance of some *tautology* here.

—DICKENS

6. (a) Determine the etymological meaning of *creosote, pirate, poet.* What semantic change does the current meaning of each reveal?

(b) Consider the expressions 'written in Greek *characters*' and 'a man of good *character*.' In which is *character* closer to its etymological meaning?

7. What is the meaning of the prefix in *diacritical*? Give an example of a *diacritical* mark.

8. What Greek-derived words are etymologically equivalent, element for element, to the Latin-derived words *aversion, carnivore, circumference, compassion, factor, Lucifer, passive*?

LESSON 17

Nouns from Verbs (*Concl'd*)

The following suffixes may be added to verb bases to form abstract nouns.

8. Verb base plus **-sis** > *-sis*, *-se*, *-sy* 'act of,' 'state of,' 'result of.'

GREEK VERB	BASE	GREEK COMPOUND NOUN	ENGLISH LOAN WORD
τιθέναι tithénai 'place'	the-	θέσις thésis 'a placing,' 'a setting'	*thesis*
διδόναι didónai 'give'	do-	δόσις dósis 'a giving'	*dose*
ἰστάναι histánai 'set'	sta-	ἔκστασις ékstasis 'displacement,' 'mental displacement,' 'madness'	*ecstasy*

Sometimes **-sia** > *-sia*, *sy* is used instead of **-sis**. This suffix is simply **-ia** (see Lesson 2) combined with the **-s-** of **-sis**.

GREEK VERB	BASE	GREEK COMPOUND NOUN	ENGLISH LOAN WORD
αἰσθάνεσθαι aisthánesthai 'feel'	aisthē-	ἀναισθησία anaisthēsía	*anaesthesia*

Abstract nouns formed with **-sis** and **-sia** are frequently paralleled by adjectives formed with **-tikos** (see Lesson 14). Thus, alongside **sýnthesis** (> *synthesis*) we have **synthetikós** (> *synthetic*), alongside **anaisthēsía** (> *anaesthesia*) we have **anaisthētikós** (> *anaesthetic*), and so on.

9. Verb base plus **-ma** > *-ma*, *-m*, *-me* 'result of.'

GREEK VERB	BASE	GREEK COMPOUND NOUN	ENGLISH LOAN WORD
στίζειν stízein 'brand'	stig-	στίγμα stígma 'a brand'	*stigma*
γράφειν gráphein 'write'	gram-	γράμμα grámma 'letter'	*gram*
τιθέναι tithénai 'place'	the-	θέμα théma 'something laid down,' 'proposition (for discussion)'	*theme*

Abstract nouns formed with **-ma** belong to the Third Declension and end in the genitive in **-matos** (see Lesson 7). Their base, found by dropping **-os** of the genitive, ends in **-mat-**. Thus, *thematic* consists of:

> *the-*, base of **tithénai** 'place'
> *-mat-* from **-ma**, genitive **-matos** 'result of'
> *-ic* from **-ikos**, adjective-forming suffix (see Lesson 2)

10. Verb base plus **-mos** > *-m* 'state of,' 'act of,' 'result of.'

GREEK VERB	BASE	GREEK COMPOUND NOUN	ENGLISH LOAN WORD
σπᾶν span 'draw out'	spas-	σπασμός spasmós	*spasm*

ETYMOLOGICAL NOTES

Metaphysics involves in its etymology no deep philosophical concepts. As a matter of fact, its origin is due to some rather unimaginative procedure on the part of Aristotle's disciples. Aristotle's manuscripts included a book on natural science (**physiká**, the 'Physics,' neuter plural of **physikós**, from **phýsis** 'nature') and, immediately following, a book on abstract philosophy. His disciples, accordingly, dubbed the latter 'after (**meta-**) the Physics.'

Graft 'a shoot inserted in the slit of another stock' is a descendant of **gráphein** 'write.' The word was earlier spelled *graff*. It came to us from the Old French *graffe*, which originally denoted a sort of pencil but also had the meaning 'grafting slip,' since such a slip resembles a pointed pencil in shape. The Old French word comes, through Late Latin, from the Greek **graphíon** 'stylus,' a derivative of **gráphein.**

Glamor, although a far cry from *graft* in meaning, also goes back to **gráphein. Grámma, grámmatos** means basically 'thing written (**gram-**, base of **gráphein** + **-ma**)' and **grammatikḗ** (**téchnē**) was the ancient Greek for 'art of letters.' The latter ultimately became *grammar* in English.   A variant pronunciation produced *glamor*, originally meaning 'magic.' *Grammar* implies learning, and learning was traditionally connected with magic.   A *glamorous* person thus is, etymologically speaking, one who 'charms' you.

EXERCISES

1. Memorize the following Greek verbs.   Analyze the English derivative listed alongside each.

γράφειν **gráphein** (**graph-** or **gram-**) 'write'	*grammatical*
κινεῖν **kineín** (**kinē-**) 'set in motion,' 'move'	*kinetic*
λαμβάνειν **lambánein** (**lēp-**, **lem-** or **lab-**) 'take'	*epilepsy*
λύειν **lýein** (**ly-**) 'loosen'	*analysis*
ὁρᾶν **horán** (**hora-** or **op-**) 'see'	*synopsis*
φαίνειν **phaínein** (**phan-** or **pha-**) 'show'	*phase*
πλάσσειν **plássein** (**plas-**) 'mould'	*plasma*
πνεῖν **pnein** (**pneu-**) 'breathe'	*pneumatic*
ῥεῖν **rhein** (**rheu-** or **rho-**) 'flow'	*rheumatic*
σχίζειν **schízein** (**schis-**) 'split'	*schism*
σπείρειν **speírein** (**sper-** or **spor-**) 'sow'	*sperm*
τάσσειν **tássein** (**tak-**) 'arrange'	*syntax*
τιθέναι **tithénai** (**the-**) 'place'	*synthesis*

2. Form an adjective from the base of the verb that appears in each of the following nouns: *catalysis, cinema, drama, ecstasy, hypothesis, periphrasis, synopsis, syntax.*

3. Analyze the words *amnesty, asphyxiate, diadem, dramaturgy, eclipse, physical, prognosticate, protoplasm, spore, stereopticon, symptom, taxidermy.*

4. Give the etymological meaning of *amnesia, aphasia, crisis, dogma, dyspepsia, genesis, schizophrenia.*

5. Analyze each italicized word and determine the meaning of the expression in which it appears: *apostasy* from one's principles, swept away by a *cataclysm, diaphanous* material, on the horns of a *dilemma, paraphrase* a significant passage, a sudden *paroxysm* of anger, the *pragmatic* value of religion, a *synoptic* view of the current political field.

6. Analyze each italicized word and determine its meaning in the context.

A "He that is accursed, let him be accursed still," was the pitiless *anathema* written in this spoliated effort of his new-born solicitousness.—HARDY

B Moreover, if one listened attentively one discovered *apophthegm* and *epigram* delivered as casually and sleepily as if they were clichés.—IRWIN EDMAN

C It is no small undertaking for a man unsupported and alone to begin a natural history from his own *autopsia!*—GILBERT WHITE

D Come, let us leave him; in his ireful mood
Our words will but increase his *ecstasy.*—MARLOWE

E He then ate kedgeree in silence. He looked like some splendid bull, and she like some splendid cow, grazing. I envied them their *eupeptic* calm.—BEERBOHM

F *Idiosyncrasy* and vicissitude had combined to stamp Sergeant Troy as an exceptional being.—HARDY

G The sight, coming as it did, superimposed upon the other dark scenery of the previous days, formed a kind of climax to the whole *panorama.*—HARDY

H *Periphrastic* methods spurning,
To this audience discerning
I admit this show of learning
Is the fruit of steady 'cram.'—W. S. GILBERT

1 He imagines, he creates, giving you not a person, but a type, a *synthesis,* and not what anywhere has been, but what anywhere might be.—BEERBOHM

7. Give the meaning of the prefix or prefixes in *apocalypse, diagnosis, metathesis, parenthesis.*

8. (a) Determine the etymological meaning of *autopsy* (cf. sentence 6c). What semantic change does its current meaning reveal?

(b) Determine the etymological meaning of *heresy*. What semantic change is revealed by its use in the expression 'convicted of *heresy* by the Inquisition'?

9. (a) Show how the expression 'yawning *chasm*' is, etymologically speaking, tautological.

(b) *Diaeresis* means etymologically 'the act of taking apart.' What does the diaeresis in *coöperate* 'take apart'?

(c) What is the difference between an *agnostic* and an *atheist*?

10. Determine the etymology, pronunciation, and meaning of the expression *dramatis personae*.

11. The following list contains nine pairs of words that are linguistically related. Select the pairs and, in each case, show what the relationship is (for example, *emblem* and *hyperbole* are related. *Emblem* contains **blē-**, a base of the verb **bállein** 'throw,' and *hyperbole* **bol-**, another base of the same verb): *aphasia, apology, apoplexy, comedy, cosmogony, diaeresis, dipody, epigraphic, genetics, gramophone, lexicon, heretical, panorama, planet, plectrum, prophet, spermaceti, spore, synopsis, syntactic, taxidermy.*

Lesson 18

Denominative Verbs. Greek Participles in English

Denominative Verbs. In its etymological note on *scholastic,* Webster's *New Collegiate Dictionary* says: "L. *scholasticus,* fr. Gr. *scholastikos,* fr. *scholazein* to have leisure, keep a school, fr. *scholé.*" In other words, a verb **scholázein** was formed from the noun **scholé,** and to **scholas-,** the base of this verb, the

adjective-forming suffix -tikos (see Lesson 14) was attached
to form **scholastikós** 'pertaining to keeping a school,' whence
our *scholastic*. *Scholastic* is just one of a sizable group of
English words that owe their origin to Greek denominative
verbs.

There are six endings commonly added to Greek noun or
adjective bases to form verbs: (1) **-an** or, deponent, **-asthai**
(with a base ending in -ē-), (2) **-ein** or, deponent, **-eisthai**
(with a base ending in -ē-), (3) **-oun** or, deponent, **-ousthai**
(with a base ending in -ō-), (4) **-euein** (-eu-), (5) -azein (-as-),
(6) **-izein** (-is-).

GREEK NOUN OR ADJECTIVE	BASE	GREEK DE-NOMINATIVE VERB	BASE	ENGLISH LOAN WORD
(1) δίαιτα **díaita** 'diet'	**diait-**	διαιτᾶν **diaitán** 'to diet'	**diaitē-**	*dietetics*
(2) ἆθλον **áthlon** 'prize'	**athl-**	ἀθλεῖν **athleín** 'to contend for a prize'	**athlē-**	*athlete*
(3) ἴδιος **ídios** 'one's own'	**idi-**	ἰδιοῦσθαι **idioústhai** 'to make one's own'	**idiō-**	*idiom*
(4) θέραψ, θέραπος **théraps, thérapos** servant	**therap-**	θεραπεύειν **therapeúein** 'to wait on,' 'to cure'	**therapeu-**	*therapeutic*
(5) μόνος **mónos** 'single,' 'alone'	**mon-**	μονάζειν **monázein** 'to live alone'	**monas-**	*monastery*
(6) Ἕλλην **Héllēn** 'a Greek'	**Hellēn-**	Ἑλληνίζειν **Hellēnízein** 'to Grecize'	**Hellēnis-**	*Hellenism*

The ending **-izein** was borrowed by Latin as *-izāre* which entered English as *-ize* 'to make into or like,' 'to subject to,' 'to put into conformity with.' Words ending in *-ize* are the only examples of English verbs regularly derived from Greek verbs; all other derivatives of Greek verbs are, with rare exceptions, nouns or adjectives.

In a great many instances verbs formed with **-izein** were combined with **-mos** to form abstract nouns (for example, **Hellēnismós** > *Hellenism*), and with **-tēs** to form agent nouns (for example, **Hellēnistḗs** > *Hellenist*). The endings *-ism* and *-ist* that resulted from this process were used as suffixes (see Lesson 2) and, along with *-ize*, freely attached in English even to non-Greek bases. For example, in *scrutinize* a Latin base has been used, in *Buddhism* a Sanskrit base, in *totemism* an American Indian base.

Verbs formed with the ending **-oun,** when combined with **-sis** or **-ma,** produce nouns that end in **-ōsis** and **-ōma.** For example, **nekroún (nekrō-)** 'kill,' denominative of **nekrós** 'corpse,' has given us *necrosis*; **sarkoún (sarkō-)** 'become fleshy,' denominative of **sarx, sarkós** 'flesh,' has produced *sarcoma*. As in the case of *-ism* and *-ist*, these endings have become suffixes in English (see Lesson 6).

Greek Participles in English. A miscellaneous group of English words derives from present active or present passive participles of Greek verbs. *Horizon*, for example, comes from **horízōn** 'bounding,' that is the circle 'bounding' the sight. **Horízōn** is the present participle of **horízein** 'to bound,' a denominative verb of **hóros** 'boundary.' *Hormone*, the secretion that stimulates an organ to action means 'impelling' etymologically. It comes from **hormón,** the present active participle of **hormán** 'impel.' *Hypotenuse* is a derivative of a present active participle in the feminine form, **hypoteínousa** 'subtending' (**hypo-** + **teínein** 'stretch'). The full expression would be **hypoteínousa grammḗ** 'subtending line.' In *ion* 'something that goes,' the neuter of the present participle of **iénai** 'go' has been used. In *ontology* we have **ont-,** the base of **ōn, ontós** 'being,' present participle of **eínai** 'to be.'

Phenomenon comes from the neuter of a present passive participle. The verb **phaínein** 'show' in the passive means 'appear,' and a **phainómenon** is 'something that has appeared.' A *prolegomenon* is 'something said in advance,' 'foreword,' from the present passive participle neuter of **prolégein.** A *catechumen,* a convert under instruction before baptism, is literally 'one who is being instructed,' from **katēchoúmenos,** the present passive participle masculine of **katēcheín** 'instruct.' The etymology of this verb throws an interesting light on ancient methods of instruction. **Kat-** comes from **kata-** 'entirely,' and **ēcheín** is the denominative of **ēchos** 'a ringing in the ears.' A close relative of **ēchos** is **ēchṓ,** the ancestor of our *echo.*

EXERCISES

1. Memorize the following Greek adjectives. Analyze the English derivative listed alongside each.

ἴδιος **ídios** 'one's own'	*idiot*
γυμνός **gymnós** 'naked'	*gymnast*
σκληρός **sklērós** 'hard'	*sclerosis*

2. Analyze the words *amphitheater, analgesic, barbarism, canonize, cathartic, evangelist, hypnotic, metamorphosis, organization, paleontology, phonetic, rheumatism, semantic, sophisticate.*

3. Analyze each italicized word and determine its meaning in the context.

A "I think, R.W.," cried Mrs. Wilfer, lifting up her eyes and *apostrophising* the air, "that if you were present, it would be a trial to your feelings to hear your wife and the mother of your family depreciated in your name."
—DICKENS

B The *apotheosis* of familiar abuses . . . is the vilest of superstitions.—COLERIDGE

C It has been therefore said, without an indecent hyperbole, by one of his *encomiasts,* that in reading Paradise Lost we read a book of universal knowledge.
—JOHNSON

D For no man lives in the external truth, among salts and acids, but in the warm, *phantasmagoric* chamber of his brain, with the painted windows and the storied walls.—STEVENSON

E The ANALOGY is a tissue of *sophistry*, of wire-drawn, theological special-pleading; the SERMONS (with the Preface to them) are . . . a candid appeal to our observation of human nature, without pedantry and without bias.—HAZLITT

4. (a) Analyze *protagonist* and *antagonist*. Is *protagonist* the antonym of *antagonist*? Explain your answer.

(b) Analyze *aphorism* and *axiom*. Distinguish in meaning between the two and give an example of each.

5. Give an example of a *euphemism*, a *neologism*, a *solecism*, a *syllogism*. What semantic change is revealed when you compare the etymological meaning of *solecism* with its current meaning?

6. Determine the etymological meaning of *cosmetic*. What semantic change does its current meaning reveal?

7. (a) In order to follow out the etymological meaning of the word, in what form ought a *diploma* be issued?

(b) What does an *onychophagist* do?

(c) What ancient Greek practice explains the semantic development of *ostracism*?

(d) Show how the expression 'biting *sarcasm*' is, etymologically speaking, tautological.

LESSON 19

Review

1. Give the Greek words, with their base or bases, meaning:
(a) blood, name, road

(b) good, bad, white, black, narrow, thick, naked

(c) bear, give, hide, judge, split, stretch, watch

2. Analyze the words *anesthetize, archetype, epithet, heretic, ideograph, mimetic, periphrasis, physiology, plastic, problem, prophylaxis, syncopation, tactics.*

3. The following list contains eleven pairs of words that are linguistically related. Select the pairs and show in each case what the relationship is (see Lesson 17, Exercise No. 11): *anecdote, apophthegm, ballistics, biology, dialectical, diarrhea, dilemma, diphthong, dose, dyarchy, epilepsy, exodus, optical, panorama, periodical, periscope, phonograph, rheumatic, skeptical, symbol, syntax, synchronize, tactics, telegram, telephone.*

4. What Greek-derived words are etymologically equivalent, element for element, to the Latin-derived words *benediction, composition, prescription, projection, resolution, supposition, transformation?*

5. What is the meaning of the proper nouns *Erasmus, Erastus, Eugene?*

· 6. Give the Greek word, with its meaning, involved in the etymology of each of the following words:

(a) *epilogue, melodrama, music, program, prologue, scene, theater*

(b) *apostrophe, colon, comma, hyphen, paragraph, parenthesis, period, semicolon*

(c) *baptistery, cathedral, Catholicism, diocese, eucharist, Episcopalian, Presbyterian*

(d) *arithmetic, axiom, geometry, logarithm, mathematics, theorem, trigonometry*

General Vocabulary

[Included are (a) words involved in the exercises, (b) words that have no common derivatives but are important in scientific terminology. Words marked with the dagger (†) have been assigned to be memorized in the exercises.]

NOUNS, ADJECTIVES, ADVERBS

ἀδελφός **adelphós** 'brother'

ἀδήν **adén** 'acorn,' 'gland'

†ἀήρ **aér** 'air'

ἀγαθός **agathós** 'good'

ἀγών **agón** 'struggle,' 'contest'

ἀγορά **agorá** 'market place,' 'assembly'

ἄγυρις **ágyris** 'assembly'

αἰγίς, αἰγίδος **aigís, aigídos** aegis (*shield of Zeus or Athena*)

Αἴολος **Aíolos** Aeolus (*ruler of the winds*)

αἰών **aión** 'space of time,' 'lifetime'

Ἀκαδήμεια **Akadémeia** the Academy (*gymnasium in suburbs of Athens where Plato taught*)

ἄκανθα **ákantha** 'thorn'

ἀκμή **akmé** 'point,' 'prime'

ἄκος, ἄκεος **ákos, ákeos** 'cure,' 'remedy'

†ἄκρος **ákros** 'topmost,' 'outermost'

ἀκτίς, ἀκτῖνος **aktís, aktínos** 'beam,' 'ray'

ἄλειφαρ, ἀλείφατος **aleíphar, aleíphatos** 'fat'

†ἄλγος **álgos** (*3rd Decl.*) 'pain'

ἀλλήλων **allélōn** (*gen. plu.*) 'one another'

†ἄλλος **állos** 'another,' 'different'

ἀμαυρός **amaurós** 'dark'

ἀμβλύς **amblýs** (**ambly-**) 'dull'

ἀμοιβή **amoibé** 'change'

ἀμφότερος **amphóteros** 'both'

ἄμυλον **ámylon** 'starch'

ἀνήρ, ἀνδρός **anér, andrós** 'man'

ἀγγεῖον **angeíon** 'blood-vessel,' 'seed-vessel'

ἄγγελος **ángelos** 'messenger'

ἄγγος **ángos** (*3rd Decl.*) 'vessel'

ἀγκύλος **ankýlos** 'bent'

ἄνθεμον **ánthemon** 'flower'

†ἄνθος ánthos (*3rd Decl.*) 'flower'

ἄνθραξ, ἄνθρακος ánthrax, ánthrakos 'coal'

†ἄνθρωπος ánthrōpos 'man'

ἀψίς, ἀψῖδος apsís, apsídos 'arch'

†ἀρχαῖος archaíos 'old,' 'ancient'

†ἀρχός archós 'chief'

ἄριστος áristos 'best'

ἀριθμός arithmós 'number'

Ἀρκαδία Arkadía Arcadia (*name of a mountainous district in the Peloponnese*)

ἄρκτος árktos 'bear'

ἄρωμα, ἀρώματος árōma, arómatos 'fragrance'

ἀρτηρία artēría 'windpipe,' 'artery'

ἄρθρον árthron 'joint'

ἄσβεστος ásbestos 'inextinguishable' (*see* sbennúnai)

ἀστήρ astḗr 'star'

ἄστρον ástron 'star'

ἄσυλος ásylos 'inviolable'

Ἀθήνη Athḗnē Athene (*goddess of wisdom*)

ἆθλον áthlon (*3rd Decl.*) 'prize,' 'contest'

Ἄτλας, Ἄτλαντος Átlas, Átlantos Atlas (*Titan who supported the heavens*)

ἀτμός atmós 'vapor'

αὐλός aulós 'flute'

αὔρα aúra 'breeze,' 'breath'

†αὐτός autós 'self'

ἄξιος áxios 'worthy'

ἄξων áxōn 'axis'

Βάκχος Bákchos Bacchus (*Greek god of wine and revelry*)

βάκτρον báktron (baktēr-) 'stick'

βάρβαρος bárbaros 'foreign'

†βάρος báros (*3rd Decl.*) 'weight'

βαρύς barýs (bary-) 'heavy'

βασιλεύς basileús 'king'

βάσις básis 'step,' 'stand' (*see* baínein)

βάθος báthos (*3rd Decl.*) 'depth'

βιβλίον biblíon 'book'

†βίος bíos 'life'

βλαστός blastós 'bud,' 'sprout,' 'germ'

βλέννα blénna 'mucus'

βλέφαρον blépharon 'eyelid'

Βορέας Boréas 'the North wind'

βοτάνη botánē 'plant'

βουκόλος boukólos 'herdsman'

βοῦς, βοός bous, boós. 'bullock,' 'cow,' 'ox'

βραχύς brachýs (brachy-) 'short'

βραδύς bradýs (brady-) 'slow'

βράγχια bránchia (*neuter plu.*) 'gills'

βρῶμος brómos 'smell'

βρόγχος brónchos 'windpipe,' 'trachea'

βροντή brontḗ 'thunder'

βρῦον **brýon** 'moss'

βύρσα **býrsa** 'hide'

χαίτη **chaítē** 'mane'

χαλκός **chalkós** 'copper'

χαμαί **chamaí** (*adv.*) 'on the ground'

χαρακτήρ **charaktḗr** 'stamp' (*see* **charássein**)

χάρις, χάριτος **cháris, cháritos** 'favor,' 'thanks'

χάρτης **chártēs** 'sheet of papyrus'

χάσμα, χάσματος **chásma, chásmatos** 'chasm' (*see* **cháskein**)

χεῖλος **cheílos** (*3rd Decl.*) 'lip'

†χείρ, χειρός **cheir, cheirós** 'hand'

χέλυς, χέλυος **chélys, chélyos** 'tortoise'

χίμαιρα **chímaira** 'she-goat,' 'chimera'

χλόη **chlóē** 'young verdure'

χλωρός †**chlōrós** 'light green'

χολή **cholḗ** 'bile'

χολέρα **choléra** 'jaundice,' 'cholera'

χόνδρος **chóndros** 'cartilage'

χορδή **chordḗ** 'gut string,' 'cord'

χόριον **chórion** 'membrane'

χορός **chorós** 'band of singers and dancers,' 'chorus'

χρόα **chróa** 'color'

†χρῶμα, χρώματος **chrṓma, chrṓmatos** 'color'

†χρόνος **chrónos** 'time'

†χρυσός **chrysós** 'gold'

χθών **chthōn** 'earth,' 'land'

χυλός **chylós** 'juice'

δαίμων **daímōn** 'god,' 'divinity'

†δάκτυλος **dáktylos** 'finger,' 'dactyl' (*metrical foot consisting of a long syllable followed by two shorts*)

δάφνη **dáphnē** 'laurel'

δεινός **deinós** 'terrible'

†δῆμος **dḗmos** 'people'

δένδρον **déndron** 'tree'

†δέρμα, δέρματος **dérma, dérmatos** 'skin,' 'hide'

δεσμός **desmós** 'band,' 'ligament'

δεσπότης **despótēs** 'absolute ruler'

δίαιτα **díaita** 'way of living,' 'diet'

διάκονος **diákonos** 'servant,' 'deacon'

δίδυμος **dídymos** 'double,' 'twin'; *in plu.* 'testicles'

δίκη **díkē** 'justice'

διφθέρα **diphthéra** 'piece of leather'

διπλόος **diplóos** 'twofold,' 'doubled'

δίψα **dípsa** 'thirst'

δίσκος **dískos** 'round plate,' 'discus'

δολιχός **dolichós** 'long'

δῶρον **dṓron** 'gift'

δόξα **dóxa** 'opinion'

δρόμος **drómos** 'course,'

'track,' 'race' (*see*
tréchein)
δρυάς, δρυάδος dryás, dryádos
'wood nymph'
δύναμις dýnamis 'force'
ἐχῖνος echínos 'sea-urchin'
εἴδωλον eídōlon 'image,'
'phantom'
εἰκών eikṓn 'image'
εἰρήνη eirḗnē 'peace'
εἴρων eírōn 'dissembler'
†ἐκτός ektós (*adv.*) 'outside'
ἔλεγος élegos 'song of mourn-
ing'
ἤλεκτρον élektron 'amber'
ἐλέφας, ἐλέφαντος eléphas,
eléphantos 'elephant'
ἔμβρυον émbryon 'foetus'
†ἔνδον éndon (*adv.*) 'within'
ἐγκέφαλος enképhalos 'brain'
ἔντερον énteron 'intestine'
†ἐντός entós (*adv.*) 'within'
†ἠώς, ἠόος ḗōs, ḗóos 'dawn'
ἐρῆμος erḗmos 'solitary'
†ἔργον érgon 'work' 'deserted'
ἔρως, ἔρωτος érōs, érōtos
'love,' Eros (*god of love*)
ἐρυθρός erythrós 'red'
†ἔσω ésō (*adv.*) 'within'
ἔθνος éthnos (*3rd Decl.*) 'nation'
ἦθος éthos (*3rd Decl.*) 'custom,' 'character,' 'nature'
εὐρύς eurýs (eury-) 'wide'
†ἔξω éxō (*adv.*) 'outside'
γάλα, γάλακτος gála, gálak-
tos 'milk'

†γάμος gámos 'marriage'
γάγγλιον gánglion 'tumor'
γάγγραινα gángraina 'can-
cerous ulcer'
†γαστήρ, γαστρός gastḗr,
gastrós 'stomach'
†γῆ gē (*base* ge-) 'earth'
γένος, γένεος génos, géneos
'race,' 'kind'
Γεώργιος Geṓrgios George
(*etymologically* 'earth-
worker,' '*farmer*')
γέρανος géranos 'crane'
γέρων, γέροντος gérōn, gé-
rontos 'old man'
γλαυκός glaukós 'sea-green'
γλεῦκος gleúkos (*3rd Decl.*)
'sweet new wine'
†γλῶσσα glṓssa (*or* glṓtta)
'tongue'
γλυκερός glykerós 'sweet'
γλυκύς glykýs (glyky-)
'sweet'
γνάθος gnáthos 'jaw'
†γωνία gōnía 'angle'
γράμμα, γράμματος grámma,
grámmatos 'something
written,' 'letter,' 'small
weight' (*see* gráphein)
†γυμνός gymnós 'naked'
†γυνή gynḗ (gyn-, gynaik-)
'woman'
γῦρος gýros 'ring,' 'circle'
†αἷμα, αἵματος haíma, haímatos (haem-, haemat-)
'blood'
ἀλκυών halkyṓn 'kingfisher'

ἅλς, ἁλός hals, halós 'salt'

ἁπλόος haplóos 'single,' 'simple'

ἁρμονία harmonía 'harmony'

ἡδονή hēdonḗ 'pleasure'

†ἕδρα hédra 'seat'

ἡγεμών hēgemṓn 'leader'

ἥλιος hḗlios 'sun'

ἕλιξ, ἕλικος hélix, hélikos 'spiral'

Ἕλλην Héllēn 'a Greek'

ἡμέρα hēméra 'day'

ἧπαρ, ἥπατος hḗpar, hḗpatos 'liver'

ἥρως, ἥρωος hḗrōs, hḗrōos 'hero'

†ἕτερος héteros 'other'

†ἱερός hierós 'holy'

†ἵππος híppos 'horse'

ἵστωρ hístōr 'learned man'

ἱστός histós 'web,' 'tissue'

†ὁδός hodós 'way,' 'road'

†ὅλος hólos 'whole,' 'entire'

ὁμαλός homalós 'even,' 'regular'

†ὅμοιος hómoios 'similar'

†ὁμός homós 'same'

ὅπλον hóplon 'tool'; in plu. 'armor'

ὥρα hṓra 'time,' 'season'

ὅρος hóros 'boundary'

ὕαλος hýalos 'glass'

†ὕδωρ hýdōr (hydr-) 'water'

ὕδρα hýdra 'water snake,' Hydra (serpent slain by Hercules)

ὑγρός hygrós 'moist'

ὕλη hýlē 'wood,' 'matter'

ὕμνος hýmnos 'song of praise'

ὕπνος hýpnos 'sleep'

ὕψος hýpsos (3rd Decl.) 'height'

ὗς hys 'pig'

ὑστέρα hystéra 'womb'

ἴαμβος íambos 'iamb' (metrical foot consisting of a short and a long syllable)

ἰατρός iatrós 'physician'

ἰχώρ ichṓr 'fluid that flows in veins of the gods'

ἰχθύς, ἰχθύος ichthýs, ichthýos 'fish'

ἰδέα idéa 'form,' 'kind'

†ἴδιος ídios 'one's own'

ἰώδης iṓdēs 'violet-like'

†ἶρις, ἴριδος íris, íridos 'rainbow,' Iris (goddess of the rainbow)

†ἴσος ísos 'equal'

ἰσθμός isthmós 'neck of land,' 'isthmus'

καινός kainós 'recent,' 'new'

†κακός kakós 'bad'

†κάλλος kállos (3rd Decl.) 'beauty'

κανών kanṓn 'rule,' 'rod'

†καρδία kardía 'heart'

καρπός karpós 'fruit'

καρπός karpós 'wrist'

κάρυον káryon 'nut'

καθαρός katharós 'pure'

καυστός kaustós 'burnt' (see kaíein)

κήλη kḗlē 'tumor,' 'rupture'

κενός kenós 'empty'

†κέντρον kéntron 'sharp point,' 'center'

†κεφαλή kephalḗ 'head'

κέραμος kéramos 'pottery'

†κέρας or κέρως, κέρατος kéras or kérōs, kératos 'horn'

κιρρός kirrhós 'tawny-yellow'

κλάδος kládos 'sprout,' 'slip'

κλέπτης kléptēs 'thief' (see kléptō)

κλίμα, κλίματος klíma, klímatos 'slope,' 'supposed slope of the earth,' 'region' (see klínein)

κλιμακτήρ klimaktḗr 'rung of a ladder'

κλῖμαξ, κλίμακος klímax, klímakos 'ladder,' 'staircase,' 'climax'

κλίνη klínē 'bed' (see klínein)

κοῖλος koílos 'hollow'

κοινός koinós 'common'

κόκκος kókkos 'grain,' 'seed'

κόλλα kólla 'glue'

κόλον kólon 'the colon'

κῶλον kȏlon 'limb,' 'clause'

κολοσσός kolossós 'gigantic statue'

κόλπος kólpos 'bosom'

κῶμα, κώματος kȏma, kȏmatos 'deep sleep'

κῶμος kȏmos 'revel'

κόγχη kónchē 'cockle,' 'mussel'

κόνδυλος kóndylos 'knuckle'

κόνις kónis 'dust'

κῶνος kȏnos 'cone'

κοπή kopḗ 'a cutting' (see kóptein)

κόπρος kópros 'dung'

κόρη kórē 'maiden'

†κόσμος kósmos 'order,' 'harmony,' 'universe'

κρανίον kraníon 'skull'

†κράτος krátos (3rd Decl.) 'power'

κρέας, κρέως kréas, kréōs 'flesh'

κρίνον krínon 'lily'

κρόκος krókos 'saffron,' 'crocus'

κτείς, κτενός kteis, ktenós 'comb'

κύανος kýanos 'dark blue mineral'

†κύκλος kýklos 'wheel,' 'circle'

κύλινδρος kýlindros 'roller,' 'cylinder'

κύων, κυνός kýōn, kynós 'dog'

†κύστις kýstis 'sac'

κύτος kýtos (3rd Decl.) 'vessel,' 'cell'

λαβύρινθος labýrinthos 'maze'

Λάκων Lákōn 'a Spartan'

Λαοκόων Laokóōn Laocoön (see Etymological Notes, Lesson 5)

λαός laós 'people'

λάρυγξ, λάρυγγος lárynx, láryngos 'larynx'

λέων, λέοντος léōn, léontos 'lion'

λεπίς, λεπίδος lepís, lepídos 'scale,' 'husk'

λεπτός **leptós** 'small,' 'weak,' 'fine'

λήθη **léthē** 'forgetfulness,' Lethe (*river of Hades*)

†λευκός **leukós** 'white'

λίπος **lípos** (*3rd Decl.*) 'grease,' 'fat'

†λίθος **líthos** 'stone'

λίτρα **lítra** 'pound'

λοβός **lobós** 'lobe,' 'pod'

λόφος **lóphos** 'mane,' 'crest'

λωτός **lōtós** 'lotus'

Λύκειον **Lúkeion** Lyceum (*temple of Apollo*)

λύκος **lýkos** 'wolf'

λύρα **lýra** 'lyre'

†μακρός **makrós** 'long'

μαλακός **malakós** 'soft'

μάργαρον **márgaron** 'pearl'

μάρτυρ **mártyr** 'witness'

μαστός **mastós** 'breast'

Μαύσωλος **Maúsōlos** Mausolus (*King of Caria in Asia Minor*)

μηχανή **mēchanḗ** 'machine'

μέδουσα **médousa** 'ruler' (*fem.*), Medusa (*name of one of the Gorgons*)

†μέγας **mégas** (**mega-, megal-**) 'great'

†μέλας **mélas** (**mela-, melan-**) 'black'

μέλος **mélos** (*3rd Decl.*) 'song'

μῆνιγξ, μήνιγγος **mḗninx, mḗningos** 'membrane'

†μέρος **méros** (*3rd Decl.*) 'part'

μηρός **mērós** 'thigh'

†μέσος **mésos** 'middle'

μέταλλον **métallon** 'mine'

μήτηρ, μητρός **mḗtēr, mētrós** 'mother'

μήτρα **métra** 'womb'

†μέτρον **métron** 'measure'

†μικρός **mikrós** 'small'

μῖμος **mímos** 'mime'

μῖσος **mísos** (*3rd Decl.*) 'hatred'

μίτος **mítos** 'thread'

μίτρα **mítra** 'headband'

μῖξις **míxis** 'a mingling' (*see* **mignúnai**)

μνήμων **mnḗmōn** 'mindful,' 'remembering'

μωρός **mōrós** 'dull,' 'stupid'

†μορφή **morphḗ** 'form'

Μοῦσα **Moúsa** 'Muse'

μυελός **myelós** 'marrow'

μύκης **mýkēs** 'mushroom,' 'fungus'

μυριάς, μυριάδος **myriás, myriádos** '10,000'

μύρρα **mýrrha** 'myrrh'

†μῦς, μυός **mys, myós** 'mouse,' 'muscle'

μῦθος **mýthos** 'word,' 'speech,' 'fable'

ναϊάς, ναϊάδος **naïás, naïádos** 'water nymph'

νάρκη **nárkē** 'numbness'

†νεκρός **nekrós** 'corpse'

νέκταρ **néktar** 'drink of the gods'

νῆμα, νήματος **nêma, nêma-
tos** 'thread'

†νέος **néos** 'new'

νεφρός **nephrós** 'kidney'

Νέστωρ **Néstōr** Nestor (*aged
and wise counselor in the
Iliad*)

†νεῦρον **neúron** 'nerve,' 'sinew'

νίκη **nī́kē** 'victory'

νόμος **nómos** 'law' (*see
némein*)

νόσος **nósos** 'disease'

νόστος **nóstos** 'a return
home'

νῶτον **nôton** 'the back'

νοῦς **nous** (**no-**) 'mind'

νύμφη **nýmphē** 'nymph,'
'bride,' 'young woman'

ὀβελός **obelós** 'spit'

†ὀδούς, ὀδόντος **odoús, odóntos** 'tooth'

ὀδύνη **odýnē** 'pain'

ᾠδή **ōidḗ** 'poem sung to music'

†οἶκος **oîkos** 'house'

ᾠόν **ōión** (**ō-**) 'egg'

†ὀλίγος **olígos** 'few'

ὦμος **ômos** 'shoulder'

ὀμφαλός **omphalós** 'navel'

†ὄνυμα, ὀνύματος **ónyma, onýmatos** (**onym-** *or* **onomat-**)
'name,' 'noun'

ὄνυξ, ὄνυχος **ónyx, ónychos**
'claw,' 'fingernail,' 'veined
gem'

ὄφις, ὄφιος **óphis, óphios** 'serpent'

ὀφθαλμός **ophthalmós** 'eye'

ὄπιον **ópion** 'poppy juice,'
'opium'

ὄπισθεν **ópisthen** (*adv.*)
'behind'

†ὤψ, ὠπός **ōps, ōpós** 'eye,'
'face'

ὀρχήστρα **orchḗstra** 'place for
dancing'

ὄρχις, ὄρχιος **órchis, órchios**
'testicle' (*wrongly inflected
órchidos when borrowed*)

ὀρειάς, ὀρειάδος **oreiás, oreiá-
dos** 'mountain nymph'

†ὄργανον **órganon** 'tool,' 'instrument'

ὄρνις, ὄρνιθος **órnis, órnithos**
'bird'

†ὀρθός **orthós** 'straight,'
'right,' 'true'

ὀσμή **osmḗ** 'smell'

†ὀστέον **ostéon** 'bone'

ὄστρακον **óstrakon** 'potsherd,'
'tile,' 'tablet used in voting'

οὐρά **ourá** 'tail'

οὐρανός **ouranós** 'sky,'
'heaven'

οὖρον **oúron** 'urine'

οὖς, ὠτός **ous, ōtós** 'ear'

†ὀξύς **oxýs** (**ox-** *or* **oxy-**)
'sharp,' 'acid'

†παχύς **pachýs** (**pachy-**)
'thick'

Παιάν **Paián** Paean (*physician
of the gods, later Apollo*);
'song of triumph'

παῖς, παιδός **pais, paidós**
'child'

†παλαιός palaiós 'old'

†πάλιν pálin (adv.) 'again,' 'back'

Παλλάς, Παλλάδος Pallás, Palládos Pallas (epithet of Athena)

Πάνδαρος Pándaros Pandarus (Trojan commander who acted as go-between for his niece and her lover)

†πᾶς pas (pan-, pant-) 'all,' 'every'

πατήρ, πατρός patḗr, patrós 'father'

πεῖρα peíra 'experiment'

πέλαγος pélagos (3rd Decl.) 'sea'

πέταλον pétalon 'leaf'

πέτρα pétra 'stone'

πέτρος pétros 'stone'

φανερός phanerós 'visible'

φάρμακον phármakon 'drug'

φάρυγξ, φάρυγγος phárynx, pháryngos 'pharynx'

φερνή phernḗ 'dowry'

φιάλη phiálē 'broad flat vessel,' 'phial'

φίλος phílos 'loving,' 'dear'

φλέψ, φλεβός phleps, phlebós 'vein'

†φόβος phóbos 'fear'

φοῖβος phoíbos 'shining'

Φοῖνιξ, Φοίνικος Phoînix, Phoínikos Phoenix (fabulous Egyptian bird)

†φωνή phōnḗ 'voice,' 'sound'

†φῶς, φωτός phōs, phōtós 'light'

φρήν phrēn 'mind'

φθόγγος phthóngos 'voice' (see phthéngesthai)

φυλή phylḗ 'tribe,' 'race'

φύλλον phýllon 'leaf'

πικρός pikrós 'sharp,' 'bitter'

†πλατύς platýs (platy-, plat-) 'broad'

πλείων pleíōn 'more'

πληθώρη plēthṓrē 'fullness'

πλευρά pleurá 'rib,' 'side'

πλοῦτος ploútos 'wealth'

πνεύμων pneúmōn 'lung'

πόλεμος pólemos 'war'

πώλιον pṓlion 'sale'

πολιός poliós 'grey'

†πόλις pólis (pol-) 'city'

πόλος pólos 'axis'

†πολύς polýs (poly-) 'much,' 'many'

πόρος póros 'passage,' 'port'

πορφύρα porphýra 'purple dye'

πόσις pósis 'a drinking'

†πούς, ποδός pous, podós 'foot'

πρεσβύτερος presbýteros 'elder'

πρωκτός prōktós 'anus'

προσήλυτος prosélytos 'one who has come,' 'stranger' (see érchomai)

προῦνον proúnon 'plum'

ψευδής †pseudḗs (pseud-) 'lying,' 'false'

ψίττακος psíttakos 'parrot'

†ψυχή psychḗ 'breath,' 'life,' 'soul,' 'mind'

†πτερόν pterón 'feather,' 'wing'

πτέρυξ, πτέρυγος ptéryx, ptérygos 'wing'

πτύξ, πτυχός ptyx, ptychós 'fold,' 'layer'

πυγή pygḗ 'rump'

πυκνός pyknós 'close,' 'compact'

πυλών pylṓn 'gateway'

πύον pýon 'pus'

†πῦρ pyr 'fire'

πυρά pyrá 'pyre'

πυραμίς, πυραμίδος pyramís, pyramídos 'pyramid'

ῥάβδος rhábdos 'rod'

ῥάχις rháchis 'spine'

ῥαφίς, ῥαφίδος rhaphís, rhaphídos 'needle'

ῥήτωρ rhḗtōr 'teacher of rhetoric'

†ῥίς, ῥινός rhis, rhinós 'nose'

ῥίζα rhíza 'root'

ῥοδῆ rhodḗ 'rose bush'

ῥύγχος rhýnchos 'snout,' 'muzzle'

σάκχαρον sákcharon 'sugar'

σάλπιγξ, σάλπιγγος sálpinx, sálpingos 'trumpet'

σαπρός saprós 'putrid,' 'rotten'

σάρξ, σαρκός sarx, sarkós 'flesh'

σαῦρος saúros 'lizard'

σχολή scholḗ 'leisure,' 'lecture,' 'place for lectures'

σελήνη selḗnē 'moon'

σῆμα, σήματος sēma, sḗmatos 'sign'

σησάμη sēsámē 'sesame'

σίδηρος sídēros 'iron'

σίφων síphōn 'siphon'

σῖτος sítos 'grain,' 'food'

σκέλος skélos 'leg'

σκηνή skēnḗ 'covered place,' 'tent'

†σκληρός sklērós 'hard'

Σόλοι Sóloi Soloi (ancient city known for its bad Greek)

†σῶμα, σώματος sṓma, sṓmatos 'body'

†σοφός sophós 'wise'

σπεῖρα speíra 'coil'

†σφαῖρα sphaíra 'ball,' 'globe'

σφήν sphēn 'wedge'

σπλήν splēn 'spleen'

σταφυλή staphylḗ 'bunch of grapes'

στέαρ stéar (stear-, steat-) 'tallow,' 'fat'

στέγος stégos 'roof,' 'house'

στήλη stḗlē 'post,' 'inscribed slab'

†στενός stenós 'narrow'

στέφανος stéphanos 'wreath,' 'crown'

†στερεός stereós 'solid'

στέρνον stérnon 'breast,' 'chest'

στῆθος stēthos (3rd Decl.) 'breast'

σθένος sthénos (3rd Decl.) 'strength'

στίχος stíchos 'row,' 'rank'

στοά stoá 'porch'

στόμα, στόματος stóma, stómatos 'mouth'

στρατηγός stratēgós 'general,' 'admiral'

στῦλος stýlos 'pillar'

Στύξ, Στυγός Styx, Stygós the Hateful River, the Styx (*river of Hades*)

Σύβαρις Sýbaris Sybaris (*ancient city known for its luxury*)

ταχύς tachýs (tachy-) 'swift'

τάλαντον tálanton 'balance,' 'that which is weighed in the balance,' 'special aptitude'

τάφος táphos 'tomb'

ταρσός tarsós 'instep'

Τάρταρος Tártaros Tartarus (*region below Hades*)

ταὐτό tautó 'the same'

†τέχνη téchnē 'art,' 'skill'

τέκτων téktōn 'carpenter,' 'builder'

†τῆλε téle (*adv.*) 'afar,' 'from afar'

τέλος, τέλεος télos, téleos 'end'

τεῦχος teúchos (*3rd Decl.*) 'tool,' 'book'

θάλαμος thálamos 'bridal chamber'

θάνατος thánatos 'death'

θαῦμα, θαύματος thaúma, thaúmatos 'miracle'

θέα théa 'sight,' 'view'

θεά theá 'goddess'

θεῖον theîon 'brimstone,' 'sulphur'

†θεός theós 'god'

θέραψ, θέραπος théraps, thérapos 'servant'

†θερμός thermós 'hot'

θησαυρός thēsaurós 'treasure'

θώραξ, θώρακος thórax, thórakos 'chest'

θρῆνος thrénos 'dirge'

θρίξ, τριχός thrix, trichós 'hair'

θρόνος thrónos 'chair of state'

θυρεός thyreós 'oblong shield'

Τιτάν Titán Titan (*one of the primeval deities*)

†τόπος tópos 'place'

τόξα tóxa 'bow' (*see Etymological Notes, Lesson 11*)

τοξικόν toxikón 'poison'

τραχύς trachýs (**trachy-**) 'rugged,' 'rough'

τραῦμα, τραύματος traúma, traúmatos 'wound'

τροχαῖος trochaíos 'running'; 'trochee' (*metrical foot consisting of a long and a short syllable*)

τροχός trochós 'wheel' (*see tréchein*)

τρώγλη tróglē 'hole'

τύλος týlos 'callus'

τυφλός typhlós 'blind'

τῦφος týphos 'smoke,' 'stupor'

τύραννος týrannos 'absolute ruler'

ξανθός **xanthós** 'yellow'
†ξένος **xénos** 'stranger'
ξηρός **xērós** 'dry'
†ξύλον **xýlon** 'wood'

ζωή **zōḗ** 'life'
†ζῷον **zôon** 'animal'
ζυγόν **zygón** 'crossbar,' 'yoke'
ζυμή **zymḗ** 'leaven'

VERBS

†ἄγειν **ágein** (**agog-**) 'lead'
ἀγωνίζεσθαι **agōnízesthai**
  (**agōnis-**) 'struggle' (*see*
  agṓn)
†αἰσθάνεσθαι **aisthánesthai**
  (**aisthē-**) 'feel,' 'perceive'
ἀκούειν **akoúein** (**akous-**)
  'hear'
ἀράσσειν **arássein** (**arak-**)
  'dash'
ἀσκεῖν **askeín** (**askē-**) 'exercise'
βαίνειν **baínein** (**ba-**) 'step,'
  'stand'
†βάλλειν **bállein** (**ball-, bol-,**
  blē-) 'throw'
βάπτειν **báptein** (**bap-**) 'dip'
χαράσσειν **charássein** (**cha-**
  rak-) 'scratch,' 'engrave'
χάσκειν **cháskein** (**chas-**)
  'gape'
χωρεῖν **chōreín** (**chōrē-**) 'go'
δεῖν **dein** (**de-, des-**) 'bind'
δηλεῖσθαι **dēleísthai** (**dēlē-**)
  'hurt,' 'injure'
διδάσκειν **didáskein** (**didak-**)
  'teach'
†διδόναι **didónai** (**do-**) 'give'
δοκεῖν **dokeín** (**dog-**) 'think'

δρᾶν **dran** (**dra-, dras-**) 'do,'
  'act'
δύειν **dýein** (**dy-**) 'enter'
δύνασθαι **dýnasthai** (**dynas-**)
  'be able'
ἐλαύνειν **elaúnein** (**elas-**)
  'drive'
ἐμεῖν **emeín** (**eme-**) 'vomit'
ἐρᾶν **erán** (**eras-**) 'love'
ἔρχεσθαι **érchesthai** (**ēly-**)
  'come'
γελᾶν **gelán** (**gelas-**) 'laugh'
†γίγνεσθαι **gígnesthai** (**gon-,**
  gen-, genē-) 'be born,' 'become'
γιγνώσκειν **gignóskein** (**gnō-,**
  gnōs-) 'know'
†γλύφειν **glýphein** (**glyph-,**
  glyp-) 'carve'
†γράφειν **gráphein** (**graph-,**
  gram-) 'write'
αἱρεῖν **haireín** (**haire-**) 'take,'
  'choose'
†ἱστάναι **histánai** (**sta-**) 'set,'
  'stand'
†ὁρᾶν **horán** (**hora-, op-**) 'see'
ὁρίζειν **horízein** (**horis-**)
  'bound,' 'limit' (*see* **hóros**)
καίειν **kaíein** (**kaus-**) 'burn'

καλύπτειν kalýptein (kalyp-) 'cover'

κεραννύναι kerannýnai (kra-) 'mix'

†κινεῖν kinein (kinē-) 'set in motion,' 'move'

†κλᾶν klan (klas-) 'break'

κλέπτειν kléptein (klep-) 'steal'

κλίνειν klínein (kli-, klin-) 'slope,' 'lean'

κλύζειν klýzein (klys-) 'wash'

κοιμᾶν koimán (koimē-) 'put to sleep'

κόπτειν kóptein (kop-, kom-) 'cut'

†κρίνειν krínein (kri-) 'judge'

†κρύπτειν krýptein (kryph-, kryp-) 'hide'

†λαμβάνειν lambánein (lēp-, lēm-, lab-) 'take'

†λέγειν légein (log-, lek-) 'speak,' 'say,' 'gather'

λείπειν leípein (leip-) 'leave'

†λύειν lýein (ly-) 'loosen'

μαίνεσθαι maínesthai (man-) 'be mad'

μανθάνειν manthánein (mathē-) 'learn'

μιγνύναι mignýnai (mik-) 'mix'

μνᾶσθαι mnásthai (mnē-, mnēs-) 'remember'

†νέμειν némein (nom-, neme-) 'deal out,' 'arrange'

ὀξύνειν oxýnein (oxys-) 'sharpen' (see oxýs)

παιειν paíein (pais-) 'strike'

†πάσχειν páschein (path-, pathē-) 'suffer,' 'feel'

πειρᾶν peirán (peira-) 'attempt'

πέμπειν pémpein (pomp-) 'send'

πέπτειν péptein (pep-) 'cook'

†φαγεῖν phageín (phag-) 'eat'

†φαίνειν phaínein (phan-, pha-) 'show'

†φάναι phánai (pha-, phē-) 'speak,' 'say'

φαντάζειν phantázein (phantas-) 'make visible' (see phaínein)

†φέρειν phérein (pher-, phor-) 'bear,' 'carry'

φράζειν phrázein (phra-, phras-) 'speak'

φθέγγεσθαι phthéngesthai (phtheg-, phthong-) 'utter'

†φύειν phýein (phy-) 'grow'

φυλάσσειν phylássein (phylak-) 'guard'

πίπτειν píptein (ptō-) 'fall'

πλανᾶσθαι planásthai (planē-) 'wander'

†πλάσσειν plássein (plas-) 'mould'

πλήσσειν pléssein (plēk-) 'strike'

†πνεῖν pnein (pneu-) 'breathe'

ποιεῖν poieín (poiē-) 'make'

πράσσειν prássein (prag-, prak-) 'do'

ψῆν psēn (psēs-) 'rub smooth'

ῥηγνύναι rhēgnýnai (rhak-) 'break'

†ῥεῖν rhein (rheu-, rho-) 'flow'

σβεννύναι sbennýnai (sbes-) 'quench'

†σχίζειν schízein (schis-) 'split'

σήπειν sḗpein (sēp-) 'make putrid,' 'rot'

σκέλλειν skéllein (skele-) 'dry up'

σκήπτειν skḗptein (skēp-) 'support'

†σκέπτεσθαι sképtesthai (skop-, skep-) 'watch,' 'examine'

σώζειν sṓzein (sō-) 'preserve'

σπᾶν span (spas-) 'draw out'

†σπείρειν speírein (sper-, spor-) 'sow'

σφύζειν sphýzein (sphyk-) 'throb,' 'beat' (used of the pulse)

†στέλλειν stéllein (stol-) 'send'

στίζειν stízein (stig-) 'brand'

†στρέφειν stréphein (stroph-, strep-) 'turn,' 'twist'

στύφειν stýphein (styp-) 'draw together,' 'contract'

†τάσσειν tássein (tak-) 'arrange'

†τείνειν teínein (ton-) 'stretch'

†τέμνειν témnein (tom-) 'cut'

θεᾶσθαι theásthai (thea-) 'behold' (see théa)

†τιθέναι tithénai (the-) 'place'

τρέχειν tréchein (troch-, drom-) 'run'

†τρέπειν trépein (trop-) 'turn'

†τρέφειν tréphein (troph-) 'nourish'

τρίβειν tríbein (trib-) 'rub'

†τύπτειν týptein (typ-) 'strike'

General Index

General Index

265

Index of Words

[Numbers refer to lessons, those numbers preceded by the symbol *G* (for "Greek") indicating lessons in Part Two. Letters indicate sections within a lesson, viz., *a* = Exposition, *b* = Etymological Notes, *c* = Exercises.]

aberrant, 22c
abjure, 19c
ablutions, 28c
aboriginal, 7a, 11c
abortive, 31c
abrogate, 19c
absolute, 19a
absolutism, 27c
absolve, 19a
abstain, 19c
abstract, 19c
abstruse, 26
Academy, G5c
acceptance, 27c
acceptation, 27c
accessible, 30c
accessory, 31c
accidental, 22a
acclaim, 19c
accommodate, 19c
accurate, 20c
acephalous, G11c
acerbity, 13c
acme, G1c
acoustic, G14a
acrimony, 14a
acrobat, G14c
acropolis, G8c
acrostic, G8c
act, 18a
action, 27a
activate, 32
active, 31a

actor, 29c
actual, 18c
actuary, 18c
actuate, 18c
acumen, 28c, 32
ad captandum, 25c
adder, 4b
adduce, 19c
adhere, 19c
ad hoc, 11c
ad infinitum, 18c
adjoin, 19b
adjunct, 19c
adjure, 19c
administratrix, 32
adolescent, 25c
adore, 19c
adrenaline, 11c
adumbrate, 19c
advent, 19c
adventitious, 31c
adventure, 32
adverbial, 11c
adverse, 19b
aegis, G5b, G5c
Aeolian, G3c
aerate, G6c
aeroplane, G5c
Aeschylus, G3c
aesthete, G16c
aesthetic, G14c
affable, 30c
affect, 20c

affectation, 27c
affection, 27c, 28c
affectionate, 32
affidavit, 17c
affinity, 13c
affirmation, 27c
a fortiori, 5c
Agatha, G8c
agelast, G16c
agelastic, G16c
agency, 23c
agenda, 25c
agent, 22a
aggravate, 19c
aggravation, 6
aggressive, 32
agile, 30c, 32
agnostic, G17c
agony, G5c
agoraphobia, G4a, G7
agrarian, 9c
album, 4a, 8c
Alcaeus, G7
alga, 1a
alias, 5c
alibi, 5a
alleviate, 19c, 23c
alleviation, 16
alliteration, 27c
allocate, 19c
allopathic, G8c
allopathy, G8c

267